Secrets of Race & Consciousness

Kamit Afrikan Cosmology and
The Spiritual Meaning of The 'N' Word(s)
Neggur - The Goose Goddess who laid the Sun Egg, the Cosmic Egg

Revealed in Ka Ab Ba (Kabala) The Tree Of Life
The Psycho/Spiritual Journey of Unfolding Consciousness
Metaphysical Oracle Key to: **Dis-spelling Illusion & Dissipating the Power To Wound**
The Ausarianization of Consciousness Tablet Series 2 – A.C.T.S. 2
From Sages to Savages to Sages
The Psycho/Spiritual Journey of Unfolding Consciousness

Dr. Terri Nelson
Nteri Renenet Elsong

John Jackson. *Man, God and Civilization.*

Hence, all men must be Negroes.

The Ausarianization of Consciousness Tablet Series 2 – A.C.T.S. 2
Metaphysical Keys To the Tree of Life & Oracle Keys to Dispelling Illusion
The Psycho/Spiritual Journey of Unfolding Consciousness

Copyright © 2000, 2003, 2005, 2008 Dr Terri Nelson. Library of Congress Cataloging in Publication

The press of Spirit causes this work to go forward now even though it is still undergoing editing phases.

Data
All Rights Reserved. No part of this book maybe used or reproduced in any manner whatsoever without written permission except in the case of brief quotations embodied in critical articles and reviews. All inquiries may be forwarded to the address below.

ISBN: 0-9659600-8-0
Printed in the United States of America

Published by: The Academy of Kamitic Education, Right Relationship Maat, Inc.
53 Cedar St.
Mattapan, MA 02126

The author is available for group lectures and individual consultations. For further information or to order additional copies contact:

АЖЕ
The Academy of Kamitic Education, Right Relationship Maat Inc.

The Academy for
Right Relationship and Right Knowledge

African Origin of The Ancient/Egyptian Wisdom
Awakening Consciousness   AfriKan Knowledge   Ausarian Enlightenment
The Knowledge & Education That Awakens 1st Eye Awareness into
The Metaphysics, Art & Science of Daily Living
Leading to Spiritual Transformation, Right Relationship, Soul Purpose Living, & Service
Seminars Held At: 53 Cedar St. Mattapan, MA 02126

www.rrrk.net   **(617) 296 - 7797**
contact@rightrelationshiprightknowledge.net

About The Author

Terri Nelson, PhD.E, L.I.C.S.W., M.S.W., M.S.E.P., Shækem RA AЖE (Reiki) Master
aka Queen Nteri Renenet Elson
The Neteru revealing Harvest to the Sons and Daughters of God

Dr. Terri Nelson is a Holistic Psychotherapist, Metaphysician, Priestess of Kamit and Teacher of the Afrikan origins of the Ancient wisdom. She is co-founder of, *The Academy of Kamitic Education, Right Relationship Right Knowledge, Maat, Inc.* where she teaches an Afrikan Centered Model for Psychological, Spiritual, and Character development which is underpinned by the History of Ancient Afrika/Kamit (Egypt) and the Diaspora as a way of Self knowledge, healing and health. Her classes on the Application of the Ancient Wisdom in Modern Daily Living are helping others find solutions to life challenges. A specialty area that she brings penetrative insight to is, *The Spiritual and Psychological Journey of Unfolding Consciousness out of Afrika*. Dr. Nteri is a gifted Wordsmith and Mtu Ntr Symbologist and has given important Keys for Dis-Spelling Illusion in her books. She has a Bachelor of Science in Psychology (B.S); a Masters in Social Work (M.S.W); a Masters in the Science of Esoteric Psychology (M.S.E.P); and a Doctor of Esoteric Philosophy (PhD.E) with a concentration in Metaphysical and Kamitic/Egyptian Studies. She is an Independent researcher of the Ancient Wisdom teachings and was a member of The Black Knostic Study Group for several years under the late Dr. Alfred Ligon. She has had the honor of traveling to Kamit (Egypt) under the guidance of Elder Dr.Yosef ben-Jochannan and Dr. Clinton Crawford; and to Ghana under the guidance of Drs. Leonard and Rosalind Jeffries and Professor James Small. She is a Shækem Ra-AЖE Master. As teacher and eternal student of the Ancient wisdom her years of experience have made her a firsthand witness to that which both fetters and liberates the Soul in its Spiritual Journey. She has been garnering and distributing the wisdom and tools for Ausarian Spiritual Transformation and Resurrection or ASTR (STAR).

She has worked in the behavioral/mental health field for the last 30 years and her training has included both traditional and alternative approaches to healing. Her working experience includes providing service within the Department of Mental Health and three Medical Associate Practices, which includes Harvard Vanguard Medical Associates where she worked as a Clinician in the Adult mental health department. She has worked many years providing psychotherapeutic services in the Massachusetts Correctional Institutions and in hospitals.

She has also had a private practice over 20 years where she uses a variety of healing methods. She provides counseling and consultation to: individuals, couples, families, groups and agencies. Co-counseling together, she and her husband, Lester Nelson, Min., specialize in Relationship work with Couples, Individuals, Families and Groups.

Dr Terri Nelson is author of: *Ka Ab Ba Building The Lighted Temple; Secrets of Race and Consciousness; On The Way To Finding Your Soulmate; The Right Relationship Workbook and The Forgiveness Process Workbook.* She has given lectures nationally and internationally which includes: the Association for the Study of Classical Afrikan Civilization (ASCAC); Indigenous Afrikan Healers Conference; First World Alliance in New York; Institute for the Study of Race and Culture; The Melanin Conference; Sankofa; Mtw Ntr; etc.

The Ausarianization of Consciousness Tablet Series 2 – A.C.T.S. 2
Metaphysical Keys To the Tree of Life & Oracle Keys to Dispelling Illusion
The Psycho/Spiritual Journey of Unfolding Consciousness

This book is dedicated to –

• *AMEN, Infinite Eternal All in All, Neter Neteru, Fount of All Possibility,*
• *Father/Mother Creator, Most High God/Goddess in Whom we live and move and have our being, Divined as AusarAuset,*
• *and to the Paut Neteru, the company of the Gods, guiding us into sacred space, imbruing us with all God qualities (Neteru), teaching us to live as Gods and Goddesses,*
• *and to the Ancestors who have gone before,*
Those who have remained steady in the Light and
Those with hard won footsteps who have trodden their way back into the Light and
Those with heavy laden footsteps who are treading their way onto the path of Light
• *In all praise and appreciation that you hear our prayers*

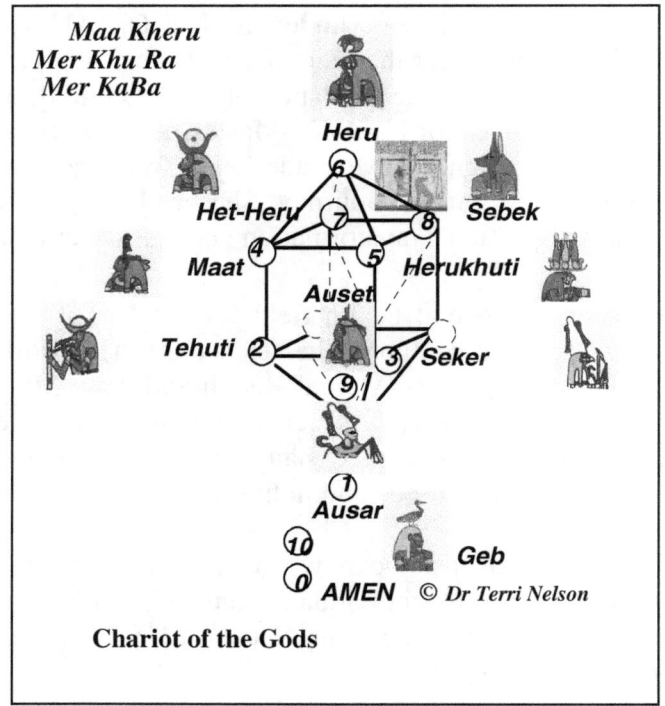

Chariot of the Gods

Secrets of Race & Consciousness Afrikan Cosmology of Kamit
with The Spiritual Meaning of The 'N' Word(s)
Neggur - The Goose Goddess who laid the Sun Egg, the Cosmic Egg

Revealed in Ka Ab Ba *(Kabala)* The Tree Of Life   Metaphysical Mysteries Meaning

Table of Contents

Chapter 1.. 9-17
  The Ausarianization of Consciousness Tablet Series 2 – A.C.T.S. 2.
  Ausar Ba.
  The Psycho/Spiritual Journey in Unfolding Consciousness & The Tree of Life.
  The Higher Spiritual Meaning of the 'N' word(s) A Metaphysician sounds an alert.

Chapter 2...18-21
  The Eldest Race On The Planet Is The Black Race.

Chapter 3..….........22-28
  Ka Ab Ba The Tree Of Life Reveals Secrets of Race & Consciousness.
  What is the Tree of Life? What is Ausarian Resurrection and Ascension?
  Metaphysical Key To: The Tree Of Life The Big MAP
  3 Primary Triangles of Ka Ab Ba
  Metaphysical Key To: Movement Within 3 primary Egoic states of Consciousness

Chapter 4...29-33
  Negroes.
  Metaphysical Key To: Metaphysical Key To: Name, Letter, and Number are Metu Neter.
  Metaphysical Key To: Oracle Keys To Dispelling Illusion

Chapter 5...…..…..…........34-37
  Vibration, The WORD & Bridging Between the Metu Neter & English Language.
  Metaphysical Law Key To: The Law of Vibration
  Metaphysical Key To: Involutionary and Evolutionary Cycles.
  The Spiritualization and Materialization in Consciousness

Chapter 6...38-40
  The Afrikan, Semitic, Aryan Root Races - The Present Planetary Consciousness.
  Metaphysical Key To: Racial Name(s), Number Physical Characteristics.
  3-4-5   AfrikanSemiticAryan - Konsciousness Admixture - ASA-KA

Chapter 7..41-44
  Metaphysical Key To: The 7 Root Races. The Number - 7 The Septenary Nature …
  The Kamitc Goddess Ta-urt and the Creative Process.

Chapter 8..45-47
  Our State of Unitive Consciousness Changed Over Eons Of Time.
  The 1st Eye and Unbroken Consciousness of the Afrikan/Lemurian?
  The Afrikan Root Race when focused in the Ba Triangle of the Tree of Life.
  Metaphysical Key To: Restoration of The 1st Eye*Overcoming impediment # 2*

Chapter 9..48-49
  Afrikans/Negroes Naturally Born Initiates Into Mysteries of the Universe Who Did. Not
  Need Temples of Initiation for Instruction on His High Origin. What is Initiation?

Chapter 10...50-54
  The So Called Pythagorean Theorem.
  3-4-5 AfrikanSemiticAryan - Konsciousness Admixture - ASA-KA Continued.
  Read from the angle of consciousness and not just from the angle of the physical form …
  Does each Root Race contribute particular qualities in consciousness?
  Metaphysical Key To: 3-4-5 unification in consciousness
  Metaphysical Key To: The Impersonality of The Cycles of Time.

Chapter 11..55-64
   Negroes and The Secret and Sacred Meaning In The Triangle. Nuhes, Neheshi
   Metaphysical Key To: Understanding the Sahu Soul Body or Vehicle

Chapter 12..65-66
   Negroes and The Secret and Sacred Meaning In The Triangle Continued.

Chapter 13..67-76
   The 7 Root Races Continued.
   Lemuria Used to Veil the Name Negro. So called Pigmy.
   Are these Racial names just Esoteric contrivances to confuse …
   Other Ways of Knowing Outside of Factual Information provided by Science …Reading the Etheric Records - What is Akasha?
   Metaphysical Key To: Past, Present, and Future Planetary Root Races

Chapter 14..77-78
   What Is Ka Ba? Divisioning into the 2.
   Metaphysical Key To: Number 1 and 2 *Ka*Ba Unity/Two-Oneness Ka and Ba/Duality Or Diad.
   On the Psycho/Spiritual Journey in Unfolding Consciousness what are you as the Sun-Son/ Daughter of God becoming fully conscious of?
   Metaphysical Key To: Spirit came down from the higher Worlds …

Chapter 15..79-83
   The First Significant Event Taking Place in Consciousness. The Outgoing Egos. What is Ego? Dispelling the Word Negroes continued.
   Metaphysical Key To: The Afrikan 3rd Root Race consciousness and the process of Individualization.
   Metaphysical Key To: What is Africa or the African?
   Metaphysical Key To: The 7 Ka-resting Steps/Stairs/Arits to become ASTR or a STAR
   The 7 Christ-ing Steps.

Chapter 16..84-87
   What is Ka Ab Ba? Divisioning Into the 3…At Work In Man And Woman
   Metaphysical Key To: The Number 3 The Trinity BaAbKa or KaAbBa
   Metaphysical Key To: The Story of Ausar, Auset and Heru

Chapter 17..88-93
   Heru as Ego. What is Manes? The Birth of Individual Self Consciousness.
   Soul or Consciousness aspect of your Spiritual equipment
   Shenit Dispelled

Chapter 18..94-95
   The 7 Planes of Consciousness.
   Metaphysical Key To: The 7 Planes of Consciousness, 7 Division of The Solar Systemic Planes. The 7 Hathors or celestial cow goddesses.

Chapter 19..96-104
   The Goose and the Golden Egg. Dispelling the word Negroes
   …Consciousness ….The Separation of the Sexes.
   Metaphysical Key To: Cosmogony and Cosmogenisis Universal Ba *To* Individualized Ba
   The Most Primal 'N' Word is Nu or Nun. The Cosmic Sun Egg? What is Khepera?
   I am the only One born of an only One.

Chapter 20..105-115
   Negroes, Goose and The Game of Hide and Go Seek.

AMEN Ra The Beautiful Goose.
Secret and Sacred Meaning of the Word Cracker.
The Egg of Earth Humanity Individual and Collective Consciousness
Geb, Nut, Shu, Bes

Chapter 21..116-126
N-G-R –The Goose-Goddess who laid the Cosmic Sun Egg. The 'N' Word For God
The R-e-n-e-g-i-n-g King or The R-e-i-n-i-n-g King
N-G K-R-I' What Does the Letter/Neter ' K ' Represent?
The Smai Tawi symbol. What Do The V's's Represent?
Metaphysical Key To: Right of Ascent and Descent of Spirit

Chapter 22..127-129
Secret and Sacred Meaning of Ham, Hamsa and Kam.
Bird of Life, The Man Swan.

Chapter 23..130-131
Afrikans/Negroes and The Secret and Sacred Meaning of The Caducceus.

Chapter 24..132-136
What is This Line You Cross in Consciousness? Crossing the Line and Death?

Chapter 25..137-139
You are The Manes Who Comes to Know Death by Degrees.

Chapter 26..140-146
3 Primary Egoic States of Consciousness Ka Ab Ba Continued.
Division into the 3 - The Nature of the Trinity at work in Man and Woman.
Metaphysical Key To: Ka Ab Ba and Western Psycholoogy/Psychoanalysis

Chapter 27..147-148
The Crossing Over in Consciousness and The Experience of Death Continued.
Higher Manes – Middle Manes – Lower Manes.

Chapter 28..149-155
The Secret and Sacred Meaning of Semitic and Aryan Consciousness.

Chapter 29..156-158
Have All Races Gone Out? Have All Races Gone Out to the Same Degree in the Materialization in Consciousness and Precipitating Outcomes on the Physical Plane?

Chapter 30..159-161
The Secret and Sacred Meaning of the Word Nigger.
Secret and Sacred Meaning of the Word Honky.

Chapter 31..162-163
Secret and Sacred Meaning of the Word English.
The Bridging Between the of Language of Metu Neter and English Continued.

Chapter 32..164-165
From Sage to Savage to Sage.
Is Evolution A Myth?
Crossing the Line in Consciousness.

Chapter 33..166-168
How are We Rounding the Corner in Our Collective Planetary Consciousness?
How might we rise as a Human Family and Together Make Earth Sacred Space?
How can we go and be At-One 'someplace' else when we can't be At-One at 'Home'?

Chapter 34..**169-170**
    The Wheel of Birth and Death.
    The Law of Reincarnation (Rebirth) & The Law of Cause and Effect-Karma.
Chapter 35..**171-174**
    The Scales of Maat The Weighing of the Heart. Standing Before The Lord Of The World.
Appendix **175-197**
    The Tree of Life *The Big Map.*
    Oracle Metaphysical Dis-Spelling Keys.
    The Story Of Ausar, Auset and Heru – The Divine Trinity Continued.
    The 7 Continents and The Super Continents.
    The Secret and Sacred Meaning of Pangea.
    The Secret and Sacred Meaning of Continent.
    What should we make of hearing about Continents Pangea, Lemuria, Atlantis…
    The Secret and Sacred Meaning of Lemuria.
    Black Race people are the Fathers and Mothers of the …What may be the impact…
    Evidences of 'Appearance' of The 6th Root Race.
    Geese Facts.
    A Hunter's Poem.
    Reascension Into Sacredness. *Song.*
    Reascension Into Sacredness. *Music*
Select Bibliography & Suggested Reading List......................................**198-199**

Chapter 1
The Ausarianization of Consciousness Tablet Series 2 – A.C.T.S. 2

As a Black Race, we are an Ancient people. As such, many stories are unfolding within *Our Story*. In my extensive research along with guidance from the Elders on the Inner realm, I have been guided not to go, 'head to head' or 'toe to toe' with the countless instances of misrepresentation, half-truths, distortions, white-washing, and racism in the reference materials. Such address and counter address would expend enormous energy as well as distract from the rhythm and flow of a story - already complex enough - a story that ponders the 'seemingly' imponderable Psycho/Spiritual Journey in Unfolding Human Consciousness.

In these collective works Titled, The *Ausarianization of Consciousness Tablet Series A.C.T.S.*, – *The Metaphysical Keys to The Tree Of Life with Oracle Keys to Dis-spelling Illusion* - I made the decision to just try to tell Our Story, doing the best I could. Many have come before me in this effort and many will come after me.

This Spirit has impelled me in presenting:
A.C.T.S. 1 Ka Ab Ba Building The Lighted Temple.
This same Spirit is now impelling me in presenting:
A.C.T.S 2 Secrets of Race & Consciousness
Afrikan Cosmology of Kamit with The Spiritual Meaning of The 'N' Word
Neggur - The Goose Goddess who laid the Sun Egg, the Cosmic Egg

It is suggested that you read *A.C.T.S 2* and subsequent *A.C.T.S.* using *A.C.T.S. 1* as a 'Key to open' what has been secret doctrine. Both reveal the Psychological and Spiritual Journey of Unfolding Consciousness.

Our Story Continues…
Eons ago our Ancestors lived in cycles of time when the Earth was in a Spiritualized state. The human, animal, plant and mineral kingdoms were more in balance and man and woman partook nurturance from the Earth, according to their need. Man and woman's consciousness was unbroken. In other words, they did not see themselves as a 'self' separated from other 'selves.' The spark of 'separative consciousness' had yet to be fanned to a flame. Instead, they saw themselves as intricately interdependent and at one with all creation. This was a state of Unity, God, All or Omniscient consciousness. It is Ausarian consciousness in the Kamitic Spiritual tradition (See Ra Un Nefer Amen, Massey, Budge).

Man and woman were in deepest communion with the divinity in all and with the Spiritual Kingdom of Celestial beings or Deities. This Spiritual Hierarchy are those helping agencies that are guiding Earth humanity into a greater measure of Spiritual Light. Known by many names which include: Neteru, Paut Neteru, Deities, Eloheem, God Kings, Kabiri, Annunaqi, Manasa-devas, Sons of Maat, Lords of the Flame, Solar Ancestors, Agniswatas, Solar Angels, Celestial Beings, Holy Ones, Angels, Orisha and so on (See *The Gods of the Egyptians; Ancient Egypt the Light of the World; Let's Set the Record Straight; Secret Doctrine; 24 Tibetan Books [A Treatise on Cosmic Fire, Initiation Human & Solar,* etc.]*; The Divine Plan; The Rosicrucian Cosmo-Conception; Lemurian Scrolls; Lost Keys of Enoch;* et. al.). These seeded and guided early humanity, both from the inner Spiritual plane or invisible realm and upon the outer physical plane or visible realm, as they walked among man and woman as God Kings. In a much later cycle of time, the Greek philosopher Hesiod (eighth century B.C) would write about this state of consciousness. According to: Robert Lawlor, *Voices of the First Day,* p. 69-70.

> A golden race of mortal men was created at the beginning of time. The golden race lived like God, pain and suffering were unknown to them, death arrived like a self-induced dream, and the earth was fruitful without human toil. Food was plentiful, no wars or strife marred the happiness of human beings.

In our unbroken Ausarian consciousness, we knew the underlying unity guiding the seamless relationship between all beings in creation. In our broken consciousness, we began to honor the 'part' more than the whole. *Hard at play* in the game of *particularization* where interconnection is not seen and upheld - man has killed, enslaved one another, destroyed and polluted the environment and violated his own nature, health and well being. In a World of separativeness and 'part-I-cularization' of consciousness, humanity is starting to glean the need and the higher aspiration to now be *hard at work* trying to make all the pieces fit back together again.

What has happened for man and woman in the Psycho/Spiritual Journey of Unfolding Consciousness over cycles of time?

Our Story Continues...
- The cycles of time would lead man and woman into an Involutionary descent
- In time a despiritualization in consciousness would occur
- The 'ways' of innate knowingness and wholeness
- Would become the veiled and concealed **'secrets'**
- Withheld from the masses of humanity
- Leaving them to *grope* in the dark
- Trying to find their way back 'Home'
- We are the prodigal Son/Daughter who has 'seemingly' left home and has
- *Gone out* on a journey as Heru
- We are likewise Son/Daughter who stayed Home - Ausar
- Yes, paradoxically, we are both Ausar and Son/Daughter called Heru
- Our I-dentification as/with both is the 'two made One' and
- The journey towards Ausarian, Unity or God consciousness
- This return journey in consciousness is Kamitically expressed as
- *"Nuk Ausar, I am Ausar"*
- This return journey in consciousness is biblically expressed as
- *"My Father and I are ONE"*

As an Ancient people, our story extends into the night of time.
- It is *Exoterically* known (more commonly) that Afrika is the cradle and birthplace of humanity some estimated 4 - 7 million years ago.
- It is *Esoterically* known (more veiled/hidden) that events in Afrikan (Lemurian) consciousness were unfolding 18 million years ago (See *Secret Doctrine; Rosicrucian Cosmo Conception; Tibetan Books; Origin and Evolution of The Human Race*).

This suggests that:
- If we are made in the Image and Likeness of God and that
- We are no less than we have always been from the beginingless beginning and endless ending
- Then we knew Unity, God or Ausarian consciousness and then *fell* from this awareness

Much in the literature says, then unsays this. To say it would mean that a more Ancient people knew, and walked upon Earth in the state of God consciousness. A consciousness that so-called, present day, advanced, 'modern man' is trying to 'get back to'. Why would we be trying to get back a state of being we never had, and cannot remember? What are people who sit and meditate really trying to achieve anyway? The Bible tells us that, 'There is nothing new under the Sun'. We are still trying to unearth the greatness of the Ancient World. What was known then dwarfs the so-called 'advances of the modern World' of today.

In some of the quotes that follow, you will at times see that language is used to esoterically 'veil' or hide meaning. In order to 'lift the veil' and reveal truer meaning, I have placed 'explanatory language' within brackets that looks like this [read here: ...'explanatory language'] after the quote in question. This practice will occur throughout this text. Our first instance of providing 'explanatory language' is to use the correct name for the Kamitic Goddess Auset and not the Greek name as expressed in the following quote accordingly: H.P. Blavatsky. *The Veil of Isis* [read here: - The Veil of Auset], *V.I*, Accordingly: *Isis Unveiled, V.I*, p. 526.

> Whenever, in the pride of some new discovery, we throw a look into the past, we find, to our dismay, certain vestiges which indicate the possibility, if not certainty, that the alleged discovery was not totally unknown to the ancients.

Nirvana which is a state of God consciousness was not first experienced by Buddha in 600 B.C.E, but thousands of years ago (Exoterically) and millions of years ago (Esoterically) by our Ancient Afrikan Ancestors. Exoterically this state of return in God consciousness was called Seket-Aarnru, Hetepu or Hotep, which means - *Peace*.

There is a *genocidal arrogance* in some of the literature that says that the 'remnant' of the Ancient tribal people of the World will die out, become extinct. Racial hatreds and tensions have led one racial group to try to destroy another. What we must come to terms with is the fact that each Root Race has its respective part to play in the great divine plan. God consciousness indwells within skins ranging in hues that are black, brown, red, yellow and white. This is expressed accordingly: Max Heindel, *Rosicrucian Cosmo Conception,* p. 311 - 312.

> Races are but an evanescent feature of evolution...Races are simply steps in evolution which must be taken, otherwise there will be no progress for the spirits reborn in them.

It is after all, a 'seeming' Journey in Unfolding Consciousness and *what goes around comes around*, full cycle - that *now is then* and *then is now* and the *serpent will put its tail in its mouth*. Today, as One Human Family, we are gathering 'closer together' due to technological advances in communication and travel which makes the Earth which is called Geb (also called Seb, Keb) - sphere 10, in the Tree of Life - seem smaller. Our future depends upon what we now choose to do in our *closer proximity*. We must now offer up the sum total of the 'parts' we have played as ONE whole humanity. In the sum total of our collective consciousness we must now work in lifting our Earth into sacredization and Spiritualization. This is expressed accordingly: *The Veil of Isis,* [read here: Auset] *V.I,* v. preface.

> Yet we do not hesitate to accept the assertion of Biffe, that "the essential is forever the same. Whether we cut away the marble inward that hides the statue in the block, or pile, stone upon stone outward till the temple is completed, our New result is only an *old idea.* The latest of all the eternities will find its destined other half-soul in the earliest.

Many of the Ancient wisdom teachings cited are from book references, which are themselves treasure chests containing the mysteries, yet requiring future research and investigation. However, let it be said at the outset that my research reveals (as amply noted by other researchers – John Jackson, Cheikh Anta Diop, et al) that there is a game that is being played. It is the game of:
1. *'saying'* and *unsaying',* and
2. *'should have been saids'* and *'should not have been saids'*

This is the game of discrediting, disappearing and degrading. In this game one must wade through a maze that has been set by authors who are skilled at both *'unsaying'*, then sometimes inadvertently *'saying',* then *'unsaying'* again, that which is ultimately revealed as *the Greatness of Black Race People.* What is astonishing in this *'double speaking'* is how even in their attempts to *'unsay',* they end up *'saying'* anyway.

My work here is to:
1. Capture the broad outlines of the Psycho/Spiritual Journey of Unfolding Consciousness in the Human Family
2. Unveil who and what the Afrikans and so called 'Negroes' are in this journey
3. Know that in time, History, Science and other related fields will come along and fill in the blanks, either disputing or confirming what is posited here. *Thus we will*
4. Move backwards in time millions of years, forward to the twenty first century and then to time cycles that take us beyond allowing us a glimpse into the future.

This work is an effort to retrieve and reclaim the image of the Black Race out of the throes and thralldom of the 'writer's pen' which has often been used as a hacksaw. As such, I focused my attention throughout this work in providing references which are the *'saying'* of the greatness of Black people while weeding through countless pages in the source material which are the *'unsayings'*, i.e., the degradation and disappearing of that greatness.

Ausar Ba
The Psycho/Spiritual Journey in Unfolding Consciousness & The Tree of Life

Man/Woman grows 'down' the Tree of Life in his long involutionary descent into matter. Man/Woman grows 'up' the Tree of Life in his evolutionary re-ascent back to the source. His climb both down and up The Tree of Life is the story of how man and woman both forget and then re-member that which they have always been - Suns - Sons/Daughters of God. The Tree of Life is your Spiritual equipment both Human and Divine and a road map in consciousness.

Who is Ausar Ba?
You are Ausar Ba.
Ausar Ba is The One True Self Realized Being-ness and Identification of man and woman. Within the raying forth from AMEN - sphere 0, Ausar - sphere 1, comes into subjective being with the divine archetypal designs and creative substance rayed forth and complete within him or her to become, the Self Realized Being-ness that he or she already is. With the emanation of Spirit into the One, we now make a descent down the Tree of Life, which is pictured at right:

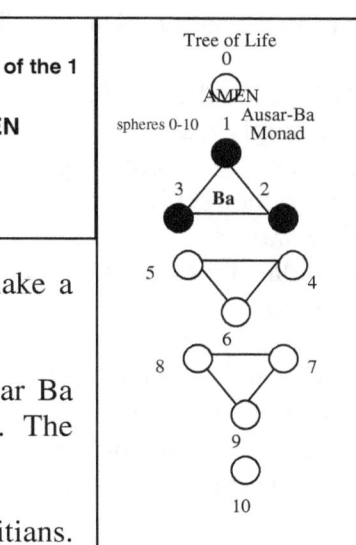

The *stirring* within AMEN, THE ABSOLUTE, gives rise to Ausar Ba who 'seemingly' leaves his ETERNAL *Home* and begins a journey. The Pilgrim called Ausar Ba, sets out on the Psycho/Spiritual Journey.

In our Eternal Home we know peace - called Hotep by the Kamitians. Peace comes from the Realization that we are made in the Image and Likeness of God. This is our One True Self Identification. As Ausar Ba we 'seemingly' leave our Eternal Home and begin a journey that we never really went on - except in appearance. This appearance, though *unreal* and called *illusion,* would eventually cause us to forget the *Real*.

Yes, this seeming appearance of leaving our Eternal Home and setting out on a journey that we never really went on would cause us to forget the *One True Self* that we are and have always been from the beginingless beginning. As we begin our Psycho/Spiritual Journey in unfolding consciousness our awareness is still AT-ONE within the Higher Spiritual realm and the full remembrance of the Supernal Light of our Eternal Home *is* our consciousness.

We are Ausar Ba, The One True Self Realized Being-ness. The Drawer from the Fount of All Possibility. Unlimited - we are The Drawer of All Power, All Wisdom, and All Pervading Presence. As we continue along the Psycho/Spiritual Journey, we gradually descend into the more material realms below and become more and more submerged in matter. From the first and highest plane, we descend as if taking an elevator through the seven planes of consciousness. The idea as we make our descent is to *remain* polarized within the Higher realms. However, we endure many impacts along the way. Impact after impact we forget the Higher planes of our birth and we come to experience a 'self' that is *less than* our One True Self. In time, we come to believe that we *are* the impacts of physical, emotional, sexual abuse, dis-ease, poverty, loss of self esteem (Self estimation), victimization, enslavement, death, and all manner of love-less conditions. Along our descent into the utmost limits of matter and material consciousness - we come to feel diminished and begin to take the illusion of these conditions as our *reality*. With continual descent, through each successive plane and *seeming* disconnection from the Higher planes, our consciousness grows successively more material, dense and dark.

So we move from our full identification as Spirit Beings into an identification with the coarse matter of our physical bodies struggling in the World for material existence. As we reach the lowest point in our descent - the 7th plane - memory of our Image and Likeness of/as God, our All in all-ness - *fades*. Our Light obscures, awareness dims. Thus we undergo a seeming obscuration or blotting out of - The One True Self.

- At last, the illusion of the Psycho/Spiritual Journey in which we
- Seemingly leave our Eternal Home
- Descend into increasingly darkening material conditions and
- Experience self diminishing impacts along the way
- *Becomes real*
- Our One True Spiritual Identity becomes
- *The unreal*
- Yet in essence
- We are no less than the Image and Likeness of God
- No less than the fullness of the One True Self
- That we have always been
- From the beginingless beginning

The Higher Spiritual Meaning of the 'N' word(s)
A Metaphysician sounds an alert.

On July 9, 2007 the NAACP took steps to - 'bury the 'N' word' - in a ritualistic and ceremonial way. This was a significant step to take in redeeming the energy of this word. A word used so negatively. A word that has been deliberately potentized to herald the delivery of insult, wounding, destruction and lethality, when uttered. After all, Whites have enslaved and killed Blacks in the name of the N word. But like the Surgeon General, a physician, who would come before the public and sound a health alert, I come before you as a Metaphysician to sound a Psychological and Spiritual alert. I come to alert you and reveal revolutionary information that has been silenced about this word and its potency.

This book is about Afrikan Cosmology and The Higher Spiritual Meaning of the N word in Kamit, Egypt. Kamit is the land of our Afrikan Ancestors. Egypt is the name later given to this land by the Greeks. Metu Neter is the name of the language of our Afrikan Ancestors – also renamed Hieroglyphics by the Greeks. Metu means 'words'. Neter and Neteru (plural) means 'qualities of divinity'. These divine words are the speech of the Gods. Metu Neter uses pictographs and letters which act as oracle to energetically convey word, symbol, idea and meaning. This name for the 'divine words and speech of the Gods' is variously spelled and some of the forms are as follows: Mtu Ntr, Mdw Ntr, Medu Neter, Mdw Netcher, Metu Neter, Medew Netjer, Mdw Net-ger, and so on. In the language itself, like the word Metu Neter, various vowels are added, substituted, and/or subtracted before or after the primal consonants used to make up a word and convey its meaning. The vowels lend themselves to facility in pronunciation.

As an Afrikan people we are millions of years old. As we made our footsteps out of Afrika we populated the world. As such, the Metu Neter have gone forth as a language that has journeyed out of Afrika also. As the Metu Neter journeyed out of Afrika it became garbled, confused and distorted by its distillation through the English language. The lower expression of the N word(s) has resulted in a concentrated pollutant of darkness and despair which has contributed to the deep psychological scarification that we experience as Afrikan and Afrikan Diaspora. Yet paradoxically, herein lies the greatest Light also.

How is this so? Words have a vibration. Words may vibrate at a higher Spiritual level, a more refined level. When Metu Neter was vibrating at this higher Spiritual and refined level this contributed to our greatness as an Afrikan people. Likewise, words may vibrate at a lower, coarse, dense and material level. As the Metu Neter went out into English, - 'words' - were negatively potenized to contribute to our demise as a people.

In my book I dispel the words Negroes, Nigger, and many others that have contributed to our deep psychological scarification, words that we must now understand and overcome. But how will we overcome? Shall we bury the Niger River too? Should we not speak the name of the Niger river? Does not the Niger river have the same Metu Neter as the N word, N-i-g-e-r or N-i-g-g-e-r? These words have Ancient origin which must be understood. Even though this potency has been used negatively if the N word did not have this potency it would not have the power to wound. Likewise this same potency, when used positively, is the power to resurrect and heal. It is this power that must be understood as we look at the journey of the N word as it moved from Metu Neter, divine speech, and became distillated through the English language. If we were to find a diamond at the bottom of a dumpster under tons of garbage - *it is still a diamond*. Herein lies the greatest Light to be discovered, a Light that has been hidden, but will be reveled once more.

The irresistible pull to give utterance to this word must be understood. After all, Black youth today both kill and greet one another in the name of the N word. There must be a reason and we must understand these reasons. And, once again Kam-unity, we will be duped if we do not look deeply into these matters. To have a half truth is to have a lie. There are two sides to every story and our story must be told in its completeness. We must look at this bridging that has occurred in language as the Metu Neter have gone out and what has happened as we crossed over that bridge. We must understand the unification in consciousness that language gives. We must also understand the fragmentation in consciousness that language can likewise give if it is used negatively. We must understand what has happened as we went from 'Kunta Kinte' to 'Tobe' and from 'Tobe' back again.

The N word brings us into an understanding of a state of Unitive consciousness and how as an Afrikan people we move from this Unitive State. This was a state of wholeness when we were with the Metu Neter, when we were with the divine speech of the Gods, when all that we built through the sounding of a 'word' reflected that divinity. As the Metu Neter moved out we began to experience fragmentation, separativeness, and brokenness in consciousness.

Understanding the N word is the pathway to understanding the resurrection of ourselves. We cannot get where we need to go using a Eurocentric paradigm that leaves many parts of our story out. We must move within an Afrikan Psychology which will tell the whole story. We cannot tell the story of Humanity's Psychological and Spiritual Journey of Unfolding Consciousness with all the necessary inclusivity unless we are willing to tell the truth about the greatness of the Afrikan Race, the Black Race. Any other story will only tell parts and pieces. As One Human Family we will move from a state of *piece and fragmentation* to a state of *peace and unification* when we see more fully and clearly.

Our day of being 'spooked up' is being concluded. Our day of confusion is being concluded. We have been told that there are secrets. But in my book, *The Secrets of Race and Consciousness,* one thing we will hopefully come to appreciate is that the *biggest secret* is that there are *no secrets*! All may be revealed to the illumined mind, to one who has a chastened heart, to one who is pure in Spirit. Have we not done the work as a people to have an illumined mind, to have a chastened heart and to be pure in Spirit?

It is time to access the secrets that were common place to us, like walking and talking and breathing - before they became the private enterprise for the few. I am called by our Ancestors to come before you to sound this Psychological and Spiritual alert. We must get ever so skillful in our treatment of the N word. Knowledge and bridging back from English to Metu Neter is the way that we will become skillful in resurrecting who we are. This is a special day and I give praise and appreciation to the initial bold steps taken by the NAACP in redeeming the N word. But we must hold an even greater awareness. In re-claiming our Kamitic Laws, the Law of Rebirth and the Law of Reincarnation, we must understand the knowledge that *there is no death*. So where there has been a so called 'burial' there must now be a process of redeeming and resurrecting. So let us come together as a Kam-unity to understand the knowledge necessary for this pathway. The Metu Neter, the Neteru are being belched up all over this Planet and they are speaking to us. They seek the redemption, the rise, the lift vibratorially that is to be accorded the divine words and speech of the Gods. Reading, *Ka Ab Ba Building The Lighted Temple* in conjunction with this book will:

1) Reveal the Spiritual and Psychological Journey of Unfolding Consciousness, the Afrikan Cosmology of Kamit and the Sacredness of the Cosmic Sun Egg, and the Higher Spiritual meaning of the N word(s).
2) Retrace, ferret out and dispel word meaning.
3) Dissipate the power to wound that the N word(s) has had as the Metu Neter have gone out into English.
4) Point the way toward healing so that we may return to the source of our greatness.
5) Offer revolution, revelation, deep thought, and resurrection out of the quagmire of confusion about words that have been used to describe, enslave, rob and kill the Black man and Black woman.
6) Wordsmith word meaning at both lower and higher spirals of vibration and dis-spell illusion so that we may reclaim and use power at its most optimal and divine Spiritual level of vibration.

Dr Nteri Renenet Elsong

Chapter 2
The Eldest Race On The Planet Is The Black Race

Our Story Continues...
We are all One Human Family. Yet, the Races within the human family do not emerge all at once during this 4th Round or World period in which we now live. The eldest Race on our Planet is the Black Race. In time other Races gradually unfolded, making their appearance on Earth. The Psycho/Spiritual Journey in Unfolding Consciousness takes us back into the night of time. Although just how far back in time continues to be debated, Esoteric estimates are giving to be around 18 million years ago •

A Round is a large cycle of time in which the human life wave progresses on our Planet.
Further description is given in a later chapter regarding the:

Metaphysical Key To:
The 7 Root Races
The Number 7 and
The Septenary Nature of Man and Creation

For now it is important to understand that:
1. As this life wave progresses the Races within the human family emerge.
2. We want to appreciate that in order to talk about Earth history and development in consciousness we must talk about Race
3. We cannot talk about the *emergence* of the human family and consciousness unless we talk about the Negroes
4. Thus we immediately confront the first major challenge within and across many fields of study

Who are the Negroes?
We must derive the Metaphysical and Spiritual meaning of the word Negroes and simultaneously the word Niger and Nigger. Let's begin to dispell the word <u>Negroes.</u>

John Jackson. *Man, God and Civilization*, p. 206.

> The fact is that the stereotype of the so-called Negro race corresponds to no reality in the World of objective phenomena. At the present time, in our own United States of America, anyone reputed to have an African ancestry, however remote, is supposed to be a Negro. Now, let us carry this thesis to its logical conclusion. Since there is overwhelming evidence that the human race originated in Africa, then all mankind has an African ancestry. **Hence, all men must be Negroes.**

★ *Negroes - Hence, All men must be Negroes.*

• See Barborka, Secret Doctrine, 24 Tibetan Books, Lemurian Scrolls, Rosocrucian Cosmo Conception., et al.

Let's take for further consideration these words by John Jackson, 'Hence, all men must be Negroes'. As we continue to dispell the name 'Negroes' we will see, *just how Metaphysically true his words ring forth.*

There is much debate within the Afrikan-American and Diaspora over the use of the 'Name' or 'word' Negroes. The names African-American, African, Black, have been adopted over time. The word Negroes will be used extensively in this text. This is not to raise any ones discomfort level. What we seek to do here is extract the Metaphysical Keys and Spiritual Meaning residing within this name. Name and word have power. This 'word' *can not* and *should not* be cast aside until we understand its deeper meanings. Then and only then can we make a more informed choice and *non-conditioned* response regarding the continuance or discontinuance in the use of this 'Name' or Neter as it is called by our Kamitic Ancestors.

As we seek to gain clarity on the name 'Negroes' and other Racial names we must continue to bear in mind that:
1. The Ancient Wisdom became 'splintered' as it was distributed throughout the World
2. There are those who have become the 'custodians' of the Ancient Wisdom
3. These custodians have had the 'stuff' of *Our Story* in places both private and public (libraries, museums, etc.)
4. In turn, these custodians have become the 'authors' of numerous 'derivative writings about the Ancient wisdom teachings. •

What are Custodians of the Ancient Wisdom?
These Custodians of the Ancient Wisdom fall into 3 distinct categories which are as follows:
1. The few who have been faithful to the care, safekeeping and appropriate transmission of the Ancient Wisdom
2. The many who offer watered down 'pop' versions that make entertaining reading for the consumer and money for the author. Many of these authors never bother to mention the more Ancient sources from which they derive ideas nor give acknowledgment to the Negroes or Black Race Ancestor from which they originate
3. The many who have hidden, obscured, refashioned and repackaged the Ancient wisdom in order to keep the masses away from it or confused by it.

Our Story Continues…
The interface of Anthropology, History, Science, Psychology, Esotericism, Social Science and related fields seeking to define issues of Race are fraught with and flawed by Western colonization. As regards Race, the 'Negro' has already been a hotly debated topic by those examining events in human history. This is revealed even in hitting the rewind over the small time frame of just 10,000 B.C.E. years into the past. A battle rages among and between these fields in terms of what to *'say or unsay'* about what they *'see or don't see,'* about the *'greatness or inferiority'* of who the Negro *'is or is not.'* Yet coming in view over the horizon are even greater debates over 'evidences' provided by these fields regarding human history dating back millions of

---

• See Secret Doctrine, 24 Tibetan Books, Lemurian Scrolls, Rosocrucian Cosmo Conception., Manly Hall et.al.

years. These evidences will likewise contain a massive amount of 'colonization'. This is expressed accordingly: John Jackson. *Man, God and Civilization,* p. 204.

> **It is of no profit to ask where the Negro came from, or to pontificate on the Negro Enigma, if we do not beforehand define the term** *Negro*; **and this, as far as we are aware, has never been done.** In Greco-Roman times the various people of Africa were known as Ethiopians. Europeans of the Middle Ages called all African Moors. In modern times certain African peoples were designated as Negroes. If you ask what is the difference between a Kushite, a Hamite, and a Negro, you can expect no concordant conclusion, for the so-called authorities on the races of mankind have never told us just what branch of the human species should be classified as Negroes.

Let's take for further consideration these words by John Jackson, 'for the so-called authorities on the races of mankind have never told us just what branch of the human species should be classified as Negroes'. There has been extensive (Esoteric) veiling of the Ancient Wisdom regarding the Races. This has contributed to much confusion and has served to hinder our ability to properly view the Psycho/Spiritual Journey of Unfolding Consciousness within the human family. We cannot wait for 'so-called' authorities. We must become the authorities
1. Through our awakening and remembering
2. Reinforced by our own research and penetrative analysis

One cannot tell the story of the Psycho/Spiritual Journey of Unfolding Human Consciousness with all the necessary inclusivity required, unless they are willing to tell the truth about the Greatness of the Black Race. One minute we are sages, the next moment we are savages. What a conundrum! Much in the literature draws a smaller circle that veils, degrades or is exclusive of the Afrikan root source and contribution. The pages that follow give insight into this journey. You will hopefully see that *Sage and Savage* belong to 'no one Race' but are inherent in the Psycho/Spiritual Journey itself.

Although fraught with racism, deceptive veiling and double speak, this literature *is not* to be disregarded. Instead it must be painstakingly mined through in order to garner the Ancient Wisdom. We must learn to read it from right to left, left to right, turning it inside out, outside in, upside down, and rightside up.

We must remember that the divine Trinity of Ka Ab Ba or Auset, Heru and Ausar (later re-named Isis, Horus and Osiris by the Greeks) is within. **Further description is given in a later chapter regarding the following Key(s):**

Metaphysical Key To: The Number 3 **The Divine Trinity** The Trinity/Triune Nature of Man/Woman and Creation Ausar, Heru, Auset BaAbKa or KaAbBa	**Metaphysical Key To:** The Story of Ausar, Auset and Heru The Divine Trinity

For now it is important to understand that:
As Heru the Karest within (later re-named the Christ) you must hold the waters or emotional body of Auset - the Divine Mother still, so that you may move past what has been inverted, distorted, and veiled in order to re-gain awareness and re-member the body of Ausar - the Divine Father, that has been broken into 14 pieces and scattered about.

What is the brokenness of the body of Ausar?
1. The brokenness of the body of Ausar is a key, symbolizing the brokenness in man and woman's consciousness of the divinity within.
2. It is likewise a symbol of the brokenness, separation and part-I-cularization in consciousness of the Divinity within the human family.
3. It is the result of the descent down the Tree of Life and the converging cycle(s) of time, which make up *The Perfect Storm,* in which we now live.

Chapter 3
Ka Ab Ba The Tree Of Life Reveals
Secrets of Race & Consciousness

The Story of Humanity's Psycho/Spiritual Journey in Unfolding Consciousness is revealed Within the Tree of Life.
As we proceed down and up the Tree of Life in our studies, acknowledgment is given to Ra Un Nefer Amen in his tremendous re-claim-ation work in the 'Naming of the Spheres' in the Tree of Life - Paut Neteru by the Kamitians. The Tree of Life is your Spiritual equipment both human and divine and a road map in consciousness. It has been veiled under Kabbalistic Names which has contributed to a disconnection with our Divine Trinity and African Deities.

What is the Tree of Life? *The Divine Cosmogram*
The Tree of Life is a divine Cosmogram to which Our Story may be appended. It acts as a template upon which the many pieces may find coherence and the dynamic movement of our divinity may be revealed.

The Tree of Life or Paut Neteru guides us in our re-ascent into Ausarian consciousness and thereby resurrection. It is our map and roadwork - back to the source - our Eternal Home. Your work in Metaphysical studies is to re-awaken to the Image and Likeness of God that 'is' and that 'you are' and have 'always been' from the beginingless beginning. You re-ascend by climbing up the Tree of Life. Each sphere on the Tree of Life is like a huge limb that you must gain firm footing upon before you can stretch up to the next limb in your climb. Firm footing is gained by your conscious experience within each sphere.

What is Ausarian Resurrection and Ascension?
Man/Woman grows 'down' the Tree of Life in his long involutionary descent into matter. Man/Woman grows 'up' the Tree of Life in his evolutionary re-ascent back to the *source*. The climb both - down and up - the Tree of Life, is the story of how man and woman both forget and then remember that which they have always been - Sons and Daughters of God. Through your study of the Tree you will learn the Metaphysical Keys to begin to *break the spell of illusion*.

1. We can make different sets of divisions within our constitution of which the Tree of Life is a symbol. This includes:
    a. Division into 3 primary triangles - KaAbBa or BaAbKa
    b. Division into 11 spheres (spheres 0 - 10) - The Neteru or qualities of the 11 Kamitic Deities
    c. Division into 7 Planes of Consciousness, 7 Divisions of Soul-Spirit - 7 Primordial Energies
2. Each division set gives us a different view and thus a variety of ways to gain a deeper understanding of the workings within our Spiritual Faculty
3. The divisions in the Tree of Life that we will examine in this and subsequent chapters will focus within the 3 primary triangles of Ka Ab Ba

4. As we will see these are the 3 Aspects of Divinity which make up our Spiritual Constitution, faculty or equipment which is both Divine and Human
5. As we examine these primary divisions, we will overlay onto the Tree of Life various systems or Metaphysical Keys for understanding the dynamic movement in the Psycho/Spiritual Journey of Unfolding Human Consciousness
6. Although each 'overlay' presents a more 'simplified' view of the Tree of Life as we go along in this text, it is suggested that the reader refer from time to time to the, 'Big Map' of the Tree of Life that is located in the Appendix -

Metaphysical Key To:
The Tree Of Life
The Big MAP

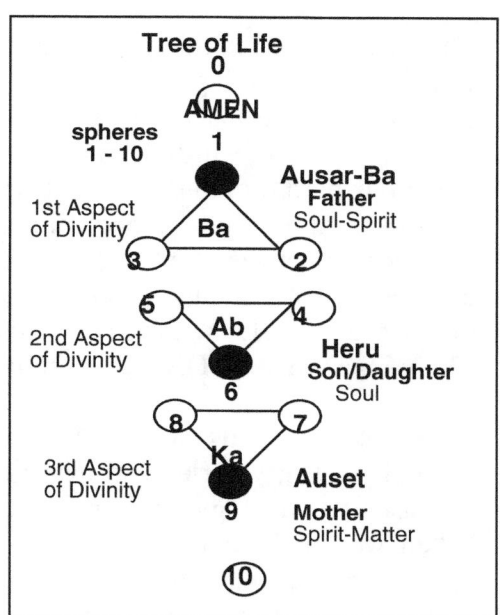

What does the divisioning of the Tree of Life into the 3 Primary Triangles or 3 aspects of Divinity look like?
We now focus within the 3 primary Triangles of Ka Ab Ba of the Tree of Life pictured at right. The Kamitians (later called the Egyptians by the Greeks) used picture images or ideographs from nature all around them to communicate ideas, which is the language called MTU NTR or METU NETER. These symbols were later called the Hieroglyphics by the Greeks. The Metu Neter, Ka Ab Ba, are pictured below.

Ka	Ab	Ba
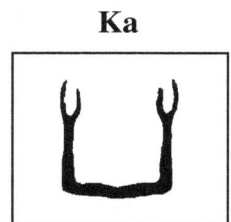	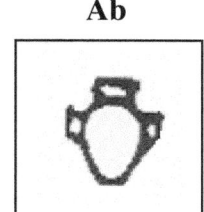	

On the Psycho/Spiritual Journey in Unfolding Consciousness what are you as the Sun-Son/Daughter becoming fully conscious of?
In the Metaphysical Keys that follow, you will see that Spirit takes of ITSELF and begins to differentiate itself in/as Spirit-matter. This is one of the many divine paradoxes. As much as Spirit is UNLIMITED and UNCONDITIONED it asserts its right to limit itself in form or matter to gain conscious experience of ITSELF. In various grades of material form, IT sees ITSELF. It is in *the seeing of ITSELF* that consciousness is born. Thus we are made human and divine, material and Spiritual.

For the Kamitians, Ka is Spirit and Ba is Soul. Soul is consciousness. Ab symbolizes the human heart. The heart is the seat of the Soul and growing Self conscious identity. The Ab Soul is the conscious experience of how Spirit and Matter are relating. It is how Father-Spirit has a conscious experience of Mother-Matter. As man's consciousness develops he must also develop a 'conscience'. This is Heru or the Karest/Christ principle within you that guides you to be and act in accord with the Universal Law of Right Relationship. Through the relating aspect of Ab, the 'seeming' duality between Spirit-Matter with its myriad objective forms in play and display as Ba Ka are seen as ONE. Thus through Ab Soul consciousness the same One True Self is seen in every other Self.

This is expressed in the diagram at right. On our Psycho/Spiritual Journey in Unfolding Consciousness as Heru - sphere 6 in the Tree of Life, we make our descent into material life conditions. As Heru we are Sun-Son/Daughter. On our return journey, we make our hard, arduous climb of re-ascent Home again, into the Spiritual realms. You are becoming fully conscious of the perfect relationship between Father and Mother and Spirit and Matter. To become fully conscious is to live the consciousness of Ausar Ba - that we are made in the Image and Likeness of God and All SELVES are but the ONE True Indivisible SELF.

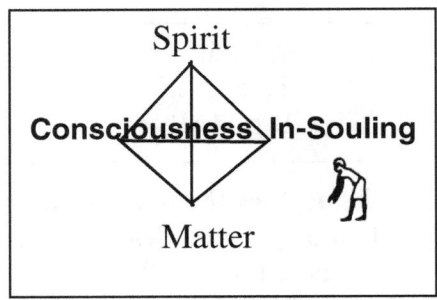

Why do we focus within the 3 Primary Triangles of Ka Ab Ba to understand the metaphysics, mysteries and meaning of Race & Consciousness?
The use of an analogy will serve as example to illustrate:
When we 'click' onto an icon on our computer Windows a whole panorama of information is opened and revealed to the awaiting and poised mind or mental field. Likewise the Metu Neter are like the icons of our Kamitic Ancestors. As we 'click' in turn onto the Ba, then the Ab, then the Ka Triangle of our Spiritual equipment, the Psycho/Spiritual Journey in Unfolding Consciousness is revealed. These ideagraphs or pictures are the 'divine idea and speech' which help open our 1st eye and aid us to glimpse within the Whole Moving Geometry in the Mind of God. Thus, as the journey unfolds, we are able to see the changing states in our consciousness that lead to changing states in our physical World. This brings us to the next -

> **Metaphysical Key To:**
> Ka Ab Ba and Movement Within
> The 3 primary Egoic states of Consciousness

The 3 Primary Egoic States in Consciousness may be observed as follows:
1. Consciousness may remain unitive
2. Consciousness can become dualized and reconciliative/combative
3. Consciousness may become separative or particularized into many parts.

Further description is given in a later chapter regarding the aforementioned Key(s):
For now let's begin to understand the *divine movement* in the Psycho/Spiritual Journey of Unfolding Consciousness by Meditating in turn within each of the 3 Primary Triangles of Ka Ab Ba.

As Afrikan Root Race man and woman you were like apprentices

Our Story Continues…

Movement within Ba consciousness
- In the divine workshop of the mind of God.
- You were witness to the *divinely intended archetypal* design
- Like a Puzzle Box Cover
- That was yet unbroken into its separate puzzle pieces
- Your 1st eye interior sightedness as - Afrikans/Negroes - Ego enabled you to see and behold
- The whole moving Geometrical Arrangement
- You beheld, as well as vibrated with the divine archetypal design and
- The divine ideation called the Khus by the Kamitians
- With your consciousness in seamless Unity of the One
- You were at play with the *simultaneity* of *All-at-once-ness* and *One-at-a-time-ness*

- With your individualization in consciousness and gradual involutionary descent down the Tree of life
- You became the Manes, as called by the Kamitians, or the Son of Mind, as called by the Esotericists.
- Manes, or mind, is the specific building material and tools needed to play the seeming game of *Go Out*
- You acquire the use of mind, thought, and imagination -
- In your descent down the Tree of Life
- From a more Spiritual consciousness into a material consciousness
- You move from the subjective to the objective World -
- You are **Master** at the dual action of *Going Out - Yet - Remaining within*
- The unbroken, seamless unity of the One
- You became co-creative apprentice
- You set out to work to fashion a World you beheld but now must co-create
- Perched here in your awareness
- All you built in the material World reflected the Spiritual
- You affirm:
- *I Know*
- *And*
- *All This is That*

Movement within Ab consciousness
- Yet cycles pass and the descent in consciousness down the Tree of Life begins
- As the game of *Go Out* further ensues
- You take long, long, loving looks at the Puzzle Box Cover
- To see if you can re-member the pattern of re-construction in the Grand Design
- In the early AfrikanSemitic Root Race consciousness cycle
- You are interiorly and Spiritually focused
- You express qualities of harmonizing, reconciling opposites, and holding the dualizing forces in nature (duality) in balance
- In your co-creative play you reference
- The Above with the *now sensed* Below and the DARK with the *now sensed* Light
- As you hold all in delicate balance you affirm:
- *I Know That I Know*
- And
- *This and That*

- Yet cycles continue to pass
- In the later AfrikanSemitic Root Race cycles
- You are gradually *Outed* in consciousness deeper into the World of physicality and materiality
- Your *Going out* upon the limited thought of lower mind would last longer and longer
- You became less and less focused on your ages long, ritual practice which
- Kept the circle in consciousness unbroken
- As you became more and more preoccupied with the play-thing-ness of thought in your awakening Mental Soul body - Het-Heru - sphere 7, (Higher Abstract Mind) and Sebek - sphere 8, (Lower Concrete Mind)
- Each thought is connected with an emotion in your awakening emotional Soul body - Auset - sphere 9
- Which would register as sensation of pleasure or pain in your awakening physical Soul body -Geb - sphere 10
- The connection was made in your circuitry to desire pleasure and avoid pain
- And the will to assert the lower self for what it wanted *grew*
- You became more dualized in consciousness and
- Less willing to reconcile seeming opposites and find harmony and balance
- As you dualized in consciousness this registered in your brain matter
- As you became more right brain hemisphere or left brain hemisphere focused
- You became less concerned about the bridging of 'This and That'
- And would now affirm:
- *This or That*

Movement within Ka (Ka-Ra-acter) consciousness
- And cycles continue to pass
- Knowing the divine archetypal design gave you play with
- The seeming Puzzle pieces against
- The backdrop of the seamless Unity and cohering, loving power of the ONE
- You could think:
- Separativeness, Multiplicity, Particularization, Division, Diversity, and
- Analyze it all
- As your desire grew you 'hung out' more and more and longer and longer in the play-thing-ness of lower mind, emotion and bodily sensation
- Your awareness became more and more trapped in your lower mental, emotional and physical Soul bodies
- These three lower bodies that you had been constructing over eons of time
- Were *just* to be your equipment, the instrument for the
- Higher Soul to do its work in the World
- They were *just* to be used as your tools for Building the Lighted Temple
- For the glory of the God indwelling you and
- To radiate Heaven on Earth and
- To reflect the Unity in all the manifest diversity in God's creation which is The Self
- So that you could affirm:
- *I Know the One and the same Self in all the seeming self appearances*
- *Approximating Ka is/as Spirit Ka*
- *I Know the One in the Many*
- *KaAbBa - I have come full circle*

- When you are as Auset you are ceaseless in your devotion
- To gather all the seemingly broken (puzzle) pieces of your beloved husband Ausar
- Into the seamless unity of the One
- You are the clear crystalline and luminous surface upon which
- The One True Self is reflected
- You are the Lighted Temple

- *Instead*
- The descent into a de-Spiritualizing cycle down the Tree of Life
- Takes you *headlong* into a more dense, materialization of consciousness
- You became encased and entombed in these lower bodies
- That became more dense and materialized upon the physical plane
- You now dangle, like a *particle* from the Higher Spiritual realms
- Through *thinking* - you *thought* - your self into less and less
- You became a part-I-cularization in your own consciousness
- And identified as/with a lesser self, that small part that you could still see
- Now that your eye has been torn out and torn into pieces by Set
- Gradually through the involutionary cycle
- Your citizenship within the Higher realms became a distant memory

Metaphysical Keys To the Tree of Life & Oracle Keys to Dispelling Illusion
The Psycho/Spiritual Journey of Unfolding Consciousness

- Forgetting the God indwelling and
- No longer seeking the treasure house of the Soul in Seket-Aarnru
- Your Heavenly Abode and Place of Peace - *Hotep*, as Gods and Goddesses
- You thought a lot about this lesser self and you thought you were 'it'
- Your citizenship upon the physical Earthly plane and the
- Seeming acquisition of all therein
- Became the treasured goal

- In your game of *Go Out* - like any game -
- There came the enthusiastic, yet wanton and childlike breaking up of the puzzle pieces
- So it is in your later AfrikanSemitcAryan Root Race consciousness cycle that you cry out, '*I can do it on my own, unaided, I need not reference or guide*'
- You are left to your own devices
- As the self is sensed more and more as separate from every other self
- You came to believe that you can *improve* upon God's design
- That you can take *some of the pieces* and *some of the laws* and put a thing called *Heaven on Earth* together
- Or was it Hell that you were intending as you fashioned
- Your own *designer and personalized World* creation
- And so it is with Man and Woman whose freedom it is to choose - *not to even* glimpse -
- The Puzzle Box Cover
- Who in blinded ignorance of the divinely intended architectural design and
- Bereft of the cohering power of Love
- Builds a World askew the divinely intended design and
- Boldly affirms:
- *This not That* and *That not This*
- Thus does mind become the *slayer of the Real* -The One True Self - Ausar
- Cut into fourteen pieces and cast apart

It is at first titillating to see the self as separate. It is a self that can take action, feel, think and use the will as power to acquire what it desires. Later, it becomes *frightful* to feel so 'seemingly' alone and isolated. How will you, 'Do it on your own' – that is, create Heaven on Earth? Or have we been creating our own Hell collectively as 3rd, 4th and 5th Root Race conscious humanity who is: 3-4-5 AfrikanSemiticAryan Жonsciousness Admixture ASA/KA. **Further description is given in a later chapter regarding the following Key(s):**

Metaphysical Key To:
Racial Name(s), and Number
3-4-5   AfrikanSemiticAryan - Konsciousness Admixture - ASA-KA

We further unveil the Secrets of Race & Consciousness *as* **Our Story Continues ...**

Chapter 4
Negroes
Name, Letter and Number are Neter – Metu Neter

This brings us to the next -

> **Metaphysical Key To:**
> Name, Letter, and Number are Neter – Metu Neter

As stated earlier the Kamitians used picture images or ideagraphs from nature all around them to communicate ideas which is the language called MTU NTR or METU NETER - a name which means, 'divine words and speech of the Gods'. The Ancient Wisdom of our Afrikan Ancestors tells us that Numbers and Letters are sacred and Divine Beings. Letters and Numbers are Oracles of God, acting as divine messages and messengers. These are the Ntr, Neter or Neteru (plural form) and known as qualities of God. Words are constructed by putting letters or Neteru together, that make up a 'name', sound a vibration and convey quality(ies) of divinity. Again it is important to remember that various vowels are added, substituted, and/or subtracted before or after the primal consonants used to make up a word and convey its meaning. The vowels lend themselves to facility in pronunciation.

These same Letters also correspond to Numbers as shown in the following table. Letter A corresponds to the number 1, B to the number 2 and so on. When numbers are double digit you add these together, then reduce them to a single digit (example: 16 = 1 + 6 = 7 = letter P).

Neteru				Number and Letter				
1	2	3	4	5	6	7	8	9
A	B	C	D	E	F	G	H	I
a	b	c	d	e	f	g	h	i
10	11	12	13	14	15	16	17	18
J	K	L	M	N	O	P	Q	R
j	k	l	m	n	o	p	q	r
19	20	21	22	23	24	25	26	27
S	T	U	V	W	X	Y	Z	
s	t	u	v	w	x	y	z	0
1	2	3	4	5	6	7	8	9

So as we begin to dispel the word, Neter or Name, 'Negroes' we start by appreciating that each Letter or Neter is a Divine Being, that is:
the 'N' is a divine being
the 'E' is a divine being,
the 'G' is a divine being
the 'R' is a divine being and so on

Every letter and every number is a divine being. When put together they act as Oracle or Messenger for the Gods. Yet, even as we begin our dispelling of the word, Neter or Name, 'Negroes', we find that the word itself is defined in the dictionary as 'sometimes offensive', something that would seemingly suggest a 'lower material vs. a Higher Spiritual vibration. This brings us to the next -

> **Metaphysical Key To:**
> Oracle Keys To Dispelling Illusion

Throughout this text the Oracle Metaphysical Keys to Dispelling Illusion will be used. A list of these Keys are located in the Appendix of this text. We begin here with –

#7. Oracle Metaphysical Dis-Spelling Key: Look up definition (dictionary, glossary, reference texts, etc.)

Definition: *Merriam-Webster Dictionary.*
Negro - 1. sometimes offensive: a member of the black race distinguished from members of other races by usually inherited physical and physiological characteristics without regard to language or culture; especially: a member of a people belonging to the African branch of the black race. 2. sometimes offensive: a person of Negro descent. Etymology: Spanish or Portuguese, from negro black, from Latin *nigr-*, *niger*. Date: 1555.

Definition: *American Heritage Dictionary.*
Negro - 1. A member of a major human racial division traditionally distinguished by physical characteristics such as brown to black pigmentation and often tightly curled hair, especially one of various peoples of sub-Saharan African. 2. A person of Negro descent: "Discrimination is a hellhound that gnaws at Negroes in every waking moment of their lives to remind them that the lie of their inferiority is accepted as truth in the society dominating them" (Martin Luther King, Jr.).

Nigger - n. Offensive. Slang. 1. Used as a disparaging term for a Black person: Used as a disparaging term for a member of any dark-skinned people.

So called 'Black people' are given many names. Accounts of the origin of the word Negro are expressed accordingly: J.A. Rogers. 100 *Amazing Facts About The Negro.* pp. 14, 40.

> The most ancient names for so-called black people are Nehesu, or Nubian; Ethiopian, and Moor from Ancient Egypt, and Negro or Nigrita from West Africa. All the above are native African words. "Negro" is probably the oldest as the Negritos are the oldest known branch of the human race. "Negro" comes from the River Niger. "Niger" found its way into Latin and since the people from that region were dark-skinned, Niger, nigra, nigrum came to mean black. Negro, Negrito, Negrita, means "the people of the great river." Black and colored, like white, are, on the other hand, European words. Ethiopian and Moor were probably used to describe the so-called black until 1500. Shakespeare uses "Negro" only once and uses it synonymously with Moor. Africa comes from the ancient Egyptian "Af-rui-ka," or Kafrica,
> the land of the Kaffir. from Proof, Miscellaneous:
>
> For the history of the word, "Niger" and "Nigrita" from which "Negro" comes, see Sir William Smith's Dictionary of Greek and Roman Geography, Vol. II, p, 429, as well as pp.296-7. Also Journal Royal Soc., Vol. II, pp. 1-28 (1832) by W.M. Leake, who says with regard to the African origin of "Niger," "More than one celebrated writer have fallen into the error of

supposing 'Niger,' a Latin word." Also Sir Rufus Donkine, "The Niger,"pp. 16, 144; and Gerald Massey, "A Book of the Beginnings," Vol. III, p. 610. For the origin of "Ethiopia," see Vol. I, p.36 of the latter work.

So we see here that the name Negro is also derivative from the word Niger, for the Niger River.

★*Negroes - Niger - the Black people of the Great River.*

Understanding the Spiritual and Metaphysical meaning of the name Negroes not only takes us into the night of time but forwards to demarcate a period in time when 'name' was given not only to Negroes, or Blacks the oldest humans (hue-mans), but also to other emerging 'races' of other 'hues'.

Fortunately, there is now a long list of Black historians who are extremely eloquent in the presentation of historical evidences over the last 10,000 years, which overwhelmingly draw the same conclusions about the Black race. You are referred to their researches as:
1. These are extensive
2. Their clarity wrests the contribution of the Black Race from its thralldom in the human heart and mind and much of the 'unsayings' by *others* have now become 'saids' by these authors
3. Such release allows all humanity to become more wholly conscious of the contribution by each Race - which together form the collective striving within the Human kingdom
4. It is this collective striving in consciousness that is being 'offered up' to The Lord of the World, The One in Whom we live and move and have our being – called Ausar Ba in the Kamitic tradition
5. The collective striving within each Root Race is the Global Consciousness - our Planetary Mind
6. Through our conscious re-collection, we are able to attain to Ausarian consciousness.

Since the works of these Chiefs should be read and meditated upon first hand I offer merest summary of some of their major conclusion and evidences. These are cited in the following accordingly:

Chancellor Williams. *The Destruction of Black Civilization,* p. 71.

> What we already know about the testimony of the Ancients proves that they did not use the vague term, "African race." From Herodotus to Diodorus, whom Maspero quotes, whenever they mentioned the Egyptian people, they specified that a Negro race was involved.

Cheikh Anta Diop. *African Origin of Civilization,* p. xiv.

> **The Ancient Egyptians were Negroes...**

Ibid. xv

> The triumph of the monogenetic thesis of humanity (Leakey)**...compels one to admit that all races descended from the Black race**, according to a filiation process that science will one day explain.

Dr Yosef A.A. ben-Jochannan. *Black Man Of The Nile And His Family,* p. 46.

> Dr Churchward attributed the entire continent of Alkebu-lan [Africa] to the so-called "PYGMY" and "NEGRO" – "True, Nilotic," and "Masaba, "Even the so-called "BUSHMEN" and "HOTTENTOT" came from the same source in Alkebu-lan where all mankind originated, including the so-called "CAUCASIAN"...

Chancellor Williams. *The Destruction of Black Civilization*, p. 77.

> According to Amelineau, this Black race, the Anu, probably created in prehistoric times all the elements of Egyptian civilization which persist without significant change throughout its long existence. These Blacks were probably the first to practice agriculture, to irrigate the valley of the Nile, build dams, invent sciences, arts, writing, the calendar. They created the cosmogony contained in The Book of the Dead, texts which leave no doubt about the Negroness of the race that conceived the ideas.

★*Afrikans/Negroes - Conceived ideas in the Book of The Dead, Prt Em Hru.*
★*Afrikans/Negroes - Charterer of cycles of time (calendar).*
★*Afrikans/Negroes - Seers into the divine architectural design (Cosmogony) and recorders.*

Cheikh Anta Diop. *African Origin of Civilization,* p. 68.

> Practically everyone agrees that until the fourth glacial epoch, flat nosed Negroids were the only humans. A South African scientist has recently declared that the first men were black, strongly pigmented, according to the proofs at his disposal. It was probably not until the fourth glaciation, which lasted 100,00 years, that the differentiation of the Negroid race into distinct races occurred, following a long period of adaptation by the fraction isolated and imprisoned by the ice: narrowing of the nostrils, depigmentation of the skin and of the pupils
> of the eyes. The four Glacial Periods of the Pleistocene Epoch include: The Gunz - 79,000 years ago, lasted 250,000; The Mindel - 480,000 years ago, lasted 50,000; The Riss - 240,000 years ago, lasted to 175,000; The Wurm -115, 000 years ago, lasted 90,000 (Cf. Palmer & Lloyd).

★*Afrikans/Negroes - the only humans until the Ice ages.*

Chancellor Williams. *The Destruction of Black Civilization*, p. 91.

> Thus, contrary to Moret's affirmation, authentic Egyptian tradition, as old as recorded time and written into the Texts of the Pyramids and the Book of the Dead, teaches us in unequivocal terms that the Egyptian deities belonged to the Black race and were born in the south. Furthermore, the myth of Osiris [read here: Ausar] and Isis [read here: Auset] points out a cultural trait characteristic of Black Africa: the cult of ancestors, the foundation of Negro religious life and of Egyptian [read here: Kamitic] religious life, just as Amelineau reports.

★*Afrikans/Negroes - Foundation of religious life and the Deities, the cult of the Ancestors.*

Cheikh Anta Diop. *African Origin of Civilization*, p. xvi.

The Ethiopians say that the Egyptians [read here: Kamitians] are one of their colonies which was brought into Egypt by Osiris [read here: Ausar]. They even allege that this country was originally under water, but that the Nile, dragging much mud as it flowed from Ethiopia, had finally filled it in and made it a part of the continent…They add that from them, as from their authors and ancestors, the Egyptians get most of their laws. It is from them that the Egyptians have learned to honor kings as gods and bury them with such pomp; sculpture and writing were invented by the Ethiopians. The Ethiopians cite evidence that they are more ancient than the Egyptians, but it is useless to report that here.

★ *Afrikans/Negroes - Law giver.*
★ *Afrikans/Negroes - Inventor of writing, sculpture.*

Chapter 5
Vibration, The WORD & Bridging Between the Metu Neter & English Language

What is the distinction between WORD and word?
Let's briefly review the following Key(s) from A.C.T.S. 1. Ka Ab Ba Building The Lighted Temple.

> **Metaphysical Law Key To:**
> The Law of Vibration

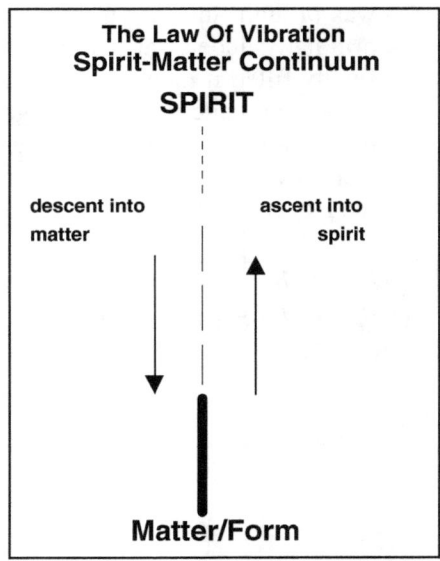

The Ancients knew that:
1. All is Spirit and that
2. Spirit periodically seeks to know ITSELF by reflecting itself into its dual aspect of Spirit-Matter
3. Spirit is matter at its lowest level of vibration and
4. Matter is Spirit at its highest level of vibration. (See *The Kybalion; Secret Doctrine*)
5. All in Universe is vibration
6. Spirit vibrates at the highest, fastest most refined level
7. Matter vibrates at a lower, slower more coarse or dense level

When we study the Kamitic Law of Vibration we understand that:
- From the beginningless beginning
- THE WORD is with GOD
- THE WORD has a Vibration
- Every Word that is derived from THE WORD, likewise has a vibration
- The Vibration carries the Neteru, the divine qualities of God
- We are THE WORD that is with God that has seemingly *gone out*
- To become the Word made flesh
- We are sounding a Word
- According to our vibration
- That is seeking to approximate the fullest measure of the WORD
- Our Temple is the manifestation of the WORD - God indwelling that we have always been from the beginningless beginning
- Our Temple is the WORD/Word made flesh

The Law of Vibration is seen operative along the Spirit-Matter continuum in what is called the involutionary and evolutionary cycles of human consciousness. This brings us to our next -

> **Metaphysical Key To:**
> Involutionary and Evolutionary Cycles
> The Spiritualization and Materialization in Consciousness

Secrets of Race & Consciousness Afrikan Cosmology of Kamit
with The Spiritual Meaning of The 'N' Word(s)
Neggur - The Goose Goddess who laid the Sun Egg, the Cosmic Egg

Revealed in Ka Ab Ba *(Kabala)* The Tree Of Life   Metaphysical Mysteries Meaning

Pictured in the diagram at right is the: **Involutionary and Evolutionary Cycles**

1. On the involutionary arc, consciousness makes its descent becoming more materialized. The vertex in the 'V' illustrates how Spirit has made its deepest descent into matter.
2. On the evolutionary arc, consciousness is making its return ascent and becomes re-spiritualized. Taken together this is the involutionary and evolutionary cycle of human consciousness.

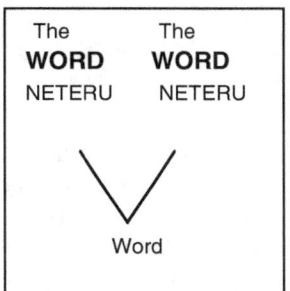

Pictured in the diagram at right we see that the WORD has *gone out* in its involutional descent into matter and returns in its evolutionary re-ascent into Spirit. **For more information see *A.C.T.S. 1. Ka Ab Ba Building The Lighted Temple* and refer to the aforementioned Key(s):**

For now it is important to understand:
Language as Unification in Consciousness
It is through language that some central unity may be realized. Language may aid this unification in consciousness that we seek in Ausarian Resurrection or it may block it. It is in language that an At-One-ing may occur between the Root Races that are running their course on the Planet. This is expressed accordingly: Albert Churchward. *Signs and Symbols of Primordial Man*, p.227.

> Gesture-signs and ideographic symbols alone preserve the early language in visible figures, and we are unable to get to the roots of all that have been pictured, printed or written, until we can decipher the figures made primarily by the early man. The latest forms of these have to be traced back to the most primary before we can get to know anything of the origins. These are the true radicals of language, without which the philologist has no final and adequate determinative; and yet these have been left hitherto outside the range of discussion by the Aryan School [read here: Aryan/European consciousness]. But the doctrine is prevalent in current philology, whilst the earlier sign-language has been ignored altogether.

> Whenever the ideographic sign of the oldest civilised nations can be compared, evidence of the original unity becomes apparent, and if we take the earliest inhabitants of any part of the World, we find from the skeletons that these were all of the same class-Negroid, just as we find in gesture-language that the further we go back the nearer is our approach towards some central unity. ...To know anything with certitude we must go back the way we came, along the track that only the evolution is free to pursue and explore. We know now that the dumb think, and that man had a gesture-language when he was otherwise dumb.

★*Afrikans/Negroes - If we take the earliest inhabitants of any part of the World, we find from the skeletons that these were all of the same class-Negroid.*
★*Afrikans/Negroes - Gesture-language that the further we go back the nearer is our approach towards some central unity...To know anything with certitude we must go back the way we came*

This quote further substantiates the erroneous assumption made by the Aryan/European mind which is that the Afrikans/Negroes did not or do not think. And continuing with above quote:

> Thus we see that the primary forms of language, so to speak, signs, symbols, ideographs, etc., were first written as a visible means of expressing articulate sounds. **This hieroglyphic language [read here: Metu Neter]** became afterwards a secret language, known and carried on from generation to generation, with secret meanings, the interpretation of which at the present day, as old, is only known to those who have worked and passed through the necessary examination to enable them to obtain that knowledge. But, inasmuch as we find the same hieroglyphics, sign, symbols, etc., in various parts of the World, also that the earliest race of beings were Negroid, it is but natural to believe that at one time these were universal, and that their birthplace must have had one common centre, which must have been Africa. "

★*Afrikans/Negroes - Metu Neter, Universal language that would become 'secret'.*
★*Afrikans/Negroes - Earliest Race of beings.*

And Likewise accordingly: H.P. Blavatsky. *The Veil of Isis* [read here: - The Veil of Auset], *V.I* p. 4.

> Max Muller states accordingly: Many things are still unintelligible to us, and the **hieroglyphic language [read here: Metu Neter]** of antiquity records but half of the mind's unconscious intentions. Yet more and more the image of man, in whatever clime we meet him, rises before us, noble and pure from the very beginning; even his errors we learn to understand, even his dreams we begin to interpret. As far as we can trace back the footsteps of man, even on the lowest strata of history, we see the divine gift of a sound and sober intellect belonging to him from the very first, and the idea of a humanity emerging slowly from the depths of an animal brutality can never be maintained again.

★*Afrikans/Negroes - Conscious and unconscious intentions.*
★*Afrikans/Negroes - Sound and sober intellect belong to him from the very first.*

The following gives reflection of the attitude toward the Afrikans/Negroes and the need to annihilate the central unity or base of language accordingly: W. Lynch. *Let's Make a Slave*.

> Cross-breeding completed, for further severance from their original beginning, **we must completely annihilate the mother tongue of both the nigger** and the new mule and institute a new language that involves the new life's work of both. You know, language is a peculiar institution. It leads to the heart of people.

★*Afrikans/Negroes - Language, leading to the heart of people.*

The Bridging Between the of Language of Metu Neter and English

We are in an ongoing process of trying to work back from the more primal symbols of the inner language and forward to that which is more exoterically expressed through Language. The Neteru called Letters and Numbers are the symbols used to give voice to the divine qualities of God. English is that language that Afrikan American and many Afrikan diaspora were forced to learn. In contrast, the Metu Neter of our Ancient Afrikan Ancestors had become a 'lost language' until the discovery of the Rosetta stone. This discovery assisted the work of Campolion in the re-translation of a language that had become silent with the destruction and closing of the Ancient mystery schools in Kamit.

English is an outer language that is both spoken and written all over the World, thus it is giving architectural design and arrangement to the World and World affairs. However, it is just a distillate of all other languages that have preceded it. English would suggest itself as the last place to look for derivation on what are '*Negroes*.' Nevertheless, someone said it well when they said, 'If you don't want someone to find something put it right under their nose.' In what follows we will use both the eldest language Metu Neter and the more recent language English to 'navigate our way Home' again - the Ausarian resurrection in consciousness. As stated in the previous quote, 'To know anything with certitude we must go back the way we came, along the track that only the evolution is free to pursue and explore'. Therefore the following diagram illustrates our movement in going back along the way we came:

Metu Neter ⟷ English

All of what I speak about - and the ability to wade through the Ancient wisdom is being guided by the Neteru. It is the Neteru who reveal themselves to me from behind the veils. From the *DARKNESS* of Unitive consciousness they cry out to us amidst all human efforts to keep the masses in the *darkness* of man's own making. The Earth itself belches up with loud retort the NETERU-*the voice of our Ancestors*.

Chapter 6
The Afrikan, Semitic, Aryan Root Races - The Present Planetary Consciousness
Racial Name(s), Number(s), and Physical Characteristics

As previously mentioned, there has been extensive (Esoteric) veiling of the Ancient Wisdom regarding the Races. This has contributed to much confusion and has served to hinder our ability to properly view the Psycho/Spiritual Journey of Unfolding Consciousness within the human family. Each Root Race is known by various Name(s), Number and physical characteristics. This brings us to the next-

> **Metaphysical Key To:**
> Racial Name(s), Number(s), and Physical Characteristics

What are the Root Races and how do the Races emerge? What is The Number and Name given by Esotericists for each Root Race?
First of all, do not become confused. We are all One Human Family. Yet, the Races within the human family do not emerge or make their appearance all at once during this 4th Round World period.

Presently, the consciousness of our Earth humanity is an admixture of Afrikan, Semitic and Aryan/European Races. Esoterically, these are also called the 3rd, 4th and 5th Root Races, with the 3rd being Ancient and elder and the 5th being recent and younger.*

1. The 3 Root Races now overlapping combine to form a consciousness admixture that I am describing in this text as:

> **3-4-5   AfrikanSemiticAryan - Konsciousness Admixture - ASA-KA**

2. Even though the 3rd, 4th, and 5th Root Races have certain physiological characteristics our focus is more about particular states of consciousness and how these are blending together at this time in our Earth history
3. Taken together they influence this World period. The Planetary *blending of consciousness* is what we confront as a Humanity in our next evolutionary steps
4. Our collective Psycho/Spiritual Journey leads us now to move from a state of separativeness and materialization in consciousness - which now dominates our Planet Earth - to that which is unitive, synthesizes and re-Spiritualizes

---

* The letter K has been substituted for the letter C in the word Consciousness. See *Metaphysical Keys to The Tree Of Life with Oracle Keys to Dis-spelling Illusion* in the Appendix for explanation.

5. We must understand the cycle of time in which we now live and the qualitative backdrop of energies available to lift us into the Ausarianization of consciousness and the re-Spiritualization of our Planet.

Racial Name(s) Number(s), and Physical Characteristics are further indicated in the diagram below:

Racial Name(s) Number, and Physical Characteristics

Racial Names/ Characteristics	Afrikan/Negro Black	Semitic Brown/Red/Yellow	Aryan/Caucasian/European White
Kamitic Naming[1]	Nehesu/Nuhes/ Nashi/Neshi/Nahsi	Aamu/Hemu	Themehu/Tamahu
Esoteric Naming[2]	3rd Root Race Lemurian	4th Root Race Atlantean	5th Root Race Aryan

Further description is given in a later chapter regarding the following Key(s):

Metaphysical Key To:
Racial Name(s), and Number
3-4-5   AfrikanSemiticAryan - Konsciousness Admixture - ASA-KA

Three Primary Races of men are depicted by the Egyptians who made no distinction between themselves and their Southern Ancestors called the Nehesu or Nubian. This is expressed in the carvings from the tomb of Rameses lll pictured at right and expressed accordingly: Anthony T. Browder. *Nile Valley Contributions to Civilization*, p. 61.

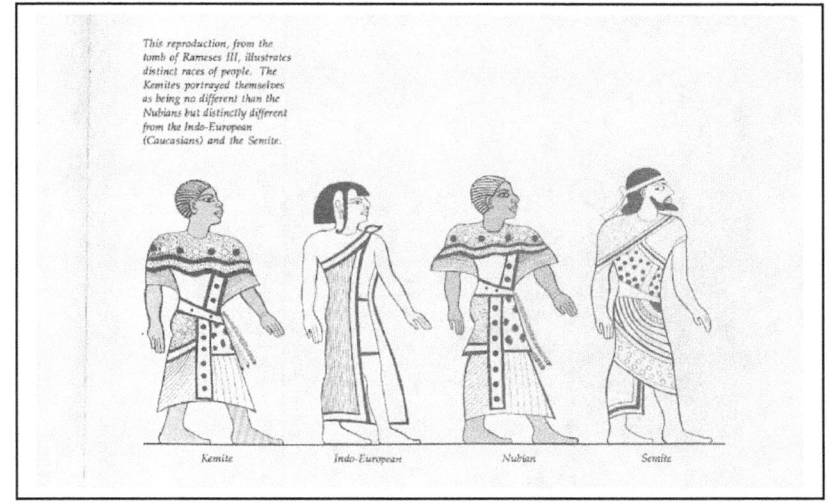

This reproduction, from the tomb of Rameses III, illustrates distinct races of people. The Kemites portrayed themselves as being no different than the Nubians but distinctly different from the Indo-European (Caucasians) and the Semite.

Historians are quick to note that the Nubians were often at odds with the people of Kemet, who often enslaved Nubian prisoners of war. But what is not commonly addressed is that the people of Kemet, while

---
[1] See Wallis. E. A. Budge. *The God of The Egyptians, V.I & II.*
[2] See Tibetan, *24 Books of The Tibetan*; Blavatsky, *Secret Doctrine;* Barborka, *Divine Plan;* Heindell, *Cosmo-Conceptions;* et al.

acknowledging geographical and political differences between themselves and the people of Nubia, did not denote any physical differences. Carvings from the tomb of Rameses lll (1200 B.C.E. portray the Nubians and Kemites as identical and Indo-Europeans and Semites as profoundly different in physical appearance and dress. It is as foolhardy to suggest that the people of Kemet were phenotypically different from their Nubian, Sudanese or Ethiopian neighbors, as it is to suggest that the people of France, Switzerland and Germany are phenotypically different from one another. With the exception of southern African countries, national boundaries have done more to distinguish cultural and political differences than racial differences.

Three primary Races of men called the Nehesu (African/Negro), the Aamu (Semitic), the Themehu (Aryan) are described by the Black Race Kamitians. In the Kamitic creation story the Nehesu has brought forth millions of men and women and this is expressed accordingly: E. A. Budge. *The Gods of The Egyptians, V.I,* p. 304.

"Ye are the tears made by my Eye in your name of 'Men.'"
The Aamu (i.e., the Semitic nomad tribes of the Eastern Desert), were created by Horus and Sekhet, and this goddess protected their souls; the Themehu, or Libyans, were also created by Horus and Sekhet, and the goddess protected their souls. Of the Nehesu, (i.e., the Negroes), Horus says, "I masturbated for you, and I have been content at the millions who have come forth from me in your name of Nehesu; Horus hath created you, and it is he who hath protected their souls."

Chapter 7
The Seven Root Races
The Number - 7 The Septenary Nature of Man and Creation

What is the Septenary Nature of Man and Creation? The Number 7.
Let's briefly review the following Key(s) from A.C.T.S. 1. Ka Ab Ba Building The Lighted Temple

> **Metaphysical Key To:**
> The Septentary Nature of Man and Creation
> The Number 7

The Septenary is 7, and 7 is Number. Number is Ntr, or Neter to the Kamitians. Neter or Number provides the vehicle through which the Deities or qualities of God may speak. The Septenate is one such numerological template in consciousness upon which unfolding events take place that express divinity. In the process of creation there is the arising of 7 primordial conditioning powers. The Ancients knew the divisioning of the nature of Man and Creation into 7 Elementary powers. These 7 discrete qualities of energy are a divine template giving geometrical arrangement and qualifying life throughout creation.

The Kamitc Goddess Ta-urt and the Creative Process
Our story is told through the Kamitic Goddess called Ta-urt. She is the first Mother who was of no sex and is called the Divine Mother and Protector. She is represented as a pregnant hippopotamus and pictured in the diagram at right. She is provider of food and life and out of her, the 7 elemental powers are born This emanation or divisioning into the 7 septenary or heptenary - is likewise later expressed as the body of consciousness of Ausar in the following accordingly: Gerald Massey, *Ancient Egypt, Light of the World. V. 1, p.* 409.

Ta–urt
Great Mother
Protector/Protractor
Hippopotamus
Goddess

> When the Supreme Being had been imaged or personified, the powers previously extant were represented as his offspring, his names, or members of his body. Hence the seven associate-gods, the Ali or Elohim, are now called the limbs, joints, the hands, the fingers, the lips, the teeth, the breath of god, or reversely stated, these parts of the one god become the associate gods, as a seven-fold emanation from Kheper-Ptah.

We see here in our story how the Great Mother and her seven elemental powers were now superseded by the combined god - Kheper - Ptah - in which both sexes were included in the one-Supreme Being who was now the Lord over all - Ausar. Accordingly: Ibid:

There was no God the father without God the mother and God the child.

Ausar expressing as Kheper and Ptah is the opener and Great Architect Of The Universe. These 7 powers qualifying all creation and guiding material expression in life are called by many names which include: 7 Elohim, the 7 Glorious Spirits, The 7 Primordial Energies, 7 African Powers, 7 Khuti, 7 Ari, Ali, 7 Spirits before the Throne, 7 Stars in Ursa Minor - The Little Bear, 7 Annuaki, 7 Angelic Powers, the 7 Ra(y)s, and the 7 Souls of Ra.

What are the 7 Root Races?
In transmitting the Ancient wisdom via the Esoteric teachings (see Secret Doctrine et. al) various writers reveal the application of the Septenary Law in Numbering the unfolding of the 7 Root Races. This brings us to the next –

> **Metaphysical Key To:**
> The 7 Root Races
> The Septentary Nature of Man and Creation
> The Number 7

This numbering is reflective of the divine Septenary template and provides much meaning as we shall see. To the extent that an Esoteric teaching looks at the 7 as it relates to creation and how the deities are qualifying *each* of the Root Races is Metaphysically *sound* and correct. We now use this Metaphysical Key to see its display as it makes 7 divisions and creates 7 Root Races within the Human Family.

We must look for the recurrence of the 7 Glorious Spirits or Neteru throughout creation. The power of the Neteru speak regardless of any author's attempt to 'doublespeak,' veil, blind, or conceal the Ancient wisdom. No veiling can conceal the Metaphysical law of the Septenary nature within creation. This law is *just as:*

1. 'Discoverable' back in the night of time in regard to - The 7 Root Races - as it is
2. 'Discoverable' in the recent present in regard to - The 7 Principles reclaimed through the works of Dr. Maulana Karenga in the Kwaanza celebration
3. 'Discoverable' as the 7 days of the week. Time is an illusion, the unreal, a structure in consciousness that keeps everything from happening 'all at once'. The Real is the Eternal Now
a. Yet we 'use time' and operate on the awareness that there are 7 days in a week, each of the 7 days has its own quality of Planetary energy, i.e. Sunday (Sun), Monday (Moon), Tuesday (Mars), Wednesday (Mercury), Thursday (Jupiter), Friday (Venus), Saturday (Saturn) and so on
4. We can appreciate for the sake of having a so called 'conscious experience', the division of time into 7 days a week
5. Likewise - we can appreciate for the sake of having a so called 'conscious experience', the simultaneous 'All-at-once-ness' and 'One-at-a-Time-ness' of the Races unfolding within the 'One' Human Family

The Ancient Wisdom tells us that in cycles of time called Rounds the following is occurring and will occur:

7 Root Races will unfold

a. These are numbered as the 1st, 2nd, 3rd, 4th, 5th, 6th, and 7th Root Races. Each Root Race has its correspondence with one of 7 Numbers or Ntrs
b. Each emerges upon the Planetary or World stage accordingly
c. Each Root Race makes its appearance against the backdrop of a specific cycle in time
d. Each cycle has its own quality of energy that conditions the degree of Spiritual versus material vibration of consciousness expressed by the Root Races
e. 5 of the 7 Root Races have made their appearance on the Planet. These are the 1st, 2nd, 3rd, 4th and 5th Root Races
f. Currently, only the 3rd, 4th, and 5th Root Races are simultaneously fully 'visible' and running their course of unfoldment on the Planet.
g. The 1st and 2nd Root Races were a more ethereal, subtle and amorphous form - therefore there is not 'evidence' that gives them 'appearance' on our Planet now
h. It is in the 3rd Root Race - Negro/Black that a more densely, compacted form emerges that is both Divine and Human

★*Afrikans/Negroes - The 3rd Root Race is the 1st form that is both Divine and Human.*

i. Insight into the Godlike and ethereal nature of the 1st, 2nd, and 3rd Root Races is revealed in the following accordingly: Thomas Burgoyne. *The Light of Egypt*, p. 97-98.

> The first race of human beings that existed upon this planet was really spiritual. Their bodies were quite **ethereal,** when compared with our gross organisms, but were sufficiently material to be objective and tangible. They were pure and innocent, true Adams and Eves, and their country was indeed a garden of Paradise. They were natural born adepts of the highest order. They played with the **Akasha** and the magnetic currents of our globe…The elementals and nature spirits were, by their art, rendered objective, and performed the duties of servants to them. This was the true Golden Age. It was the first spiritual race of human beings; the progenitors of humanity upon our Earth. The race which followed them was termed the Silver Age in the arcane doctrine… Both these races, and also **the third [read here: Afrikan/Negro],** viz., the people of the Copper Age, when they wished to die passed peacefully away, and their bodies were immediately disintegrated by the currents of vril. This, the Copper Age, was the last remnant of those **who inherited the Divine Wisdom of the Gods of the Golden Age.**

★*Afrikans/Negroes - Inheritor of the Divine Wisdom of the Gods of the Golden Age.*

Let's dispel the word <u>ethereal</u>:

#7. Oracle Metaphysical Dis-Spelling Key:

Look up definition (dictionary, glossary, reference texts, etc.)
<u>Ethereal</u> - Of the celestial spheres; heavenly. Not of this World; spiritual. Characterized by lightness and insubstantiality; intangible. 2. Highly refined; delicate.

Before going forward, let's take for closer examination in this quote the words, 'both these races, and also the third…the last remnant of those who inherited the Divine Wisdom of the Gods of the Golden Age.' This reference to the third is the 3rd Negro/Black Root Race. This is an obvious admission that the Afrikans/Negroes are the inheritor of the Divine Wisdom. We will not be able to discern what is unfolding in consciousness within the Root Races until we lift the veil on both Name and Number.

Further description is offered on the 5 Root Races who *have* unfolded accordingly: The Tibetan. *The Treatise On Cosmic Fire*, p. 121.

> The Secret Doctrine teaches us that in this evolution or Round on this planet the Jivatma [read here: Ba - Soul - according to the Kamitians] - **the human soul - passes through seven main types or "rootraces."** In the case of the two earliest of these, known as the "Adamic" and the "Hyperborean," the forms ensouled were astral and etheric respectively: "huge and indefinite" they were with a low state or outward-going consciousness exercised through the one sense (hearing) possessed by the first race, or through the two senses (hearing and touch) possessed by the second. **But with the third race the Lemurian [read here: Afrikan/Negro], a denser and more human type was evolved,** this being perfected in the fourth or Atlantean race [read here: Semitic]. The fifth race, the Aryan [read here: Aryan/European], is now running its course on this globe concurrently with a large part of the fourth race and a few remnants of the third. For it must be noted that, although each race gives birth to the succeeding race, the two will overlap in time, coexisting for many ages. Of existing peoples the Tartars, Chinese and Mongolians belong to the fourth race, the Australian aborigines and Hottentots to the third.

Before going forward, let's take certain notices in this quotation:
Firstly - With the pervasiveness of the Negro/Black Race on the Planet to call the 3rd Root Race a remnant can only be construed as a racist term which serves to feed a policy of genocide. Likewise we witness a case of 'seeing but not saying' the obvious when H.P. Blavatsky mentions the Australian, and Hottentot, but fails to mention the Afrikans/Negroes as genesis of both.
Secondly - Let's take for closer examination the words, 'But with the third race the Lemurian [read here: Afrikan/Negro], a denser and more human type was evolved'. This is obvious reference to the Negro/Black Race in which God indwelling is now expressing through a Spiritual Constitution (Vessel/Temple) that is both Divine and Human.

★*Afrikans/Negroes - God indwelling is now expressing through a Negro/Black Race Spiritual Constitution (Vessel/Temple) that is both Divine and Human.*

j. The last two Root Races have yet to make their 'full appearance' within the World cycles of time. These are the 6th and 7th Root Races
k. Each Root Race in turn expresses 7 sub-races, and the sub-races further divide into branch Races and family Races until the Earth is variously populated

Further description is given in a later chapter regarding the following Key(s):

Metaphysical Key To:
The 7 Root Races
The Septenary Nature of Man and Creation
The Number 7

Chapter 8
Our State of Unitive Consciousness Changed Over Eons Of Time
The 1st Eye and Unbroken Consciousness of the Afrikan/Lemurian?

What was this Unbroken Consciousness of the Afrikan/Lemurian?
Our state of Unitive consciousness changed over eons of time and so did our relationship with ourselves, nature and the World around us. This consciousness is called by many names which includes: Unitive, All Consciousness, God or Ausarian Consciousness, Omniscient Consciousness. According to: Max Heindel, *Rosicrucian Cosmo-Conception,*
p. 216.

> Before the beginning of the Saturn Period the virgin spirits who are now man, were in the World of Virgin Spirits, and were "All-conscious" as God in whom (not from whom), they were differentiated. They were not "self" conscious however. The attainment of that faculty is partly the object of evolution which plunges the virgin spirits into a sea of matter of gradually increasing density which eventually shuts it from the All-consciousness.

★ *Afrikans/Negroes - Are All consciousness then they become self consciousness*
★ *Afrikans/Negroes - Virgin Spirits who differentiate out of the All Conscious to become conscious virgin spirits.*

And Continuing: Ibid. p. 278:

> The Lemurian [read here: Afrikan 3rd Root Race consciousness] knew no death because when, in the course of long ages, his body dropped away, he entered another, quite unconscious of the change. His consciousness was not focused in the physical World, therefore the laying aside of one body and the taking of another was no more to him than a leaf or twig drying and falling away from the tree and being replaced by a new growth.

★ *Afrikans/Negroes - Knew no death.*

What was the consciousness of the Original Humans? The Afrikan Root Race when focused in the Ba Triangle of the Tree of Life.
Our Black Race Ancestors saw interiorly and in wholeness. This is a consciousness of Unity and Synthesis. Their consciousness was poised within the Higher Ba and Ab Triangles of their Spiritual equipment, symbolized by the Tree of Life. This is later described. They went out as *knowers* and populated the World. They possessed the 1st, or inner eye, which gave them innersightedness and revealed to them the whole moving geometry within the Mind of God. Thus they were poised within Divine Mind, which is symbolized as the Kamitic deity Tehuti - sphere 2. This sphere has correspondence with the 2nd Soul body called the Khu and is pictured in the diagram at right. Within this sphere resides divine ideation or the archetypal lives

called the Khus by the Kamitians. This is divine intelligence. As Divine Mind, Tehuti is like the Puzzle Box Cover of a 'seemingly' multitudinous piece puzzle.

Innersightedness allows you glimpses of the Puzzle Box Cover of the great architectural design and plan of creation and manifestation. Our Ancestors had inner-sight of the underlying unity in nature. Within the whole moving geometry of the Puzzle Box Cover of the Great Design of Creation, the seamless unity, interconnection and interdependence throughout creation is viewed. Wholeness and unbrokeness in consciousness is the Reality. This inner wisdom or Tehuti faculty within is the Synthesizing Power Of Love and Wisdom. This power holds and coheres the seeming myriad pieces or part-I-cularizations of the to-be created forms in *the seamless unity of the One*. This power keeps the *circle in consciousness unbroken*. This brings us to the next –

Metaphysical Key To:
Restoration of The 1st Eye
Overcoming impediment # 2
Blindness

The Afrikan 3rd Root Race - later described - had inner-sight of the underlying unity in nature. The latter Races would lose this innersightedness which is registered through the power of the 1st eye. Today we are working to restore our 1st eye. This is indicated accordingly: H.P. Blavatsky. *Secret Doctrine, V.II*, p. 306.

> The possession of a physical third eye [read here: first eye], we are told, was enjoyed by the men of the Third Root-Race [read here: Afrikan/Negro] down to nearly the middle period of Third Sub-race of the Fourth Root-Race, when the consolidation and perfection of the human frame made it disappear from the outward anatomy of man. Psychically and spiritually however, its mental and visual perceptions lasted till nearly the end of the Fourth Race [read here: AfrikanSemitic] when its functions, owing to the materiality and depraved condition of mankind, died out altogether before the submersion of the bulk of the Atlantean continent.

What is the 1st Eye?

As previously stated, this eye is erroneously called the 3rd eye. The 1st eye in man and woman has its correspondence with the eye of Ra. As Creation arises within the waters of space, called Nun by the Kamitians, it is the eye that *sees and knows*.

We have been using the more imperfect geometric square or Puzzle Box Cover to give example of the 1st eye. In order to understand the 1st eye we now move to the more perfect geometrical figure of a sphere. Imagine holding a soccer ball and noting its outer design of polygon shapes. Now imagine standing in the center within the soccer ball with each polygon shape in its patterning acting as a mirror. The 1st eye is like a sphere of reflecting mirrors. It is what gives us full circumference or full circle seeing – that we may s*ee* from all sides and in all directions. Standing within this magnificent mirrored spherical 1st eye, you are increasingly able to see that each mirror reflects its relationship to every other mirror. As you scan all around this sphere you are simultaneously able to:

1. Survey each mirror - seeing each individuated reflection, perspective and point of view it holds and

2. Glimpse the synthetic wholeness held in the full spherical sight of the entire moving geometry

When your awareness is poised within the unbroken Omniscient consciousness of the Tehuti faculty - sphere 2, you are moving within 3rd Root Race consciousness and are able to behold in fullness - the whole moving geometry of the Divine Design. When poised within Unbroken Omniscient consciousness, our Ancestors were guided by this invisible inner patterning. The higher impress of Divine mind and ideation was at work within them. The way to arrange the affairs of life is revealed in order to manifest the divinely intended archetypal design. They were able to intuit the design and to instantaneously *know* how the pieces fit. Thus, divinity was made manifest in all that was constructed. They walked as Gods and Goddesses and Heaven and Earth were made one.

The latter Races would lose this innersightedness which is registered through the power of the 1st eye. Events would occur where man began to experience a 'brokeness in consciousness'. Man's consciousness gradually became more exteriorly focused. His reality moved from:
1. Being one of inclusiveness, Spiritually and interiorly focused in the Spiritual World to
2. Becoming one of separativeness, exteriorly focused and materially driven by the outer World
3. He began to lose innersightedness and thus the ability to glimpse the Puzzle Box Cover of the grand design. In other words, he suffered a gradual loss of the whole or 'bigger picture'.

In his increasingly narrowing focus, he came to see separateness more and more among the puzzle pieces. He saw himself as separate from other created beings. Changes already abrew in the Afrikan/Black 3rd Root Race would be starkly registered during the later part of the Semitic 4th Root Race, where the balance would be tipped before their deepest registration within the Aryan/European 5th Root Race. The quality of consciousness would gradually shift from being Unitive to Separative. Not only would man lose sight of how to arrange or put back the puzzle pieces. Equally important, an increasing perception of separation between *all* entities would diminish the cohering, vitalizing power of *L-o-v-e* that holds all in unity and sees *all things as new*. In the cycles to come Might would win over Right.

★*Afrikans/Negroes - The 1st eye, apprentice in the workshop of Divine Mind.*
★*Afrikans/Negroes - Witness and observer of the whole moving geometry in the Mind of God.*

Consciousness is unfolding as we move from Afrikan, to Semitic, to the Aryan Root Race. Personal will is being exercised and each Root Race can choose to build in accord with the divine architectural design for creation Each may likewise choose to fashion its own 'designer World' without even making reference with the 'Puzzle Box Cover' of the grand archetypal design. Thus do we build a World askew the divinely intended design.

Today we are working to restore our 1st eye in order to avert World catastrophe.

We further unveil the Secrets of Race & Consciousness as, **Our Story Continues …**

Chapter 9
Afrikans/Negroes Naturally Born Initiates Into Mysteries of the Universe Who Did Not Need Temples of Initiation for Instruction on His High Origin

How has each Root Race used this power and what has been the cost?
Accordingly: HPB. *The Secret Doctrine V.l,* p. 318-319.

> Civilisation has ever developed the physical and the intellectual at the cost of the psychic and spiritual. The command and the guidance over his own psychic nature, were with early Humanity innate and congenital, and came to man as naturally as walking and thinking... But they have become **"Secrets"** only in our race, and were public property with the Third [read here 3rd/Afrikan Root Race].

Accordingly: *Secret Doctrine, V. ll.* p.134.

> It is that Third [read here: Afrikan], the last semi-spiritual race, which was also the last vehicle of the divine and innate Wisdom...The Fourth, which had tasted from the fruit of the Tree of Good and Evil-Wisdom united already to earthy, and therefore impure, intelligences-had consequently to acquire that Wisdom by initiation and great struggle.

These are key words here.
Let's take for a closer examination the words: '...civilisation has ever developed the physical and the intellectual at the cost of the psychic and spiritual.' These statements do not seem to be readily acknowledged by the so-called modern Western World. People of the World who try to hold onto the 'unbroken consciousness' of the 3rd and even early 4th Root Races are called primitive, backwards, underdeveloped. Yet the Spiritual poverty of the so called 'modern' World must be viewed in counterbalance with the material poverty of the so called 'underdeveloped' World.

Let's take for a closer examination the words: '...Secrets...were public properly with the Third. This is reference to the 3rd/Afrikan Root Race. Only by finding such balance are we made 'inner-sensed' and in a state of 'innocence'. Thus, are we attuned to or given 'secrets'.

Let's take for a closer examination the words: 'The command and the guidance over his own psychic nature, were with early Humanity innate and congenital, and came to man as naturally as walking and thinking...' This may make us take stock that *Omniscient* consciousness is our natural state of consciousness. This consciousness is known by various names. It is called Ausarian, or Ba consciousness by the Kamitians, Monadic consciousness by the Esotericist, and Nirvanic consciousness by the Hindus.

And finally -
Let's take for a closer examination the words: '...But they have become "Secrets" only in our race,' The reference here in the Secret Doctrine to 'our race' means the 5th Aryan Root Race - the most recent Race to make its appearance on our Planet. The statement attests to how man and woman must trod back up the Tree of Life through a process called 'stages of initiations.' There is

an admission here that the Afrikan/Negro had no need for 'initiation' into the so called 'mysteries', that s/he just lived and breathed Omniscient consciousness as a stabilized conscious awareness.

What is Initiation?
Initiation is the successive process of expansion in consciousness, which is our return to the inner-sightedness of the whole. It is your growing awareness upon 'each' of the 7 planes of consciousness (latter described) as you make your 'conscious re-ascent.' Initiation by initiation you ascend the 'rungs of the ladder' up the Tree of Life. With each 'rung' upward you are sounding a Higher Spiritual vibration, a higher appeal. Each sounding is the release of the encapsulated 'lesser self' on the way to embracing more - the One True Self. It is through these stages of initiation that so-called secrets are again revealed whereby man 're-members' how to put his 'broken consciousness' back together again - thus realizing, the Unity of Spirit. Today the disciple must move through stages of initiation in his re-ascent up the Tree of Life. Ausarian resurrection is a return to Unity or God consciousness. A consciousness we left when we 'seemingly' left our Father's Home.

- In the ages that would lead man and woman in their
- Involutionary descent and despiritualization in consciousness.
- The 'ways' of innate inner knowingness and wholeness
- Would become the veiled and concealed 'secrets'
- Withheld from the masses of humanity
- Leaving them to *grope* in the dark
- Trying to find 'their way Home.

Accordingly: Max Heindel, *Rosicrucian Cosmo-Conception,* p. 280-281.

> The Lemurian [read here: Afrikan/Negro] was a born **magician.** He felt himself a descendant of the Gods, a spiritual being; therefore his line of advancement was by gaining not spiritual, but material knowledge. The Temples of Initiation for the most advanced did not need to reveal to man his high origin; to educate him to perform feats of magic; to instruct him how to function in the desire World and the higher realms. Such instruction is necessary today because now the average man has no knowledge of the spiritual World, nor can he function in super physical realms.

★ *Afrikans/Negroes - Born magicians. A Spiritual being who did not need Temples of Initiation for instruction of his high origin. Naturally born initiates of the Mysteries of the Universe.*

Do you still think you are part of an advanced humanity living in the modern Western World? So let's see if we get this. As 3rd Root Race Afrikans/Negroes we were 'outed' from our unbroken contemplation of the Divine so that as we 'advanced' to become 4th Root Race Semitic and later 5th Root Race Aryan consciousness we would gain mastery in the physical realm. But in the state of Aryan consciousness something has gone horribly *Awry*. Instead of Earth being seen as the manifold Glory of God and its resources being used in reverence and dance of that Glory our Mother Earth is looked upon as a whore to be pillaged, plundered and raped of all that can be greedily taken from her.

Chapter 10
The So Called Pythagorean Theorem
3-4-5   AfrikanSemiticAryan - Konsciousness Admixture - ASA-KA

For now we return to a previous -

> **Metaphysical Key To:**
> Racial Name(s), and Number
> **3-4-5   AfrikanSemiticAryan - Konsciousness Admixture - ASA-KA**

Now where have we seen the Numbers or Neteru 3-4-5 before? The so called 'Pythagorean theorem.
The so called 'Pythagorean theorem' states that in a right triangle the sum of the square of the legs is equal to the square of the hypotenuse. This is expressed accordingly: Anthony Browder. *Nile Valley Contributions to Civilization.* p. 108.

> The dimensions of the King's Chamber (34'f'' in length x 17'2" in width x 19'1" in height) are most significant because they express two ratios of the "Pythagorean Triangles"
> ($A^2 + B^2 = C^2$). The pyramid builders were obviously familiar with these sacred triangles thousands of years before Pythagoras was supposed to have introduced them. These same basic geometric principles were referred to by Plato as the building blocks of the cosmos.

This is expressed in the diagrams below. In the first diagram we see the 3-4-5 right triangle which was well known to the Ancients. It is seen reflected in the construction of the 3 Pyramids of Giza in Kamit, which are the Great Pyramid or Khufu, Khafre and Menkaure.

This is pictured in the second diagram.(See William Eisen. *The Cabalah of Astrology*, p.102 -104 for greater detail. The Kamitic deity Min is pictured in the third diagram. He is the God of fertility and power and is further described later.

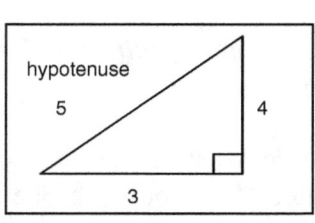
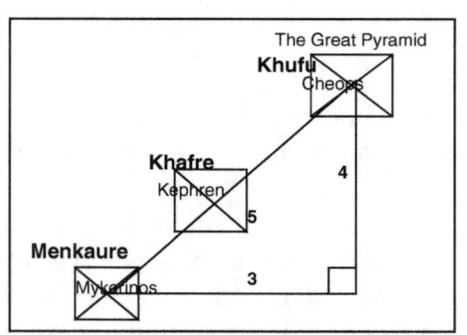
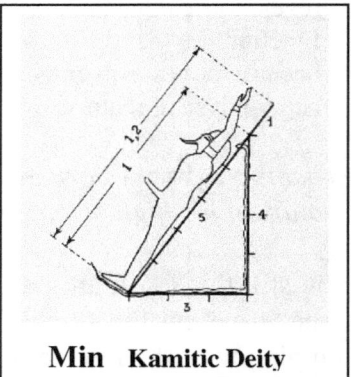

Min   Kamitic Deity

Furthermore, we see the mathematical derivation of the number 7 in this formula.
$$3^2 + 4^2 = 5^2$$
$$9 + 16 = 25$$

25=25
(2+5) = (2+5)
7 = 7

Race and the Psycho/Spiritual Journey of Unfolding Consciousness
This brings us to the next -

> **Metaphysical Key To:**
> Read from the angle of consciousness and not just from the angle of the physical form that each Root Race is manifesting through.

Presently, the consciousness of our Earth humanity is an admixture of Afrikan, Semitic and Aryan/European Races. Esoterically, these are also called the 3rd, 4th and 5th Root Races, with the 3rd being Ancient and elder and the 5th being recent and younger.* The 3 Root Races now overlapping combine to form a consciousness admixture that I am describing in this text as:

> **Metaphysical Key To:**
> Racial Name(s), and Number(s)
> 3-4-5   AfrikanSemiticAryan - Konsciousness Admixture - ASA-KA

In *The Ausarianization of Consciousness Tablet Series - The Metaphysical Keys to The Tree Of Life with Oracle Keys to Dis-spelling Illusion,* passages will be quoted which have been written by authors who have had access to the Ancient wisdom. These authors have made a link between Race and Consciousness. I did not make this link. It was made long before these present writings. What I do is make an earnest attempt to unscramble, ungarble and unveil what has been said, in order to wade through the tremendous racism, secrecy and veiling that has occurred in these reference sources. As we sift through the splinters of the Ancient Wisdom we must discern what is a veil.

On the one hand - a veil is used to both conceal and reveal the Ancient Mysteries to the poised and awakening consciousness.
On the other hand - a veil is often used as a heavy cloak of racism that pervades and separates so that the underlying unity is obscured. Thus, consciousness remains separative and isolative.

Does each Root Race contribute particular qualities in consciousness?
The different racial groups have responded differently to the event of 'individualization' in consciousness, which is described later. Although first occurring in the Afrikan 3rd Root Race this event of individualization, would have its greater impact on the later Semitic 4th and Aryan/European 5th Root Races, who made their appearance on the Planet in a *later* and

---

*This Name and Numbering is described in greater detail in, *The Ausarianization of Consciousness Series 2*. The letter K has been substituted for the letter C in the word Consciousness. See *Metaphysical Keys to The Tree Of Life with Oracle Keys to Dis-spelling Illusion* #10 in the Appendix for explanation.

descending cycle of time. What is key in understanding these passages is to read them from the *angle of consciousness* and *not just from the angle of physical form/manifestation*. In other words, an individual who belongs to or identifies with a racial group and *tends to* express one of the three primary Egoic states of consciousness i.e. Unitive, Dual, or Separative, may likewise express all primary Egoic states of consciousness. Full consciousness in all its states belongs to no individual Race. **Further description is given in a later chapter regarding the following Key(s):**

> **Metaphysical Key To:**
> The Afrikan 3rd Root Race consciousness and the process of Individualization

> **Metaphysical Key To:**
> 3 primary Egoic states of Consciousness

For now it is important to understand the next –

> **Metaphysical Key To:**
> 3-4-5 unification in consciousness.

We are now in a major 3-4-5 unification in consciousness.
Among all that has been said in the writings of these authors that would divide, a *major hint* is given in the following particularly about what unites us *now*. The Tibetan. *Treatise on Cosmic Fire,* p. 696.

> Finally, the student should very carefully study here the significance of the numbers **three, four and five** in the evolution of consciousness. Numerology has hitherto been studied primarily, and rightly, from the substance aspect, but not so much from the standpoint of conscious energy. The Triad, for instance, is usually looked upon by our students as the triangle formed by the manasic-buddhic and atmic permanent atoms [read here: Ka Ab Ba -the Spiritual aspects or soul bodies for Building the Lighted Temple] the cube stands for the lower material man, and the five-pointed star has frequently a very material interpretation. All these angles of vision are necessary, and must precede the study of the subjective aspect, but they lay the emphasis upon the material rather than upon the subjective; **the subject nevertheless should be studied psychologically. In this solar system, the above numbers are the most important from the angle of the evolution of consciousness.** The five-pointed star on the mental plane signifies (among other things) the evolution, by means of the five senses in the three Worlds (which are also capable of a fivefold differentiation) of the fifth principle, the attainment of self-consciousness, and the development of the fifth spirilla.

This brings us to the next -

> **Metaphysical Key To:**
> The Impersonality of The Cycles of Time.

This Key reminds us to seek to understand the *impersonality of the cycles* of time that *rise and fall*. It is important to see that whenever we look upon an event in Human history, we must simultaneously look at it upon the backdrop of time in which the event is occurring. Each Root Race has made its appearance upon a backdrop of time. Within each cycle certain qualities (Neteru) of energy are available that qualify events. The Root Races and the process of Individualization are further described later in this text. This brings us to the next -

Metaphysical Key To:
Oracle Keys To Dispelling Illusion

Let's dispell the name <u>Pythagoras</u>:

 # 1. Oracle Metaphysical Dis-Spelling Key: Put letters of word or words together in a circle, like a serpent putting its tail in its mouth. Coming full Circle.

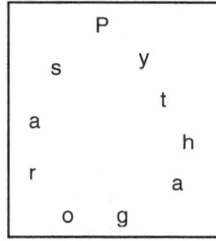
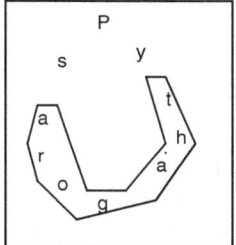

#2. Oracle Metaphysical Dis-Spelling Key: Read letters, putting together words, going forwards, backwards and in zig-zag patterns.
#3. Oracle Metaphysical Dis-Spelling Key: You may crossover in order to use a letter more than once. Place re-used letter in parenthesis ( ).
#4. Oracle Metaphysical Dis-Spelling Key: You may add a letter to complete a word. Place added letter in parenthesis ( ).
#5. Oracle Metaphysical Dis-Spelling Key: Letter substitution-you may substitute a letter. Place substituted letter in parenthesis ( ).
#13. Oracle Metaphysical Dis-Spelling Key: You may abrade a letter so that it is changed to another letter as in 'h' to 'n'. Notice the loping off of the top of the 'h' to make 'n'.

Definition:
Abrade - 1. To wear down or rub away by friction; erode. See synonyms at chafe. 2. To make weary through constant irritation; wear down spiritually. (Latin abradere, to scrape of: ab -, away;)

#6. Oracle Metaphysical Dis-Spelling Key: Make a list of derived words.

Derived Word List:
Ar(r)oga(n)t Spy - arrogant spy

#7. Oracle Metaphysical Dis-Spelling Key: Look up definition (dictionary, glossary, reference texts, etc.)

Definition: We turn to one of our great Chiefs for definition accordingly: George James. *Stolen Legacy,* p. 5-6.

> "The dishonesty in the movement of the publication of a Greek philosophy, becomes very glaring, when we refer to the fact, purposely that by calling the theorem of the Square on the Hypotenuse, the Pythagorean theorem, it has concealed the truth for centuries from the World, who ought to know that the Egyptians [read here: the Kamitians] taught Pythagoras and the Greeks, what mathematics they knew."

Ibid: p. 9.

> "According to history, Pythagoras after receiving his training in Egypt, returned to his native island, Samos, where he established his order for a short time, after which he migrated to Croton (540 B.C.) in Southern Italy, where his order grew to enormous proportions, until his final expulsion from that country."

Ibid: p. 43.

> "The teaching of Pythagoras seem to have been so comprehensive that nearly all his successors embraced and taught a portion of his doctrine, which we are told he obtained by frequent visits which he made to Egypt for the purpose of his education. Two things are at once obvious, (1) that the Greek philosophers practiced plagiarism and did not teach anything new and (2) the source of their teachings was the Egyptian Mystery System, either directly through contact with Egypt, or indirectly through Pythagoras or tradition."

Ibid: p. 155-156.

> This I suggest should be done by World wide dissemination of the truth, through a system of re-education, in order to stimulate and encourage a change in the attitude of races toward each other. In combining their efforts, both races must not only preach and teach the truth that the Mystery system of the African Continent gave the World philosophy and religion, and the arts and sciences, but they must see to it that all false praise of the Greeks be removed from the textbooks of our schools and colleges: for this laid the foundations for the deplorable race relations of the modern World. (a) The name of Pythagoras, for instance, should be deleted from our mathematical textbooks: in Geometry, where the theorem is called the pythagorean, because this is not true…"

#8. Oracle Metaphysical Dis-Spelling Key: Meaning. See the relationship and oracle or story of the Neteru – Put word list together to tell a story.

Meaning:

The Kamitians used the word 'Ren' for Name. Here the oracle of the Neteru speak *very* clearly, revealing in the Name Pythagoras, an 'Arrogant Spy.' This Neter yields the longest continuous unbroken string of words. There is just one doubling of a letter that is already present which is Neter 'r.' Lastly, the letter 'h' is abraded to yield the Neter 'n'. Notice, to abrade is to wear down spiritually. The oracle is revealing to us that this man who studied extensively in the temples of Kamit is much overrated. He has both taken and been given by the Western World *credit* for Ancient Wisdom that both far precedes and exceeds him.

Chapter 11
Negroes and The Secret and Sacred Meaning In The Triangle

Let's Dispell the word <u>hypotenuse</u>:
 # 1. Oracle Metaphysical Dis-Spelling Key:
Put letters of word or words together in a circle, like a serpent putting its tail in its mouth. Coming full Circle.

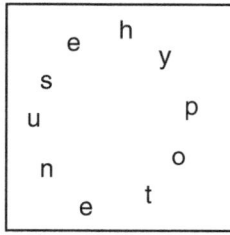 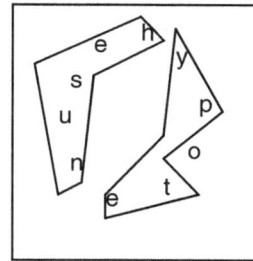 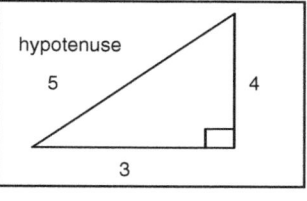

#2. Oracle Metaphysical Dis-Spelling Key: Read letters, putting together words, going forwards, backwards and in zig-zag patterns.
#3. Oracle Metaphysical Dis-Spelling Key: You may crossover in order to use a letter more than once. Place re-used letter in parenthesis ( ).
#4. Oracle Metaphysical Dis-Spelling Key: You may add a letter to complete a word. Place added letter in parenthesis ( ).
#5. Oracle Metaphysical Dis-Spelling Key: Letter substitution-you may substitute a letter. Place substituted letter in parenthesis ( ).
#6. Oracle Metaphysical Dis-Spelling Key: Make a list of derived words. Try to make the longest continuous unbroken word or string of words.

Derived Word List:
<u>Nuhes, type, o</u>   Types o(f) Nuhes

> Lets dispel the word <u>Nuhes</u>
> **Definition:** In continuing to dispell the word Negroes, the next key meanings come from the Kamitic language directly accordingly: E.A. Wallis Budge. *An Egyptian Hieroglyphic Dictionary, V.l,* p. 355.
> <u>Nuhes</u> - Negro

#8. Oracle Metaphysical Dis-Spelling Key: Meaning. See the relationship and oracle or story of the Neteru - Put word list together to tell a story.
Meaning:
<u>Nuhes, type o</u> - The word <u>hypotenuse</u> reveals the Neteru – 'Types of Nuhes' *which is* 'Types of Negroes'. We derive the word(s), 'Types of Negroes' from within the Triangle. This suggests that the word Negroes relates to mathematical formula which in turn relates to the architectural design of man and woman. It is the process of creating the 'outgoing "NEGROES" 'or as we shall see, "EGOS" who are man and woman. This is the *point* in creation where Negroes are no longer

associated with "landmass" which does not seem to exist, as there is no Negroland, but to Divine Archetypal Design and Ideation *in* the Mind of God.

★*Afrikans/Negroes - The hidden meaning in the Triangle.*
★*Afrikans/Negroes - Hypotenuse is 'Types of Negroes'.*
★*Afrikans/Negroes - Divine Archetypal Design and Ideation in the Mind of God.*
★*Afrikans/Negroes - Divine architectural and mathematical design.*
★*Afrikans/Negroes - Mathematics - the enumeration or numbers that come from the M(a)th-e(r), M(o)th-e(r) and the Father.*
★*Afrikans/Negroes - The point in creation where Negroes are no longer associated with "landmass" which does not seem to exist as there is no Negroland, but to Divine Archetypal Design and Ideation in the Mind of God.*

Let's continue to dispel the word <u>hypotenuse</u>:

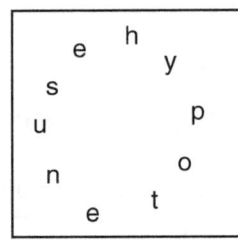 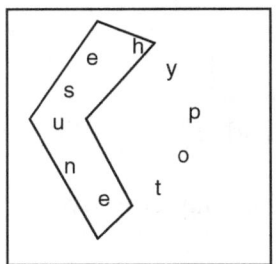

Derived Word List Continued:
#13. Oracle Metaphysical Dis-Spelling Key: You may abrade a letter so that it is changed to another letter as in 'h' to 'n'. Notice the loping off of the top of the 'h' to make 'n'.

>**Definition:** Dictionary
>Abrade –1. To wear down or rub away by friction; erode. See synonyms at chafe. 2. To make weary through constant irritation; wear down spiritually. (Latin abradere, to scrape of: ab-, away.

<u>Neheshi, Neshi, N(a)shi</u> – Here the Neter 'u' is abraded into an 'i'

Derived Word List and Definition Continued: Ibid: *V. I.* p. 386.
<u>Neheshi, Nehsi</u> - He of the Sudan. Negro.
<u>Nehesu</u> -Tuat V, the Sudani tribes in the Tuat, the results of the masturbation of Ra.
<u>Nehesit</u> - Title of the Sudani Hathor.
<u>Nehes</u> - To mutter incantations, to be restless, to kick out with the legs.
<u>Nehsi</u> - To wake up, to rouse oneself.
<u>Nehsu</u> - To cover oneself.

Meaning:
The One True Self takes of the substance of Itself - and - covers Itself in 'coats of skin' in order to see Itself reflected in form. Ra is the Kamitic Sun God. The Nuhes, Neheshi, Nehsi, Neshi, Nehesu, Negro are the results arising from the fedundating (impregnating power) of.the fire (seed) of Ra. The Negro as 'outgoing Ego' begins to: wake up, arouse the Self, become restless, mutter incantations, kick out with the legs and take 'out going' steps in consciousness.

Let's dispel the word <u>Neshi:</u>
Nehsi, he of the Sudan, Sudani, Negro.

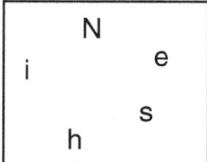

Derived word list:
Shine
Hi nes - Hi(g)(h)nes - as in Your Highness.

#8. Oracle Metaphysical Dis-Spelling Key: Meaning. See the relationship and oracle or story of the Neteru - Put word list together to tell a story.

Meaning: The Neshi or Nehesu is the Shining Star - the Sun-Son/Daughter of God. The 5 pointed Star is seen in the diagram at right. This is called the *Amsu Heru* by the Kamitians. It is a divine symbol that has been *so* falsely glamorized by Hollywood - as in the 'Hollywood stars'. To become a 5 pointed STAR - Amsu Heru, is to measure up, become the <u>Sum</u> or the fullest measure of what you have always been from the beginningless beginning. The Seker - sphere 3 aspect of our Spiritual equipment teaches us to 'measure up' and (a) achieve the fullest measure of the divinely intended design and to (b) sound the fullest measure of THE WORD we are and have always been from the beginningless beginning.
See A.C.T.S. 1. Ka Ab Ba Building The Lighted Temple for further information.

★Afrikans/Negroes - Your hi- nes, Highness.
★Afrikans/Negroes - The Shining Ones, the Shining Stars, One among The Shining Ones, a Shining Star.
★Afrikans/Negroes - Amsu Heru.

Derived Word List Continued:

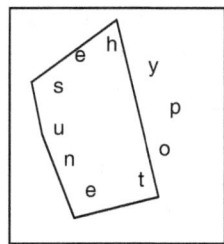

#11. Oracle Metaphysical Dis-Spelling Key: What does the word sound like? Say the word out loud and then silently in a meditative state.
Derived Sounds Like List:

H(i) p(p)o(p)ota(m)us - Hippopotamus sounds like hypotenuse. Recall from our previous chapter that Ta-urt is the Great Protector, Great Mother, and Hippopotamus Goddess. She brings, protection, childbirth, and good fortune.

Let's dispell the word <u>Ta-urT</u>:
This brings us to a new Oracle Metaphysical Dis-pelling Key:
#9. Oracle Metaphysical Dis-Spelling Key: Take each letter one at a time or in combination with one or more letters and derive its meaning.
Derived letter or Neter list:
<u>T</u> – As the vertical and the horizontal line intersect to form the cross bar, we have creative potential arising within the Divine Mother
<u>Au</u> – Divine Breath
<u>Ra</u> – Fire of Ra, power of fecundation (impregnation) of the Mother substance
<u>T - T</u> - Ring of creation – Measure of fecundation of the Mother, the expanse of the Universe or manifested form. Enclosing 'ring pass not'.

#8. Oracle Metaphysical Dis-Spelling Key: Meaning.
See the relationship and oracle or story of the Neteru – Put word list together to tell a story.
Meaning:
The fecundating (impregnating) fiery breath of 'Ra' which is breathed 'Au' throughout the Mother within the manifesting ring 'T – T' giving rise to creation. This manifesting ring or 'ring pass not' is wherein we achieve the greatest measure. This symbol upon which her hand and foot rest (indicated by the arrow) has been described as the Great Protector.

Let's dispel the word <u>protector</u>:
#11. Oracle Metaphysical Dis-Spelling Key: What does the word sound like? Say the word out loud and then silently in a meditative state.
Derived Sounds Like List Continued:
<u>Protractor</u> - Protector sounds like protractor.

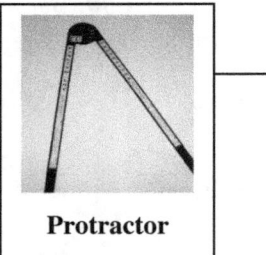

Protractor

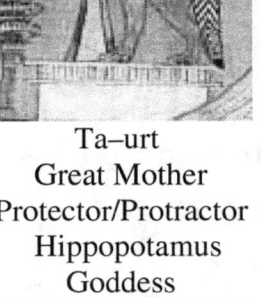

Ta–urt
Great Mother
Protector/Protractor
Hippopotamus
Goddess

Meaning:
<u>Protector</u> sounds like <u>protractor.</u> This is also a symbol of measurement i.e. the protractor used to measure circumference. Protection comes as Ta-urt insures that we are the fullest measure of the Image and Likeness of God that we have always been from the begningless beginning. She draws and assures that we are birthed within the circle that contains the Greatest Good, without truncation or collapse into a lesser measure.

★*Afrikans/Negroes - The Nehesu (i.e., the Negroes), Hours say, " I masturbated for you, and I have been content at the millions who have come forth from me in your name of Nehesu; Horus hath created you, and it is he who hath protected their souls." Ibid. p. 304.*
★*Afrikans/Negroes - Birthed by Ta-urt, Divine mother*

★*Afrikans/Negroes - To be fullest measure of the Image and Likeness of God without collapse into a lesser measure.*
★*Afrikans/Negroes - The measure of man/woman.*
★*Afrikans/Negroes - Veils many Names - Hypotenuse, Nuhes, Type O, Neheshi, Neshi, N(a)shi Nehesu,*

Derived Word List Continued:

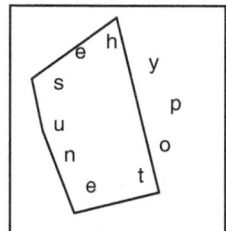

Definition: Accordingly: E.A. Wallis Budge. *An Egyptian Hieroglyphic Dictionary, V.1*, p. 355.
Nuh - To diminish, to bind, to tie, tie on, to fasten. String, cord, rope, cordage, measuring cord, traces, harness - Tuat V, a cord, endowed with reason, used in measuring the estates of the blessed in the Tuat. To be drunk with joy or drink
Nuhu - bonds, fetters
Nuheh - Eternity

#11. Oracle Metaphysical Dis-Spelling Key: What does the word sound like? Say the word out loud and then silently in a meditative state.
Derived Word Sounds Like List:
Noose - that which binds.

Derived Word Sounds Like List Continued:
Nu sh(u) - Nu Shu sounds like 'New Shoes'.
Nu se, Nu see -

Meaning:
The ALL takes within the LIMITLESS UNCONDITIONED SUBSTANCE of ITSELF called the NU. The NU brings us to the most primal meaning of the N word. The letter N in Metr Neter is represented by a symbol of water. The Nu is the waters of space. It is AMEN - sphere 0, ABSOLUTE ALL AND ALL in the Tree of Life, and is called Mulaprakriti by the Hindus.•. It is the INFINITE FOUNT OF ALL POSSIBILITY from which creation stirs forth. Shu is the Kamitic Deity of air, light and heat. Shu is derivative of the Neter Khu, which is the divine ideation in the mind of God. 'Nu shu' sounds like 'new shoes'. The Nu Shu as Negroes are the divine idea(tion) that begin 'outgoing footsteps' into physical manifestation. The 'Nu see' is *what* the *eye* of Ra, which has now arisen upon the surface of Nu - *sees* - as the reflected Self. The 'Nu see' or that which is 'Nu ly' seen, may become a 'Noose', that which binds when we come to identify as a self

---
• See H.P. Blavatsky, *Secret Doctrine*.

that is less than the fullness of the One True Self. We come to know the eternal/infinite Self through the finite sightings of the self that we have 'projected'. We can become caught on the 'hook' of the pro-J - ected self, like a fish. Lets dispel the word Self.

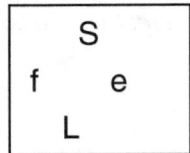 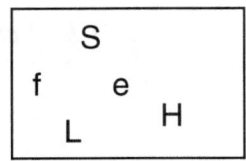 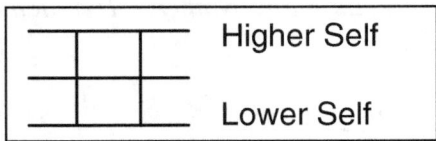

Derived Word List:
Fles(H)

Meaning:
The letter 'H' reflects the Spirit-Matter continuum as the Higher Self and the Lower Self. It corresponds to the number 8, which is the Karesting of Matter or Christing of matter as expressed according to Christianity. The lower self which has become flesh, may come to identify as flesh, forgetting the Higher Self, which is Spirit.

★*Afrikans/Negroes - The Nu Shus (new shoes), the divine idea(tion) that begins 'outgoing footsteps' into physical manifestation.*
★*Afrikans/Negroes - The 'Nu see' is that which the eye of Ra which has arisen upon the surface of Nu now sees as the reflected Self.*
★*Afrikans/Negroes - The Nu see or that which is Nu ly seen may become a Noose, that which binds when we come to identify as a self that is less than the fullness of the One True Self that we are and have always been from the beginingless beginning.*

Let's return to the dispelling of the word hypotenuse:
Derived Word List Continued:
Hetepu, Hotep - Kamitic word for peace
Honey steps - Steps leading to the land of Honey
Nest - place of birth
Noose, Nusee
Ship Top Mu - Ship on top of the waters, the mother
One
Poten - as in potency
Tune, Tone - Vibration
Nose
Shen(i)t - a word derived from Neshi.

Let's dispell the word Shenit:

#7. Oracle Metaphysical Dis-Spelling Key:
Look up definition (dictionary, glossary, reference texts, etc.)
Definition:
Shenit - A class of divine beings. E. A. Wallis Budge. *Prt Em Hru. (The Egyptian Book of The Dead)*, p. 258. May the Shenit, who make men to stand fast… Ibid. p. 309

Special ministers to the king, officials of the Court of Ausar. (*Osiris and the Egyptian Resurrection*, V.1), p. 333.

Definition Continued: As the Disciple moves through the Halls of Amenta he or she beseeches the Gods that his/her name is not made to 'stink'. This is expressed accordingly: E.A. Wallis Budge. *The Prt Em Hru. (The Egyptian Book Of The Dead)*, p. 258, Chapter xxxb.

> "Ausar, the scribe Ani, saith: "My heart my mother, my heart my mother, my heart my coming into being! May there be nothing to resist me at [my] judgment; may there be no opposition to me from the Tchatcha. May there be no parting of thee from me in the presence of him who keepeth the scales! **Thou art my Ka within my body [which] knitteth** and strengtheneth my limbs. Mayest thou come forth to the place of happiness to which I am advancing. **May the Shenit not cause my name to stink**, and may no lies be spoken against me in the presence of the god. Good is it for thee to hear."

1. Oracle Metaphysical Dis-Spelling Key:
Put letters of word or words together in a circle, like a serpent putting its tail in its mouth. Coming full Circle.

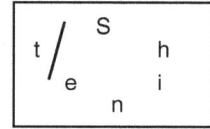 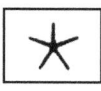

#2. **Oracle Metaphysical Dis-Spelling Key:** Read letters, putting together words, going forwards, backwards and in zig-zag patterns.

#3. **Oracle Metaphysical Dis-Spelling Key:** You may crossover in order to use a letter more than once. Place re-used letter in parenthesis ( ).

#4. **Oracle Metaphysical Dis-Spelling Key:** You may add a letter to complete a word. Place added letter in parenthesis ( ).

#5. **Oracle Metaphysical Dis-Spelling Key:** Letter substitution-you may substitute a letter. Place substituted letter in parenthesis ( ).

#6. **Oracle Metaphysical Dis-Spelling Key:** Make a list of derived words. Try to make the longest continuous unbroken word or string of words.

Derived Word List:
Shine

Derived Word List Continued:
Het Sun - Het means house in Kamitian, so here we have the house of the Sun, or that which houses the Sun.

#8. Oracle Metaphysical Dis-Spelling Key: Meaning. See the relationship and oracle or story of the Neteru – Put word list together to tell a story.

Meaning: As stated, the Neshi (Negroes) are the Shining Ones, the shining stars. They symbolize the Shenit who are the special Ministers to the King, officials of the Court of Ausar. If we dispel the word <u>Minister</u> we see it reveals the words, Min-I-star and the Kamitic Deity, Min.

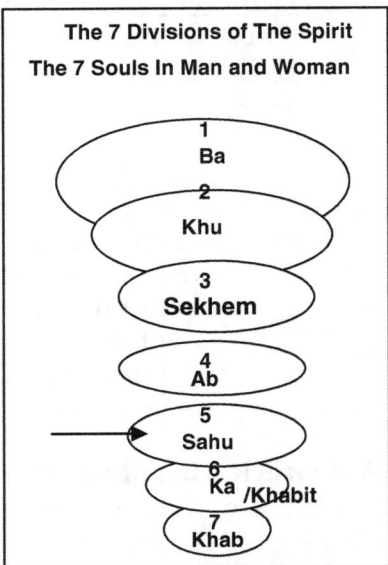

- We are all Mini-Stars of the One and Only Star
- We are all the Mini-Stares that we have projected as the
- One and Only same Self everywhere present that is *doing* the looking
- We are all the Mini-Stairs upon/within which we descend from and re-ascend to Heaven

Within the 3-4-5 triangle the relationship of the 3 and the 4 produces types of Negroes or Egos. It is a process of relating Spirit and matter. This perfect relationship produces the Sahu or *Glorified body of 'Light'*.* The Sahu Soul body is 5th of the 7 divisions of the Spirit or 7 Soul bodies or vehicles and is pictured at right. This is not to be confused with the *body of 'White'* - the European. The Aryan/Europeans are 'types of Negroes' and out going Egos in consciousness that Black Race people have produced and have erroneously - at times - fallen victim to 'glorifying'. To idolize is to create an idol. It is a 'false god'. This is mesmerism, a kind of spell, that must be broken.

For more information see *A.C.T.S. 1. Ka Ab Ba Building The Lighted Temple*
and refer to the following Key(s):

Metaphysical Key To:
Understanding the Sahu Soul Body or Vehicle

Meaning Continued:
For now it is important to understand:
The Sahu body is not a body of White, it is a body of Light. It is the Spiritual Soul body produced by the treasure garnered by you the knower, called Manes by the Kamitians. The agent of Manes or mind brings about right conscious relationship between Spirit and Matter. It is the essence of what is learned about living in accord with the Universal law of right relationship - Maat. The reincarnating Soul dons garment after garment - until these lessons are re-membered. The Sahu body is the body in which man arises to live and take form again, after he appeared dead in the grave. You undergo an initiatory process which resurrects the Spiritual man and woman within - that you may be born Anu (anew). Sa means wisdom and Hu means matter. In contrast, the White (Caucasian) body has made its appearance during the deepest downspiral into material consciousness during a coarse, dense vibratory period in our Earth history. We have become

---

* (see *The Ausarianization of Consciousness Series - The Metaphysical Keys to The Tree Of Life with Oracle Keys to Dis-spelling Illusion* for ealier description.

confused about which is which. The literalization of a White Jesus figure has contributed to our profound psycho-spiritual confusion. Television and other media, replete with White images, have also exacerbated this confusion. Instead, we should seek to become a being whose 'whole body is full of Light' - one refined, solarized, and divinised with the substance of God.

We must remember the Key -

> **Metaphysical Key To:**
> Read from the angle of consciousness and not just from the angle of the physical form Each Root Race is manifesting through.

Let's briefly review the following Key(s) from A.C.T.S. 1. Ka Ab Ba Building The Lighted Temple

> **Metaphysical Key To:**
> **The Number 7**
> The 7 Souls of Ra, The 7 Soul Divisions or 7 Divisions of Spirit
> The Septenary Nature of Man and Creation

The 7 Souls of Ra, The 7 Soul Divisions, 7 Divisions of Spirit
Within the Kamitic Spiritual tradition there are Seven divisions of the Spirit or 7 Souls or 7 Soul bodies or vehicles. These are also called the 7 Souls of Ra (See works of Budge, Massey, Ra Un Nefer Amen). Each corresponds with and gives qualities to 1 of the 7 planes of consciousness. The 7 Divisions of Spirit - Soul are pictured in the diagram at right and briefly described below.

The Seven Divisions of Spirit-The Seven Souls of Ra
1. **Ba** – Soul.
2. **Khu** – Intelligence. The Divine ideation in the Mind of God. Luminous Beings of Light revealing the Divine archetypal design. Divine wisdom.
3. **Sekhem** – Power to achieve the fullest co-measure of God's divinely intended design in manifested/ing form.
4. **Ab** – Heart expressing Higher Divine Will and/or lower personal will and desire.
5. **Sahu** – Spiritual Body. (The Mental Body - a. Higher Abstract Mind b. Lower Mind). This is the body that has become the incorruptible body through its accumulation and attainment of a degree of knowledge, wisdom and intelligence.
6. **Ka/Khaibit**
   a. **Ka** – The double, Spirit. (The Emotional/Astral Body)
   b. **Khaibit** - The shadow or overshadowing body. The Khaibit Soul division of Spirit may be thought of as an interpenetrating web between the 6th and 7th plane of consciousness. *See A.C.T.S. 1. Ka Ab Ba Building The Lighted Temple for further information and diagrams.* The Khaibit is the scaffolding upon which the dense Physical body is built and the vitalizing source of the dense body. It is called the Astral or Etheric body by the Esotericists.

c. The Ka and the Khaibit are viewed as closely linked. This is expressed in the following quotes accordingly: Donald Mackenzie, *Egyptian Myths and Legends,* p. 90.

> The Khaybet [Khaibit], or shadow, is evidently the survival of an early belief. It is really another manifestation of the Ka.

And likewise expressed in the following accordingly: E.A. Wallis Budge, *The Gods of The Egyptians. V. 1,* p. 39.

> ...the "double" [the Ka] was an integral part of a man, and was connected with his shadow [the Khaibit], and came into being when he was born, and lived in the tomb with the body after death...

7 Khab – The dense living Physical body. (see also Khat – body of the deceased)

We further unveil the Secrets of Race & Consciousness

Our Story Continues ...

Chapter 12
Negroes and The Secret and Sacred Meaning In The Triangle Continued

The following is said about the 3-4-5 Triangle accordingly: G.R.S. Mead. *The Book of Tehuti,* p. 234.

1. "And one might conjecture that Egyptians [also revered] the fairest of the triangles, likening the nature of the universe especially to this; for Plato also, in his Republic, seems to have made additional use of this in drawing up his marriage scheme.

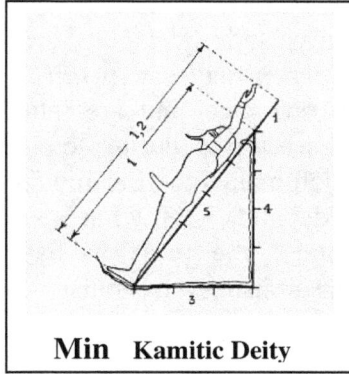

Min Kamitic Deity

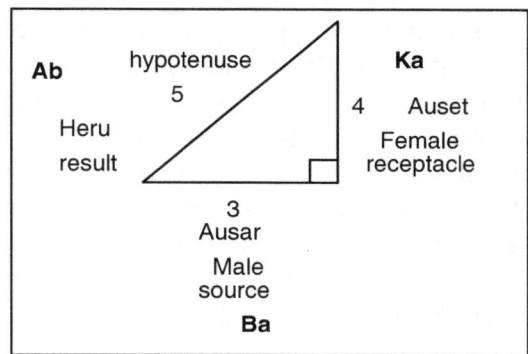

2. We must, accordingly, compare its perpendicular to male, its base to female, and its hypotenuse to the offspring of both; and [conjecture] Osiris [read here: Ausar] as source, Isis [read here: Auset] as receptacle, and Horus [read here: Heru] as result.
3. For the "three" is the first "odd" and perfect; while the "four" is square from side "even" two; and "five "resembles partly its father and partly its mother, being composed of "three" and "two".

Pictured above at right is another view into the Tree of Life. Here we see KaAbBa as one Triangle and not 3 separate Triangles. Likewise we see the divine Trinity of Auset, Heru and Ausar revealed.

The Kamitic deity Min is pictured above at left. As the ityphallic Ausar, Min symbolizes regeneration and the sublimation of the sexual energy. Here the energy is directed interiorly so that there is 'intercourse' with Spirit and the divine ideation of God. This ability to be Spirit directed is then reflected in the outer World in what man and woman create. This is the power of not only man and woman but of collective humanity. In this 'intercourse' with Spirit we make reference to the architectural design for creation and we build in accord with the divine plan. Without this 'intercourse' with Spirit we are without reference to the architectural design for creation and we build askew. It is the power to be and manifest the fullest measure of the divinely intended design. What is suggested here in the 3-4-5 AfrikanSemiticAryan Konsciousness Admixture Triangle (ASA KA) is that we have the golden opportunity to measure up as a Human Family - putting all the parts together *again*.

★ *Afrikans/Negroes - Hypotenuses, Types of Negroes, who have gone out on the Psycho/Spiritual Journey of Unfolding Consciousness, becoming Racial Types who in consciousness are becoming the full measure of the One True Self.*

Again as previously stated, what we must come to terms with is the fact that each Root Race has its respective part to play in the divine plan. God consciousness indwells within skins ranging in hues that are black, brown, red, yellow and white. Accordingly: Max Heindel, *Rosicrucian Cosmo Conception,* p. 311- 312.

> Races are but an evanescent feature of evolution… Races are simply steps in evolution which must be taken, otherwise there will be no progress for the spirits reborn in them.

It is after all, a 'seeming' Journey in Unfolding Consciousness and *what goes around comes around*, full cycle - that *now is then* and *then is now* and the *serpent will put its tail in its mouth*. You will hopefully see that *Sage and Savage* belong to 'no one race' but are inherent in the Psycho/Spiritual Journey itself. Today, as One Human Family, we are gathering 'closer together' due to technological advances in communication and travel which makes the Earth which is called Geb - sphere 10, in the Tree of Life - seem smaller. Our future depends upon what we now choose to do in our *closer proximity*. We must now offer up the sum total of the 'parts' we have played as ONE whole humanity. In the sum total of our collective consciousness we must now work in lifting our Earth into Sacredization and Spiritualization.

All of what I speak about and the ability to wade through the Ancient Wisdom is being guided by the Neteru. It is the Neteru who reveal themselves from behind the veils. From the DARKNESS of Unitive or Ausarianization of consciousness they cry out to us amidst all human efforts to keep the masses in darkness (see Metaphysical Key to DARKNESS and darkness, ***A.C.T.S. 1. Ka Ab Ba Building The Lighted Temple)***. I do not consider myself a mathematician; I am a seeker of truth. At the same time I do feel my work is suggestive for others to engage in deeper research. This 3-4-5 mathematical relationship is suggestive of 'turning an important corner' in the consciousness of our present Earthly inhabitants.

Chapter 13
The 7 Root Races Continued –
Lemuria Used to Veil the Name Negro
Are these Racial Names Just Esoteric Contrivances to Confuse Our Everyday Exoteric Understanding and Experience of 'Who We are' and 'Where We Come From?

We return now to a previous –

> **Metaphysical Key To:**
> The 7 Root Races
> The Septentary Nature of Man and Creation
> The Number 7

Simultaneous with the Numbering of the 7 Root Races is the Naming of the 7 Root Races. Names are given in the Esoteric literature, yet prove inadequate if we are going to build bridges in consciousness. These names are inadequate because they convey little by way of meaning and practical day to day experience in our World. Furthermore, these names continue to cause considerable debate.

> **Metaphysical Key To:**
> The 7 Root Races
> Numbering and Name

The Number and Name given by Esotericists for each Root Race is as follows:

Number	Name
1st Root Race Consciousness	Adamic
2nd RootRace Consciousness	Hyperborean
3rd Root Race Consciousness	Lemurian
4th Root Race Consciousness	Atlantean
5th Root Race Consciousness	Aryan
6th Root Race Consciousness	Unnamed
7th Root Race Consciousness	Unnamed

Are these names just Esoteric contrivances to confuse our everyday Exoteric understanding and experience of 'who we are' and 'where we come from?
Our interest here in posing this question is to look at how names are used as esoteric veils to obscure. These Esoteric names are *off-putting a*nd must first be addressed. For example, 3 out of

the 5 'Named' Root Races are named after continents which have allegedly 'sunken' (i.e. Hyperboria, Lemuria, and Atlantia). So then where is/was the continent called, Adamic or Aryan? Like any veil, it can be selectively used to both reveal *and* conceal. How much we penetrate beneath any veil depends on our level of conscious awareness. It is important to extricate every splinter of the Ancient Wisdom wherever it may be found, no matter how buried beneath the rubble of human motive or machinations.

In this next diagram, I have made the following substitutions in Name:

Number	Name
1st Root Race Consciousness	Adamic
2nd RootRace Consciousness	Hyperborean
3rd Root Race Consciousness	**Afrikan/Negro**
4th Root Race Consciousness	**Semitic**
5th Root Race Consciousness	**Aryan/European**
6th Root Race Consciousness	Unnamed X
7th Root Race Consciousness	Unnamed Y

Despite the atmosphere that would confuse, there are those like Albert Churward and Gerald Massey who express far greater clarity on who the Negro is *and* without the double speak of H. P. Blavatsky et. al. They have made significant contribution to our study of the Ancient Wisdom, origin and evolution of man. Their work likewise provides direction for further research. It is a pity that Blavatsky and other Esotericists who were some of the 'custodians' of and 'writers' on the Ancient Wisdom, could not use the word 'Negroes,' but veiled it instead by calling it the 3rd Root Race Lemurian and 4th Root Race Atlantean. The splinters of the Ancient wisdom where being gathered up at the time the Black Race was steeped in slavery and/or reeling from the impact of post slavery. What dilemma must have presented itself for these writers in:
1. Trying to present Ancient truths of the Black Race Humans while
2. Seeing them enslaved by their own White Race Humans

Lemuria Used to Veil the Name Negroes
Striking Similarities In Description of Afrikan Pigmy and Lemuria
The differences between these authors becomes apparent in the quotes that follow. You will see in the next two quotes by Churchward that he is straightforward in naming the Negroes. Yet in the third quote from the Secret Doctrine the Negro is veiled by the name Lemuria. This is expressed accordingly: Albert Churward. *Origin and Evolution of The Human Race.* p. 65-66:

> The original Pigmy [read here: Negro/Black Race] was "born" in Central Africa and spread throughout this World over a million years ago, and remnants of this first race are still found in

the forests of Africa, in the forests of Bolivia, South America, in New Guinea, the New Hebrides. The mountains of China and the Philippine Islands (particularly the North Island of Luzan). With the Pigmy religion dawned, by the propitiation of Elementary Powers, propitiation of departed spirits and a belief in a Supreme Being. **Theirs was the first articulate language; from the Pigmy, the human race has gradually developed in body and mind up to the present White Man, and the Christian doctrine, by evolution, from the various cults preceding it.** From the Pigmy and Bushman and Masaba Negroes, who have no Totemic ceremonies, we gradually pass to the Nilotic Negroes, in various tribes of a higher type of the Nilotic Negroes, in whom we find Totemic ceremonies with Hero Cult finally established and practiced.

That these Nilotic Negroes followed the Pigmy all over the World there can be no doubt, because these Nilotic Negroes have the same signs and symbols, **the same Totems and Totemic ceremonies everywhere, which must have been derived from a common center, and could not possibly have been developed from their own ideas and own surrounding in each case, and yet be so widely distributed as we find them at the present day.** By these Nilotic Negroes in Egypt the old Astro-Mythology was first developed, followed by the Stellar Mythos, and carried throughout the World (except in Australia, Tasmania, Patagonia, and Oceania). After that came the Lunar and Solar Cults. The Solar Cult was not universal, and only in a few countries, comparatively speaking, can remains of the same be found, vis., Egypt, Europe generally, except the extreme North, the South of Asia as far as Japan, but not the North of Asia, in America only in Yucatans, a little North and West of this, and South as far as Peru.

According to Albert Churhward there is no reason to locate the origin of man, outside of the continent of Africa. The human race begins with the Negro who over time has variously populated the Earth. The original man and woman, the Negro 'Pigmies', migrated all over the World - populating it as they went. This is expressed accordingly: Albert Churchward. *The Origin and Evolution of the Human Race*, p. 123.

The Pigmy, starting from Africa, could, in the ancient World, make his way across to Sicily, into Italy, across Europe to Greenland and the East of North America, or he could cross over to Asia and then into Western America by the North, where the Aleutian Islands are now. If he turned South when in Central Asia, it was possible for him to reach India, the Malay Peninsula and the East Indies, united here and there by land connections, and with the help of his frail canoe he would be able to cross over into Australia and then on to Tasmania. Some, no doubt, went North by the Icelandic Bridge-Greenland-others via the Alaskan Isthmus and other South to Australia and Tasmania.

Yet interestingly enough -
When we read and contrast the above quote of, 'where the Negroes went', with the quote below on, 'where the continent of Lemuria was' striking similarities cause a halting in conversation as to *what*, if any distinctions there may be. Similarity, if not indeed 'sameness' is revealed. A description of the Northern and Southern regions of the Continent of Lemuria are given accordingly: Geoffrey Barborka. *The Divine Plan*, p. 291-293.

In regard to Northern Lemuria: "…Lemuria, which served as the cradle of the Third Root Race [read here: Negro/Black Race], not only embraced a vast area in the Pacific and the Indian

> Oceans, but extended in the shape of a horse-shoe past Madagascar, round 'South Africa' through the Atlantic up to Norway. In regard to Southern Lemuria: It covered from the foot of the Himalayas [Tibet, Mongolia, and Gobi were under water at that time]…From thence, it stretched South across what is known to us as Southern India, Ceylon, and Sumatra; then embracing on its way, as we go South, Madagascar on its right hand and Australia and Tasmania on its left, it ran down to within degrees of the Antarctic circle; when from Australia an island region on the mother continent in those ages, it extended far into the Pacific Ocean, not only beyond Rapa-nui {Easter Island…(S.D. ll, 333-334).

> {Australia being part of a remain of Lemuria.}…since it (Lemuria) stretched, during the Third Race, E and W, as where the two Americas now lie, and since the present Australia is but a portion of it, as are also a few surviving islands sown hither and thither on the face of the Pacific and a large bit of California, which belonged to it. (SD ll 328).

How should we conclude?
Given the above striking similarities between these two descriptions of:
a.) Where the Negroes traveled and
b.) The span of the Continent Lemuria -

One would be left to conclude that:

c.) The 'so called Negroes' traveled throughout 'so called Lemuria'!

★ *Afrikans/Negroes - Lemurian, Lemuria.*

Once we lift the veils, we see that as much as H.P. Blavatsky and others are caught 'unsaying' the greatness of the Black Race, they are equally caught in the 'saying' of that greatness as evidenced accordingly: *Secret Doctrine, V. ll,* p. 172.

> That Third [read here: Afrikan Root Race] and holy Race consisted of men who, at their zenith, were described as, "towering giants of godly strength and beauty, and the depositories of all the mysteries of Heaven and"… **The Third race became the vehicle of the Lords of Wisdom.**

★ *Afrikans/Negroes - Pigmy.*
★ *Afrikans/Negroes - Towering giants of godly strength and beauty.*
★ *Afrikans/Negroes - Every measure of man.*
★ *Afrikans/Negroes - The depositories of all the mysteries of Heaven and Earth.*
★ *Afrikans/Negroes - The Third race became the vehicle of the Lords of Wisdom.*

And likewise:

Accordingly: Barborka. *The Divine Plan* p. 290:

> People today are inclined to believe that the peak of civilization has only now been reached in our day and age, and declare that never has there been such prosperity. They also hold the

opinion that mankind has steadily advanced in culture up to its present status from the era of the cave-dweller, some thousands of years ago. Those who maintain such notions will naturally reject the idea that there could have been any civilization worthy of the name some millions of years ago, not to mention city dwellers. To offset these opinions there is the ancient record, as narrated in the Stanzas of Dzyan, telling of the cultural activities of the Third Race, or Lemurians [read here: Black Race/Negroes]...

★*Afrikans/Negroes - Civilization and city dwellers millions of years ago.*

In the quote that follows you would perhaps think that what is being said here applies to the later 3rd Root Race Kamitians, the Egyptians, but read what is said about the Negro/Lemurian 3rd Root Race millions of years earlier in human history who are the Ancestors of the Kamitians. This is testimony that the later Egyptian/Kamitic civilization *was a culmination, fed by the consciousness and streams of the spiritual greatness that preceded it.* It is also a testimony to the recapitualization of the Root Races in that:
- The earlier Race 'Knows'
- What the later Races come to 'Know that they Know'

According to *The Secret Doctrine V.ll*, p. 317.
> They (the Lemurians) [read here: Afrikan Root Race Consciousness] built huge cities. Of rare earths and metal they built. Out of the fires (lava) vomited." Stanza xl. Sloka 43)...under the guidance of their divine Rulers, [the Lemurians] built large cities, cultivated arts and sciences, and knew astronomy, architecture, and mathematics to perfection...we find the Lemurians in their sixth sub-race [read here: sixth sub-race under the 3rd Root Race, see explanatory diagram later in this chapter] building their first rock-cities out of stone and lava. One of such great cities of primitive structure was built entirely of lava some thirty miles west from where Easter Island now stretches its narrow piece of sterile ground, and was entirely destroyed by a series of volcanic eruptions. The oldest remains of Cyclopean buildings were all the handiwork of the Lemurians of the last sub-races...The first large cities, however, appeared on that region of the continent which is now known as the Island of Madagascar. There were civilized people and savages in those days as there are now.

★*Afrikans/Negroes - Builders of large cities, cultivators of arts and sciences, and knowers of astronomy, architecture, and mathematics to perfection.*

And likewise:

Ibid. p. 194.

> But that which is preserved in unanimous traditions, only the willfully blind could reject. Hence we believe in races of beings other than our own in far remote geological periods; in races of ethereal, following incorporeal "Arupa," men, with form but no solid substance, giants who preceded us pigmies; in dynasties of divine beings, those Kings and Instructors of the Third Race [read here: Afrikan/Negro] in arts and sciences, compared with which our little modern science stands less chance than elementary arithmetic with geometry.

Other Ways of Knowing Outside of Factual Information provided by Science and Direct Observation
Reading the Etheric Records - What is Akasha?

Krummenaker points out a descriptive problem which arises in that Esotericists speak from the angle of consciousness, and Scientists speak from the angle of matter. Thus, they do not always agree to certain data regarding Lemuria and Atlantis (See Daniel Krumenaker. *Where Were Atlantis and Lemuria?*). We have probably all heard the expression, 'left without a trace.' But how does this expression apply to Science, Anthropology, and related fields, whose methods of investigation rely upon:
1. 'some-thing' of 'substance' that
2. 'leaves a trace of evidence' for
3. 'discovery and examination'

According to Krumenaker, Esotericists have introduced the idea that the Earth is a sphere that moved from a more etherealized state to a more dense state. This means a progressive and simultaneous densification of the Planet, Man and species, as a process of cooling and hardening took place on Earth. Over time, soft bodies of living entities have become the more skeletal forms. They are then rendered as 'discoverable and observable' through the outer five senses of man/woman, the examiner.

Are There Other Ways of Knowing Outside of Factual Information provided by Science and using direct observation? What is Akasha?
There are other methods of investigation such as the sense of 'subtle sight' used by clairvoyants which allows them to read the Akasha or astral records and thereby access 'other' ways of 'knowing'.

An analogy may best serve to give explanation:
Just as one is able to:
- Download data from the activity in their computer files due to the storage of memory, there are methods from which *to*
- Download from the 'Planetary storage files' outlines in the happenings and events of human history and Planetary consciousness. These are the Planetary Etheric records called Akasha.

Science has been 'behind' in these fields of 'discovery'. This is not new. The *difference* in the methods of 'knowing' is illustrated for example in the fact that Science does not as yet acknowledge the existence of the *Soul*. This is expressed accordingly: Tibetan. *Externalization of the Hierarchy,* p. 369.

> The next step ahead for science is the discovery of the soul, a discovery which will revolutionize, though not negate, the majority of their theories.

Imagine, where we would be if we felt we had no Soul just because scientists could not as yet observe, measure, quantify, tincture, dissect, or cryogenically freeze (preserve) the Soul?

As indicated in, *A.C.T.S. 1. Ka Ab Ba Building The Lighted Temple* the journey of the Soul was well understood by our Afrikan/Kamitic Ancestors, and their Spiritual/Religious practices were of the highest development. This is expressed accordingly: George James. *Stolen Legacy,* p. 1.

> The ancient Egyptians [read here: Kamitians] had developed a very complex religious system, called the Mysteries, which was also the first system of salvation. As such, it regarded the human body as a prison house of the soul, which could be liberated from its bodily impediments through the disciplines of the Arts and Sciences, and advanced from the level of a mortal to that of a God. This was the notion of the summum bonum or greatest good, to which all men must aspire and it became the basis of all ethical concepts.

To further compound the matter regarding discrepancies between Science and Esotericsm, the problems confronting these fields of discovery do not vanish even when they may 'consult' with one another as expressed in the following accordingly: Krummenacher. *Atlantis and Lemuria,* p. 3.

> We have here the first discrepancy, which we think is perhaps due to the fact the number of years given by H.P.B. were borrowed from the scientific estimates at the end of the last century. Indeed the powerful tool of radioactivity, which now allows precise, scientific geological dating, was not yet discovered at the time of H.P.B.

To tell Our Story is to attempt to tell the story of the Psycho/Spiritual Journey in the Unfolding Consciousness of humanity. This is Ausarian Spiritual Transformational and Resurrection or ASTR. To always find the 'traceable substantiality' that history and science *exact* cannot pose delay, as we grapple to make sense of our human experience. Our Story is the story of human consciousness, and consciousness is *Soul.* Science will perhaps discover 'Soul' when humanity as a whole becomes more Ba Soul conscious which is to undergo the Ausarianization of Consciousness.

Our Story continues…
We are told by the Ancient Wisdom accordingly: *The Secret Doctrine. V.ll*, p.132.

> The Lemurian 3rd Root Race [read here: African/Negro] dates back to the Miocene period, twenty five million years ago.

Advancing discoveries in the field of Esotericism, Science and related fields will continue to try to understand the origin and the migration of the human family on our Planet - Geb - sphere 10 in the Tree of Life. While all the debating *back and forth* goes on, nothing substantial changes in *Our Story* due to double speaks, or haggling between Scientists and some of the 'custodians' of the Ancient Wisdom. These custodians are called by many names which includes - Esotericists, Masons, Spiritualists, etc. One may spend considerable time in debate about; who the 'Negroes' are, when did they appear and whether or not these Continents really existed.

What is important to note here is that Black 3rd Root Race people are millions of years old. *Just how many million continues* to be debated with scientific estimates upwards of 7 million years. Science estimates the Earth to be approximately 5 billion years old (See Encyclopedia Britannica 2002). The age of the Earth would suggest that even 7 million years may be too puny an estimate. Is Science ready to accept the view of the Esotericists? I think not. Again, key to understanding these passages is to read them from the angle of consciousness and not just from the angle of physical form/manifestation. **Further description is the Appendix regarding the following Key(s):**

> **Metaphysical Key To:**
> The 7 Continents and The Supercontinents
> The Septentary Nature of Man and Creation
> The Number 7

For now it is important to understand:
Past, Present, and Future Planetary Root Races
The Number 7 The Septentary Nature of Man and Creation

This brings us to the next –

> **Metaphysical Key To:**
> Past, Present, and Future Planetary Root Races
> The Septentary Nature of Man and Creation
> The Number 7

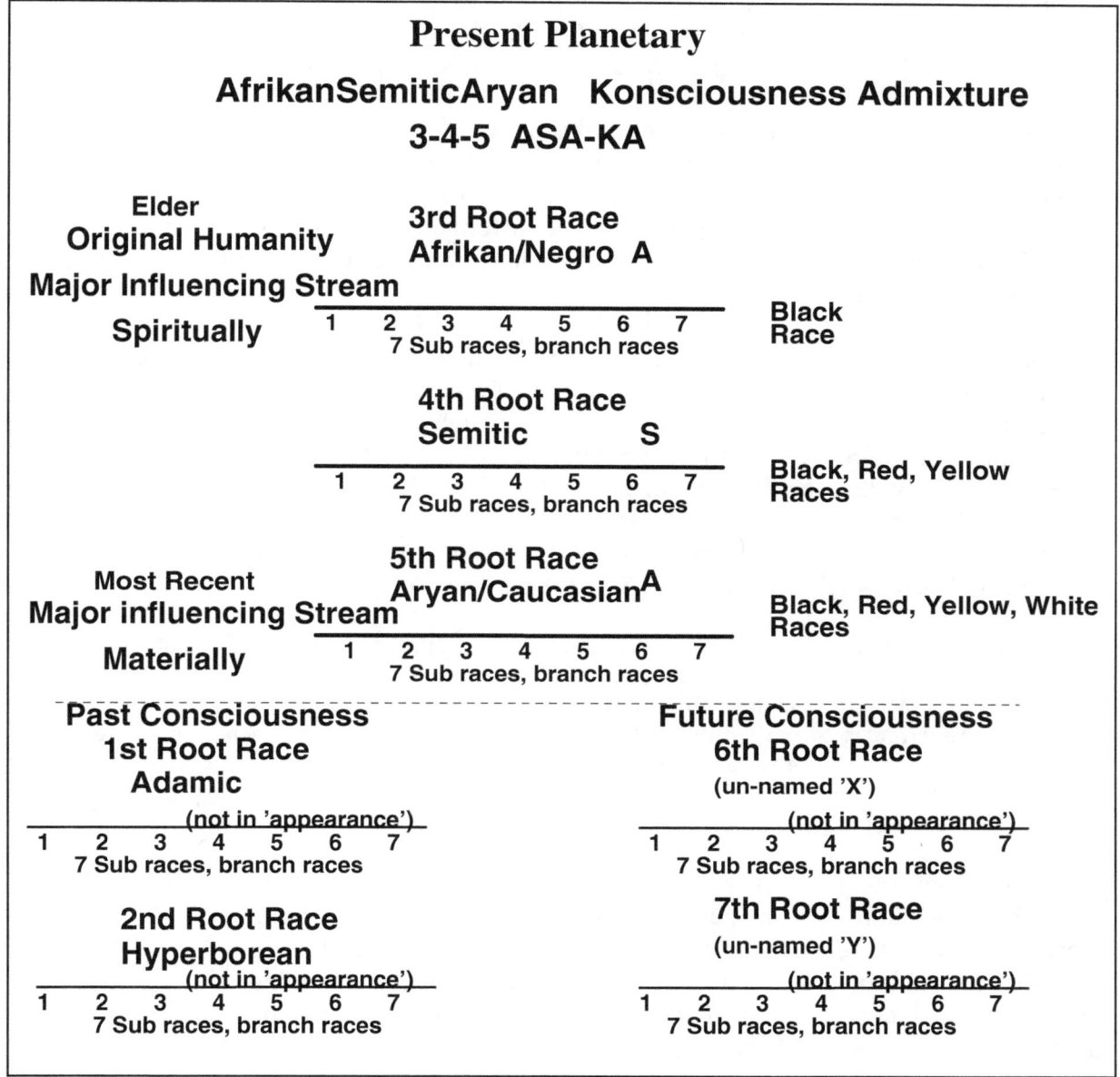

In the diagram on the opposite page we see that:
1. Presently, the consciousness on our Earth is an admixture of the 3rd Afrikan/Black, the 4th Semitic and the 5th Aryan/European Root races. Taken together they comprise and influence the consciousness in this 4th Round or World period.
a. The Afrikan/Black consciousness which is more Ancient is a major influencing stream Spiritually on the Planet.
b. The Aryan/European consciousness which is more recent is the major influencing stream materially on the Planet.

c. This more material influence of the Aryan/European Root Race consciousness has been able to dominate Planetary consciousness with great impact, given the cycle of time that we now live in but is undergoing a shift (See **A.C.T.S. 1. Ka Ab Ba Building The Lighted Temple** - *Chapter 17 - The Spiritual Implications Of The Perfect Storm - Where are we today?).*

2. The past or remote consciousness of the Adamic 1st Root Race and the Hyperborean 2nd Root Race that are no longer in 'appearance' on our Planet. These two Root Races occurred at a period on Earth far too subtle and times much to remote in the past to warrant much more than mere mention for our present purpose here. Nevertheless having *no-thing* substantive by way of 'appearance' of the 1st and 2nd Root Race in no way negates their ancestral influence upon our unfolding consciousness.

3. The future and remote consciousness of the 6th and 7th Root Races which have not made their full 'appearance.' The 6th and 7th Root Races referred to as 'X' and 'Y' in the diagram are 'not yet in full manifestation' and are un-named, although we see evidence today which gives us a 'glimpse' of the 6th Root Race'. The 'evidence' today reflecting the 'appearance' of 6th Root Race is briefly described in the Appendix. *(See Appendix).* The 6th and 7th Root Races are not necessarily 'new'. They are synthesizing of the five Root Races that have gone before. So in this regard their effect in collective Planetary consciousness is experienced as 'new'. This is expressed accordingly: The Tibetan. *Treatise On Cosmic Fire,* p. 164.

> I would here point out a fact that is little realised, that in this fivefold evolution of man and in this solar system, the two remaining rounds in any planetary cycle, and the sixth and seventh root-races in those cycles are always synthetic; **their function is to gather up and synthesise** that which has been achieved in the earlier five. For instance, in this root-race, the sixth and seventh sub-races will synthesise and blend that which the earlier five have wrought out.

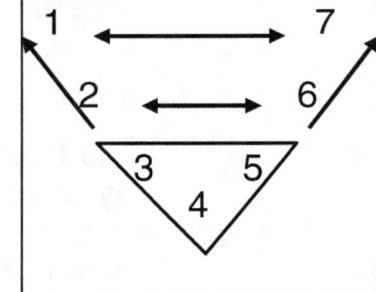

These two Root Races are likewise remote in the future to warrant any more than mention for our purposes here. Again, having no-thing substantive by way of 'full appearance' of the 6th and 7th Root Race consciousness in no way negates their influence upon our unfolding consciousness. Pictured in the diagram at right and indicated by the arrows, we see Root Races 1 through 7:

4. The 1st and 2nd Root Races where Divine/Etheral/Godlike, the 3rd Afrikan/Negro is Divine and Human.
    a. Root Races 3, 4, and 5 indicated by the triangle and forming a critical core in Collective Planetary Human Consciousness.
    b. Root Races 1 and 2 are Divine/Godlike and find their respective resonance with Root Races 6 and 7 which are synthesizing of the whole Psycho/Spiritual Journey in Unfolding Consciousness.
    c. Through this resonance in our Collective Consciousness (3,4,5) we come to see that we are in our return journey in consciousness (6,7) what we are in the beginning (1,2).

Chapter 14
What Is Ka Ba? Divisioning into the 2

Let's briefly review the following Keys from A.C.T.S. 1. Ka Ab Ba Building The Lighted Temple

> **Metaphysical Key To**:
> Number 1 and 2
> ***Ka*Ba Unity/Two-Oneness Ka and Ba/Duality Or Diad**
> Out of the '0', Zero –
> Whenever:
> There is the arising of the 1 as unity Ba (Monad)
> There is the arising of the 2 of Duality – BaKa or KaBa (Diad)

As earlier described, for the Kamitians, Ka is Spirit. Spirit takes of ITSELF and begins to differentiate itself in/as Spirit-matter. This is one of the many divine paradoxes. As much as Spirit is UNLIMITED and UNCONDITIONED it asserts its right to limit itself in form or matter to gain conscious experience of ITSELF. In various grades of material form, IT sees ITSELF. It is seen as having a double nature. Ka is therefore called the 'double' because it is reflected as both:
1. Spirit Ka - the essential and eternal Image and Likeness of God and the
2. Approximating Ka - the specific 'snapshot' of how much you have been able to put together in consciousness of the right relationship between Spirit and matter.

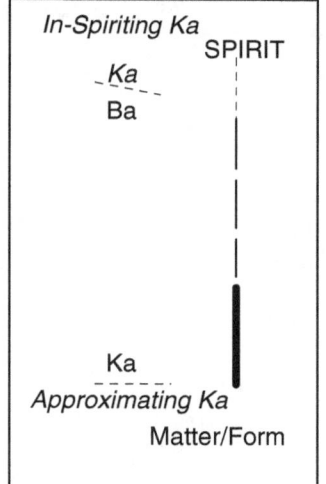

It is in *the seeing of ITSELF* that consciousness is born. Ba is Soul. Soul is consciousness. Thus we are made human and divine, material and Spiritual.

On the Psycho/Spiritual Journey in Unfolding Consciousness what are you as the Sun-Son/Daughter of God becoming fully conscious of?

As Heru - sphere 6, we are Sun-Son/Daughter. We make our descent into material life conditions. On our return journey, we make our hard, arduous climb of re-ascent Home again, into the Spiritual realms. You are becoming fully conscious of the perfect relationship between Father and Mother, between Spirit and Matter. To become fully conscious is to live the consciousness of Ausar Ba - that we are made in the Image and Likeness of God and All SELVES are but the ONE True Indivisible SELF. This is expressed in the diagram at right.

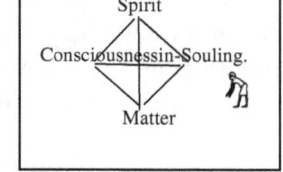

You will recall from *A.C.T.S. 1. Ka Ab Ba Building The Lighted Temple* that:

> The Ba comes forth upon earth to do the will of its Ka.

The Ausarianization of Consciousness Tablet Series 2 – A.C.T.S. 2
Metaphysical Keys To the Tree of Life & Oracle Keys to Dispelling Illusion
The Psycho/Spiritual Journey of Unfolding Consciousness

This is restated as: The Soul-Ba comes forth upon the Earth to do the will of its Spirit-Ka. *Ka*Ba is Unconscious-Consciousness and cannot be separated. This Unity is expressed in the previous diagram at right. As seen, *Ka*Ba enfold and circle upon each other, like the serpent that bites its own tail. Where one ends and the other begins, challenges our ability to discern. All 'seeming' divisions between Ka and Ba are arbitrary and merely useful for helping us to find our way back *Home* from a Psycho/Spiritual Journey in Unfolding Consciousness that we never really went on, except in an illusion, we came to believe as 'Real.' (Whenever we see the word Ba in a diagram the word Ka is always present or implied). This is seen in the three diagrams below:

1. The diagram at left reveals KaBa as One, the Primal couple or Two-Oneness. The Middle diagram reveals the Spirit-Matter continuum or the descent of Spirit into matter
2. The diagram at right is overlay of diagrams 1 and 2 as revealed in the Tree of Life

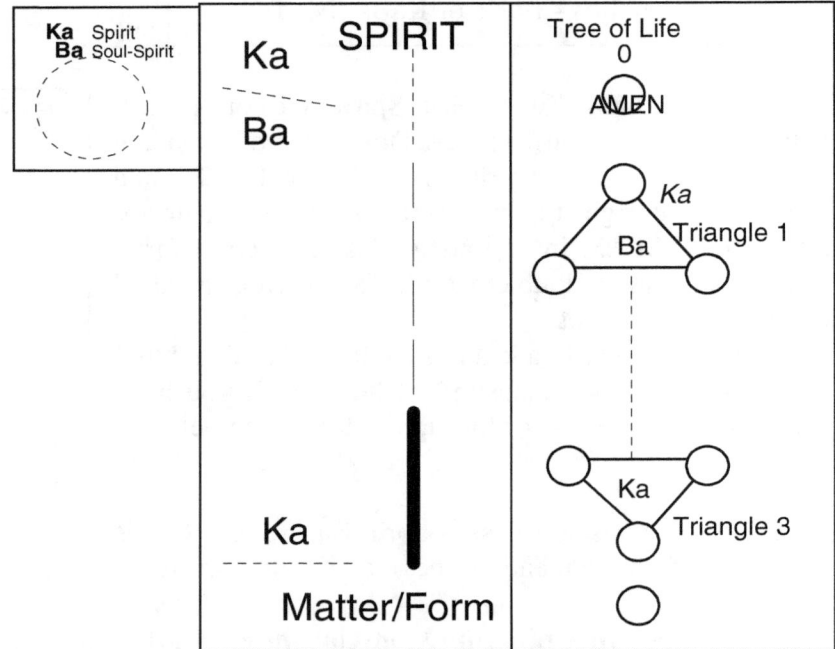

This brings us to the next –

> **Metaphysical Key To:**
> Spirit came down from the higher Worlds and by concurrent action are the bodies built upward.

Max Heindel. *The Rosicrucian Cosmo-Conception*, p. 266-269.

> The Spirit came down from the higher Worlds during involution; and by concurrent action, the Bodies were built upward in the same period. It is the meeting of these two streams in the focusing Mind that marks the point in time when the individual, the human being, the Ego, is born - when the Spirit takes possession of its vehicles.

Chapter 15
The First Significant Event Taking Place in Consciousness
The Outgoing Egos
What is Ego?

This meeting of these two streams is indicated by the arising of the middle triangle. It is the meeting of these two streams in the focusing Mind that marks the point in time when the individual, the human being, the *Ego*, is born - when the Spirit takes possession of its vehicles'. It is marked by the arising of a third or middle triangle which is called the Ego, or Ab Soul. This is the Ab Soul consciousness. The progression from Unity, Duality to Trinity is expressed moving from left to right respectively in diagram 1 - 3 below. The 3 primary Triangles revealed within the Tree of Life are the 3 Aspects of Divinity. In diagram 4 we see the event of 'self consciousness' arising as **Our Story Continues...**

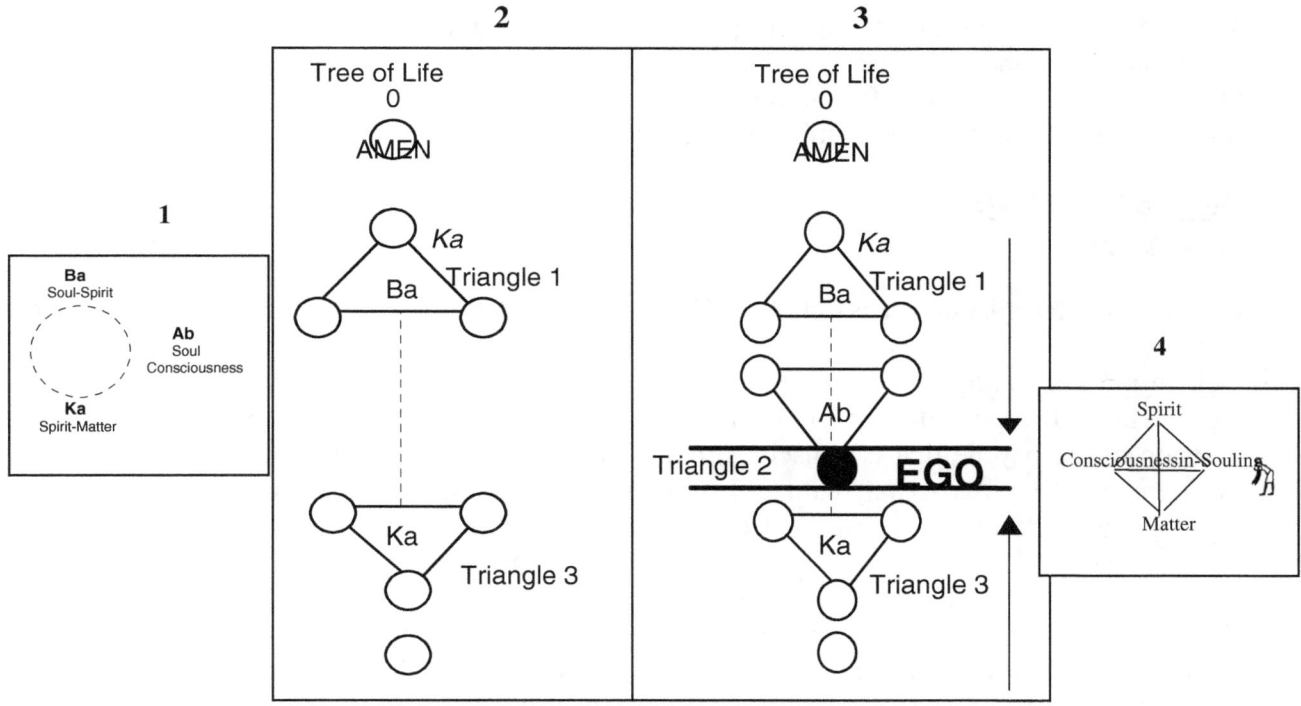

For now it is important to understand that -
This brings us to continue to dispel the word <u>Negroes</u>:

The Ausarianization of Consciousness Tablet Series 2 – A.C.T.S. 2
Metaphysical Keys To the Tree of Life & Oracle Keys to Dispelling Illusion
The Psycho/Spiritual Journey of Unfolding Consciousness

1. Oracle Metaphysical Dis-Spelling Key:
Put letters of word or words together in a circle, like a serpent putting its tail in its mouth. Coming full Circle.

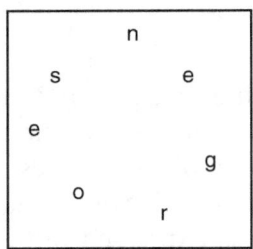

#2. Oracle Metaphysical Dis-Spelling Key: Read letters, putting together words, going forwards, backwards and in zig-zag patterns.

#3. Oracle Metaphysical Dis-Spelling Key: You may crossover in order to use a letter more than once. Place re-used letter in parenthesis ( ).

#4. Oracle Metaphysical Dis-Spelling Key: You may add a letter to complete a word. Place added letter in parenthesis ( ).

#5. Oracle Metaphysical Dis-Spelling Key: Letter substitution-you may substitute a letter. Place substituted letter in parenthesis ( ).

#6. Oracle Metaphysical Dis-Spelling Key: Make a list of derived words. Try to make the longest continuous unbroken word or string of words.

Derived Word List:
Ego, ego, egos

#7. Oracle Metaphysical Dis-Spelling Key: Look up definition (dictionary, glossary, reference texts, etc.)

Definition: *Dictionary.*
Ego - The self, especially as distinct from the World and other selves. 2. In psychoanalysis, the division of the psyche that is conscious, most immediately controls thought and behavior, and is most in touch with external reality. 3.a. An exaggerated sense of self-importance; conceit. b. Appropriate pride in oneself; self-esteem. [New Latin, from Latin, I.] Important derivatives of eg are *I* and *ego*.

Definition: H.P. Blavatsky. *Theosophical Glossary,* p. 111.
Ego - (Lat.) "Self"; the consciousness in man "I am I" - or the feeling of "I-am-ship". Esoteric philosophy teaches the existence of two Egos in man, the mortal or personal, and the Higher, the Divine and the Impersonal, calling the former "personality" and the latter "Individuality."

★*Afrikans/Negroes - Outgoing Egos*

What is this significant event taking place in consciousness? The Outgoing Egos?

The significant event occurring in consciousness within the Afrikan Root Race is called Individualization or Self Conscious Development. Esoteric sources on the Ancient wisdom• tell of this event occurring during the Negro (Lemurian) Root Race approximately 21-18 million years ago. This brings us to our next -

> **Metaphysical Key To:**
> The Afrikan 3rd Root Race consciousness and
> the process of Individualization

These dates given by Esotericist are debatable by science. The debate will no doubt continue between the 'evidences' of the Scientific realm and the 'subtleties' of the Spiritual realm as previously described and as it relates to:
a. When humans appeared and
b. What events were unfolding in consciousness

We are told by the Ancient Wisdom that along the Psycho/Spiritual Journey of Unfolding Consciousness man and woman of the 3rd Root Race underwent a process of *individualization* wherein the 'spark of mind' was implanted.• This 'spark' is called Manes by the Kamitians.

What is Ego - Continued? What is the meaning of the Ego in the Kamitic Spiritual tradition?

The implantation of the spark of mind is the birth of self-reflective consciousness in man and woman. As man and woman became self-reflective beings, the great game of subject-object was begun and entered into. Gradually they began to experience the self as separate from all other selves. This represents the great 'entification', 'objectification' or 'particularization' in consciousness. The birth of self-reflective consciousness is the power to *Know* That You *Know*. It is the Ego expressing as the Higher Self and the ego expressing as the lower self. The birth of self consciousness is called by many names or Neteru which include the following:

-Ego (as Higher Self) and ego (as lower self)
-Manes - a Kamitic term that is further defined later in this chapter
-Karest/Christ Principle - Karest is a Kamitic term - *See **A.C.T.S. 1. Ka Ab Ba Building The Lighted Temple***
-self reflective consciousness
-individualized self consciousness
-individualized man/woman
-I am ness
-Soul
-Son of Mind
-Intelligence Principle

• Cosmic Fire, Secret Doctrine, Rosicrucian Cosmo-Conception, Divine Plan, et. al.
• See Secret Doctrine, Tibetan Books, Rosicrucian Como Conception.

- Solar Angel
- Agnishvattas

#8. Oracle Metaphysical Dis-Spelling Key: Meaning. See the relationship and oracle or story of the Neteru – Put word list together to tell a story.

Meaning:
As you can see, the word Ego is derived from the word or Neter <u>Negroes.</u> In the Psycho/Spiritual Journey of Unfolding Consciousness there is the Higher Ego that is perched within the Higher division of your Spiritual Faculty or the Ab and Ba triangles. Then there is that which takes flight from the Higher Ego and can appear as the lower ego and identifies *with* and *as* the lower mental, emotional and physical bodies. The idea as we make our descent down the Tree of Life is to *remain* polarized within the Higher realms as we use the lower Soul vehicles or bodies as our instrument to do our work in the World. Instead we lose sight of our higher origin and begin to identify as/with the lower vehicles and thus lose sight and identification with our divine and Higher Soul *mooring*, purpose, origin and plan. As Afrikan people we have also been given the name *Moors*.

Let's dispel the word <u>Moor</u>:

#7. Oracle Metaphysical Dis-Spelling Key: Look up definition (dictionary, glossary, reference texts, etc

Definition:
<u>Moor</u> - To make fast (a vessel, for example) by means of cables, anchors, or lines. Moor a ship to a dock. To secure a place;

Meaning Continued:
Negroes became the Outgoing Ego's. As Moors, Negroes were to stand fast or fastened in the Will of God as they made their outward pilgrimage in consciousness. However, we endured many impacts along the way. Impact after impact caused us to forget the Higher planes of our birth and we came to experience a 'self' that is *less than* our One True Self. In time, we came to believe that we *are* the impacts of physical, emotional, sexual abuse, dis-ease, poverty, loss of self esteem (Self-estimation), victimization, enslavement, death, and all manner of loveless conditions. Along our descent into the utmost limits of matter and material consciousness – we came to feel diminished and begin to take the illusion of these conditions as our *reality*. With continual descent, through each successive plane and *seeming* disconnection from the Higher planes, our consciousness grew successively more material, dense and dark. When we began to lose our conscious stationing within THE BLACK, THE DARKNESS, THE DEEP, we then needed Religion (re –ligare, re tie, to tie fast) to tie us back together again. In this descending cycle of time we let go of the Moor (More) to become less.

★*Afrikans/Negroes - In this descending cycle of time we let go of the Moor (More) to become less.*

This brings us to our next

> **Metaphysical Key To:**
> What is Africa or the African?

Secrets of Race & Consciousness Afrikan Cosmology of Kamit
with The Spiritual Meaning of The 'N' Word(s)
Neggur - The Goose Goddess who laid the Sun Egg, the Cosmic Egg

Revealed in Ka Ab Ba *(Kabala)* The Tree Of Life   Metaphysical Mysteries Meaning

Let's dispell the word Africa:

#10. Oracle Metaphysical Dis-Spelling Key: Letter replacement. Here we have replaced the 'k' which had been substituted by the letter 'c.'

#11. Oracle Metaphysical Dis-Spelling Key: What does the word sound like? Say the word out loud and then silently in a meditative state.

Derived Word List:

A Free Ka, A Fri Ka

    Definition: *Thesarus.*

    Free - Unbound. Boundless. Limitless. Emancipated.

A Freak Ka

    Definition:

    Freak – 1. A thing or occurrence that is markedly unusual or irregular.

#8. Oracle Metaphysical Dis-Spelling Key: Meaning. See the relationship and oracle or story of the Neteru – Put word list together to tell a story.

Meaning:

Africa, or Afrika dispelled is A free Ka, a free Spirit. It is return to a state of peace which is Ba - hotep. The word Continent dispelled is 'contentment' (See Appendix on Continents) 'A-Fre(I)e-Ka' is not just a geographical land mass, it is a state of consciousness. When the approximating Ka is united with Ba, - *KaBa* – then it is *free and unfettered* in reflecting Spirit Ka – the Image and Likeness of God – *without flaw or distortion*. When we live out of accord with the divinely intended design and purpose for our lives, we look in the mirror and see 'A Freak Ka' – an image full of distortion. When the two eyes represented by 'ee' in the word Free are made One, which is the single or 1st eye then we may affirm, I am 'A Fri Ka'. This is biblically expressed: 'If thine eye is made single then thy whole body is full of Light.' This is further expressed accordingly: Albert Churchward. *Signs and Symbols of Primordial Man*, p. 211.

> The Ka or spirit after death separated from the Ba or soul and went before the Divine Creator to be judged, and, if justified, then returned to the Soul and could travel after throughout the universe.

For more information see *A.C.T.S. 1. Ka Ab Ba Building The Lighted Temple* and refer to the following Key(s):

> **Metaphysical Key To:**
> The 7 Ka-resting Steps/Stairs/Arits to become ASTR or a STAR
> The 7 Christ-ing Steps

For now it is important to answer -
What are The Three Primary Triangles?
This question brings us to the next -

Chapter 16
What is Ka Ab Ba? Divisioning Into the 3.
The Nature Of The Trinity At Work In Man And Woman - The Story of Ausar, Auset and Heru

Again, the Tree of Life is the divine symbol of our Spiritual Equipment which is both Divine and Human. We will begin our descent down the Tree of Life describing consciousness within the Three primary Triangles of Ba Ab Ka. We look within the Number or Neter 3 - the 3 Primary Triangles that form the Divine Trinity. These are the 1st, 2nd and 3rd Aspects of Divinity in Tree of Life. ***Let's briefly review the following Keys from A.C.T.S. 1. Ka Ab Ba Building The Lighted Temple.***

> **Metaphysical Key To:**
> The Number 3
> **The Divine Trinity**
> The Trinity/Triune Nature of Man/Woman and Creation
> Ausar, Heru, Auset
> BaAbKa or KaAbBa

Our story gives us an important archetype and geometrical design revealed in Number. Neter or Number provides the vehicle through which the Deities or qualities of God speak. The Trinity is one such numerological vehicle or template, upon which the events of unfolding consciousness are taking place and expressing divinity. The divisioning of the nature of creation and man/woman into 3 discrete qualities of energy is the story of the Divine Trinity. These 3 powers qualify and guide our Psycho/Spiritual Journey of Unfolding Consciousness. In the two diagrams at right we simultaneously see:

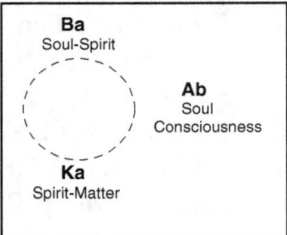
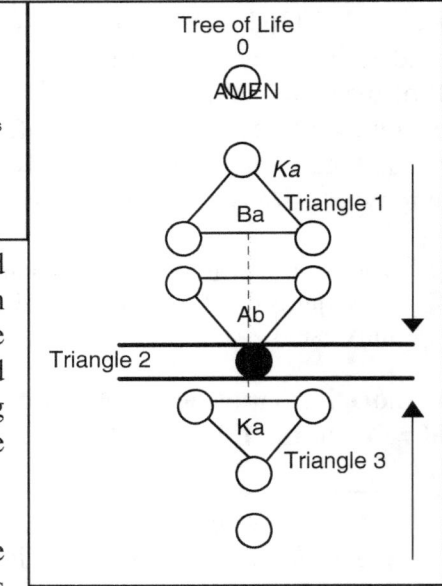

1. KaAbBa as a circle and KaAbBa revealed in the Tree of Life and visually laid out in a straight line as three triangles
2. The division of the Tree of Life into 3 primary triangles is called KaAbBa or BaAbKa depending upon which direction up or down the Tree of Life we move in
3. The three triangles combined express the Divine Trinity within you whose name is Ka Ab Ba
4. When consciousness is poised within the Higher or Ab and Ba Soul then the temple you fashion is the Lighted Temple.
5. The Ba Triangle is the 1st Aspect of Divinity and is comprised of spheres 1, 2 and 3

6. The Ab Triangle is the 2nd Aspect of Divinity and is comprised of spheres 4, 5 and 6
7. The Ka Triangle is the 3rd Aspect of Divinity and is comprised of spheres 7, 8 and 9, with sphere 10 completing the square or quarternary, described later.

This brings us to the next -

Metaphysical Key To:
The Overlay of The Divine Trinity
Within The Tree of Life

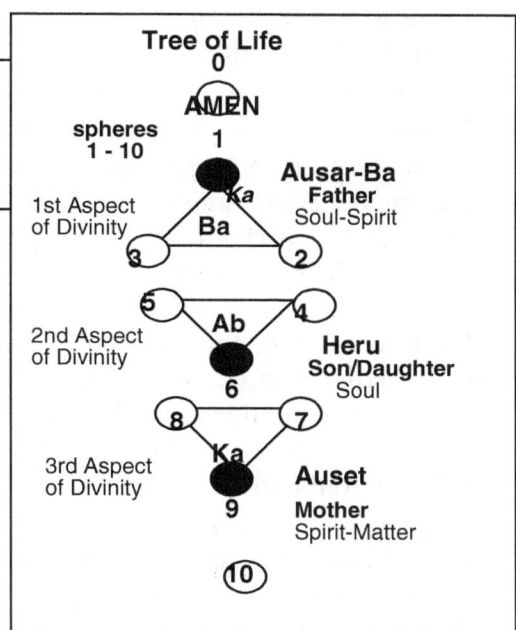

In the diagram at right, we see the overlay of the Divine Trinity revealed within the Tree of Life. This Divine Trinity is shown in the 3 colored spheres. Ausar and his wife Auset are pictured as sphere 1 and sphere 9 and their Son/Daughter Heru as sphere 6, respectively. These are the 3 aspects of Divinity within our Spiritual make-up or equipment which are Father (Spirit-Soul), Son/Daughter (Soul), and Mother (Spirit-Matter). The story of the Divine Trinity pre-dates Christianity by what is exoterically known as thousands of years (and what is esoterically known as millions of years).[3] As the Eldest Race, *Our story* is an ancient story. Furthermore, within Our story other stories have been enfolded and encoded and have evolved over time. Thus Our Story is *story, within story, within story*.

The story of **Ausar, Auset and Heru** is one such story. Ausar, Auset and Heru are later called Osiris, Isis, and Horus, respectively by the Greeks. In this story Ausar and Auset harmoniously rule their kingdom as king and queen of Kamit. Egypt is the name later given to Kamit by the Greeks. The Greeks and others re-named much of our story. To the Kamitians, Numbers and Letters were called Ntr or Neter, which are qualities of God or Deity. Quality is vibration.

For our purposes now the question is:
How does the Story of Ausar, Auset and Heru contribute in telling *Our story* about the Psycho/Spiritual Journey of Unfolding Consciousness in man and woman?

We are told by the Ancient Wisdom in the story of Ausar, Auset and Heru, that:
1. Ausar and Auset harmoniously rule their kingdom as King and Queen.
2. Heru is the son of Ausar and Auset.
3. Ausar is slain by his jealous brother Set.
4. A fierce battle ensues between Heru and Set in which Heru must avenge his Father's death and be restored as the rightful heir to the throne. This symbolizes the re-establishing of the Kingdom of God on Earth.

---
[3] See *Secret Doctrine. 24 Tibetan Books* under the name Asauras, Kumaras, Sanat Kumara.

If you are unfamiliar with the story of Ausar, Auset and Heru see Appendix A and refer to Key(s):

> **Metaphysical Key To:**
> The Story of
> Ausar, Auset and Heru
> The Divine Trinity

For now it is important to understand that -

In the diagram at right we see the Ka triangle within the geometric figure of the square or quaternary. These are spheres 7-10, the third triangle in the Tree of Life. This *triangle* and *square* are illustrated in the diagram at right. These are spheres 7, 8, 9, and 10 within the Tree of Life and comprise the Ka triangle.

The lower self or ego when 'disconnected' from the Higher Self or Ego 'thinks:
1. 'I am my thoughts'- sphere 7 & 8 – Mental or Sahu Soul body.
2. 'I am my emotions' - sphere 9 - Emotional or Ka/Khaibit Soul body.
3. 'I am my body' - sphere 10 – Physical or Khab Soul body.

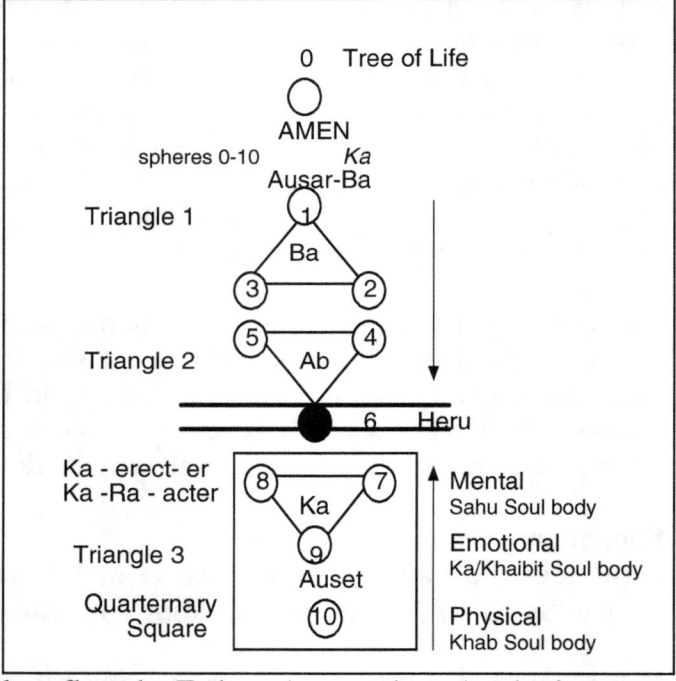

It is within the 'square' or the quarries of life that character or the temple is built. Character dispelled is Ka-erect-er and Ka-Ra-acter (See **A.C.T.S. 1. Ka Ab Ba Building The Lighted Temple** for further description). These words are used interchangeably in this text. Ka-erect-er is how you are erecting the son/daughter within you. As the developing Self conscious entity, Ka-Ra-acter is what is erect-ing the Sun/son within you. As the Ra-acter, you are trying to *act* like Sun-Son/Daughter who at first can only approximate the Sun. It is through your efforts as Heru - sphere 6, that you are striving to be fully Self Conscious. As Heru, the Son/Sun is fully *erected* to then fully reflect the Father- Ausar sphere 1, who is now *re-surrected*. It is within this aspect of your Spiritual equipment that you must fashion a temple, which will bear the light from the higher two triangles, the Ab and the Ba. In the diagram at right we see that:

1. This concurrent action of the Spirit coming down from the Higher Worlds during involution and the bodies being built upward is indicated by the arrows.
2. *As* the consciousness *remained* focused within the higher triangle, it used the lower Ka triangle which is comprised of the physical, emotional and mental Soul bodies in order to do its work in the World.
3. These are the Soul 'bodies that are built upwards'.

4. It is likewise Heru - sphere 6, which is the 4th plane of consciousness which mediates between the Higher Spiritual World and it's vehicles of manifestation in the dense physical World.

It is only later, through a series of events, over the passage of time that this focus begins to shift. This shift in focus would precipitate the following:
1. Leave man and woman forgetful of their residence within the Higher Soul realms
2. Move the conscious awareness into the lower spheres which comprise the more material and human aspect of man and woman's Spiritual equipment
3. Instead of knowing that we are *Spirit Ka*, we would forget the fullness of our identity or 'ID' and wander in the World as an *approximating Ka* - trying to re-member and reconstruct our proper ID-entification (See ***A.C.T.S. 1. Ka Ab Ba Building The Lighted Temple*** for further description)

Chapter 17
Heru as Ego
What is Manes? The Birth of Individual Self Consciousness

Heru (sphere 6) as Soul or Consciousness aspect of your Spiritual equipment
Our Story Continues…

In the story of Ausar, Auset and Heru we turn now to a discourse that is occurring between Auset and her son Heru. In it she is teaching him how to come into maturity so that he may avenge his Father's death and come into his rightful inheritance of the throne of his/her Kingdom. She speaks about this *spark of mind* or power *'to know'* and use the mind accordingly: *Virgin of the World.* (G.R.S Mead, *Thrice Greatest Hermes;* Dr. Muata Ashby, *Ausarian Resurrection).*

> O Heru, these were the souls, created out of God's very being. In time they came to be conscious of themselves and looked up at the Father of All. Being sparks of their creator as sun rays are emanations of the sun, souls have the power to create due to their ability to **know and use the mind**.

> O Heru, **this power became the source of pride and conceit.** The souls thought themselves to be equals to The God, and as their punishment, were enclosed in watery encasements. This is the nature of human existence and it is the reason why human **beings are a blend of what is physical and what is Divine.**

Again, in the discourse between Auset and Heru: Accordingly:

> For taking breath from His own Breath and blending this with **knowing Fire-consciousness**, He mingled them with certain other substances which have no power to know; and having made the two together, with certain hidden words of power, He thus set all the mixture going thoroughly, until out of the compost smiled a substance, as it were, far subtler, purer far, and more translucent than the things from which it came; it was so clear that no one but The Artist could detect it.*

As Our Story continues we learn more about:
1. How we come to be a blend of that which is physical and Divine
2. How these 'Souls' have 'the power to create due to their ability to know and use the mind' which is called Manes by the Kamitians
3. How this power became the source of pride and conceit

This blending of the two together reflected in the discourse between Auset and Heru is the - 'Two-Oness' *(see Lawlor),* i.e., the unconscious-conscious as the primal couple, at the origin of creation. The entirety of creation comes into existence through the interaction of these two. In the beginning, this is the Consciousness that is Conscious of ITSELF. This knowing, fire-consciousness is referred to as Manes by the Kamitians which is the power to know.

★*Afrikans/Negroes - Manes, knowing fire consciousness.*

---

* *The Virgin of The World*

The game of consciousness is to gain conscious awareness of the *seeming selves* against the backdrop of the *Seamless Unity of The One True Self*. This is accomplished as your awareness remains perched in your higher Spiritual equipment of the Ba and Ab Soul triangles, as/while you perform your work in the World using your Ka-erector or Lighted Temple as an instrument.

However, when the One True Self as Ausar is forgotten then 'particularization' is seen and mistaken as the *self*. In our lesser self identifications we choose to build askew or out of alignment with *the divinely-intended design*. This leads to the accumulation of regret, remorse, greed, fear and anger which weighs the heart like lead so that it is heavier than the feather of Maat - sphere 4. Upon her scales of justice the heart is weighed against the lightness of the feather. When the scales of balance tip, we incur Karma and become bound upon the wheel of birth and death. This is expressed accordingly: Ra Un Nefer Amen. *Metu Neter VI,* p. 228.

> Heru corresponds to our will, which is the freedom to follow or reject divine law, and our emotions. This freedom is the crux of our divinity. Without it, man would be compelled to follow the structural shaping forces of order which manifest in the 10th sphere as the "instincts" that compel all other creatures to obey the law, in which case he could not be held accountable to law, human or divine, let alone be considered the "likeness of God".

What is Manes?
Man and woman are developing the power of manes. The work in the return Home of the Manes is to articulate the fullness of the One Sound of your being. This is to become One with Universal Ba.

Let's dispel the word or Neter, <u>Manes</u>: (Spelling of Manes and Manas is used interchangeably)
#7. Oracle Metaphysical Dis-Spelling Key: Look up definition (dictionary, glossary, reference texts, etc.)

<u>Definition</u>; An important key is revealed in the following which describes the ritual of Coming Forth by Day which guides Ausarian Resurrection. According to Gerald Massey. *Egypt the Ancient Light of the World, V. l,* p.194.

> The **Manes** enters Amenta with a papyrus roll in his hand corresponding to the one that was buried in his coffin. This contains the written word of truth, the word of magical power, the word of life. The great question now for him is how far he has made the word of god Ausar truth and established it against the powers of evil in his lifetime on the earth. The word that he carries with him was written by Taht-Aan, [read here: Tehuti] the scribe of truth. Another word has been written in his lifetime by himself, and the record will meet him in the Hall of Justice on the day of weighing words, when Taht will read the record of the life to see how far it tallies with the written word and how far he has fulfilled the word in truth to earn eternal life. The sense of sin and abhorrence of injustice must have been peculiarly keen when it was taught that every word as well as deed was weighed in the balance of truth on the day of reckoning, called the Judgment Day. The question confronting the **Manes** on entering Amenta are whether he has laid sufficient hold of life to live again in death?

<u>Definition Continued</u>: Dictionary definition: G.de Purucker. *Occult Glossary,* p. 95.

<u>Manes</u> - (Sanskrit) The Sanskrit root of this word means "to think,", "to cogitate," "to reflect" - mental activity...**The center of the ego-consciousness** in man and in any other quasi-self-conscious entity...Manas itself is mortal, goes to pieces at death - in so far as its lower parts are concerned. All of it that lives after death is only what is spiritual in it and that can be squeezed out of it, so to say - the "aroma" of the Manas; somewhat as the chemist takes from the rose that attar or essence of roses....What we know of each principle...the Manas, is what we have so far assimilated of it in this Fourth Round. The Manas will not be fully developed in us until the end of the next Round....What we now call our "Manas" is a generalizing term for the Reincarnating Ego, the Higher Manas.

As we briefly recall from *A.C.T.S. 1. Ka Ab Ba Building The Lighted Temple* -

Ka-erect-er is built or 'erected. *It is the blended essence or bouquet of fragrant qualities* that arise once the personality structure is blended, coordinated and balanced. After even a partial dispelling of the words Ka-erect-er and Ka-Ra-acter, the vital importance of its development can not be overemphasized in the Psycho/Spiritual Journey of Unfolding Consciousness and Ausarian Resurrection. You can not get where you think you are going without great moral Ka-erect-er. This is why the Manes in his/her prayers to the Gods beseeches them '*not to make his/her Name to Stink*'. (Refer to page 172 of this text for *Ritual* verse from, *The Prt Em Hru (The Egyptian Book Of The Dead)*. The Lotus petals unfold as Ka-Ra-acter is developed. The story of Ausar and Auset reveals insight into the meaning of:
1. Scent or odour of Ka-Ra-acter
2. Re-gaining immortality by passing through the purificatory fires in order to transmute the more coarse, material substance of your vehicles into a more refined, *fragrant* Solar substance.

Insight into the meaning of odour or scent is revealed as Auset travels to Byblos in search of her deceased husband Ausar. This is expressed accordingly: E. A. Budge, *Osiris. The Egyptian Religion and Resurrection,* p. 5.

> When this news reached Auset she set out at once for Byblos, and when she arrived there she sat down by the side of the fountain of the palace and spoke to no one except the queen's maidens, who soon came to her. These she treated with great courtesy, and talked graciously to them, and caressed them, and tired their head, and at the same time transferred to them wonderful **odour** of her own body. When the maidens returned to the palace the queen perceived the **odour** which emanated from their hair and bodies, and learning from them that it was due to their contact with Auset, she sent to her and invited her to come to the palace.

What's the matter with our lives is our density, coarseness, and lower vibration. You will overcome your descent into matter and begin your re-ascent into Spirit by clearing up the matter(s) within your own vehicles. In Ausarian Spiritual Transformation and Resurrection ASTR, you are striving to be resurrected in Ausarian consciousness. Within this acronym is another which is AST. AST is another name for Auset. Ast and Ausar are synonymous with Ka and Ba. Likewise, Ast and Ausar and Ka and Ba are inseparable. ASTR is doing the work to raise your vibration by transmuting (changing) the substance of your vehicles from a more dense, coarse material nature which has a lower vibration, into a more refined and luminous solar substance of a higher vibration. To become a STAR. When someone is told that they have a Ka-Ra-acter or Ka-erect-er that 'stinks' or is 'lousy' they are being told that they are reflecting a more 'materialized' Ka-Ra-acter which falls short in its approximation to the in-Spiriting Ka, the true Image and Likeness of God in which we are made. As the Disciple moves through the Halls of Amenta he or she beseeches the Gods that his/her Name is not made to 'stink'.

May the Shenit not cause my name to stink, and may no lies be spoken against me in the presence of the god. Good is it for thee to hear.

Let's revisit and continue to dispel the word <u>Shenit</u>:

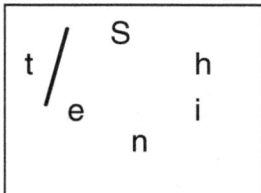 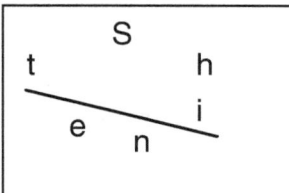

<u>Derived Word List Continued</u>:
<u>Shine</u>
<u>Shit</u>
<u>Het</u> - Kamitic word for house
<u>Sin</u>
<u>S(u)n</u>
<u>Neshi</u> - Negroes

<u>Meaning</u>:
By transmuting the matters of our life into luminous Light we Shine. We have become one among the Shining Ones, we are the house of the Sun. By failing to transmute the matters of our life into luminous light we are filled with foul odour, stink, and have become as shit We are the house of sin. One of the more painful expressions for a Black Race people of High Stationing to hear stated is, 'niggers ain't shit'.

Lets continue to dispel the word <u>Manes:</u>
 # 1. Oracle Metaphysical Dis-Spelling Key:
Put letters of word or words together in a circle, like a serpent putting its tail in its mouth. Coming full Circle.

```
    m
s       a
  e   n
```

#2. Oracle Metaphysical Dis-Spelling Key: Read letters, putting together words, going forwards, backwards and in zig-zag patterns.

#3. Oracle Metaphysical Dis-Spelling Key: You may crossover in order to use a letter more than once. Place re-used letter in parenthesis ( ).

#4. Oracle Metaphysical Dis-Spelling Key: You may add a letter to complete a word. Place added letter in parenthesis ( ).

#5. Oracle Metaphysical Dis-Spelling Key: Letter substitution-you may substitute a letter. Place substituted letter in parenthesis ( ).

#6. Oracle Metaphysical Dis-Spelling Key: Make a list of derived words. Try to make the longest continuous unbroken word or string of words.

Derived Word List:

Names - As we have become the particulated self, we became involved in the game of naming. We are trying to articulate our way back – *HOME*. Manes = name. As namer, Manes is the invoker of his return in Spirit by scaling the mount.

Mane - hair. The Ancients used the Metu Neter of the lion as symbol for the power of Heru - sphere 6. Heru is ruled by the Sun, which is a symbol for Ra, and the constellation Leo, which is symbolized by the Lion. We may derive the following by analogy:

1. Just as many hairs arise from the one scalp, so do the many 'seeming' lesser selves arise from the One True Self.
2. Just as there are many rays that emanate from the one Sun, so do the many 'seeming' lesser selves arise from the One True Self.

Man, men - this is a game played by man and wo/man.

Mean - as in mean-ing.

Men(e)s - King Menes (Narmer) - The King of Egypt who founded the first dynasty uniting Upper and Lower Kamit (Egypt). This symbolizes the work of the manes or mind in uniting the Higher and lower aspects of the Spiritual Faculty which is both Human and Divine.

Sane, Same - Our ability to see how much the 'Same' we all are will determine how sane we really feel.

Meas(ure) the mouth. The lion opens his mouth and makes the *Rrrraaaa* sound, invoking God.

AMEN - is known by many names: THE NAMELESS, ABSOLUTE, the ALL IN ALL, NETER NETERU. DARKNESS, BLACKNESS, BEGININGLESS BEGINNING, THE FOUNT OF ALL POSSIBILITY, THE SUPREME BE-NESS, THE ROOT CAUSELESS CAUSE, THE INFINITE, THE ETERNAL. THAT WITHOUT POINT OR CIRCUMFERENCE, THE BOUNDLESS ALL, THE EVERYTHING AND NO-THING. LIMITLESS POTENTIAL, THE ALL, GOD, SPIRIT, AIN, are just a few names for the ABSOLUTE REALITY in which – *CREATION Stirs..* This is sphere 0 in the Tree of Life. Within this awareness of ABSOULUTE BE-NESS feel your access to all potential, all power, all wisdom, all creativity.

sem(a)n - a man who is crossing the sea

seam(e)n - the male fluid through which sperm, the creative fire of Ra travels. Thoughts contain the vital fire. They impregnate the waters of Auset - sphere 9 within our emotional nature, what the Kamitians call - Nu. The vibration of the thought is what contributes to what is imaged in Auset upon her watery surface. Thus the fire of mind impregnates the waters of the emotional vehicle or body.

amnes(i)a - When no 'I' or individual self is remembered, forgetfulness. In forgetting all the individual selves we identified with in the game of *self and others* or *subject and object* - we remember the SELF.

#8. Oracle Metaphysical Dis-Spelling Key: Meaning. See the relationship and oracle or story of the Neteru – Put word list together to tell a story.

Meaning:
- As Negro/Ego consciousness descended down through lesser planes of self awareness
- Manes is the power of mind to know, to think or cogitate, to discriminate, to differentiate this from that' and to *Name*.
- A developing sense of a separated self is a self that is developing personal thoughts (mind), desires (emotions) and sensations (physical body).
- This is the approximating Ka reflecting through the Ka-erect-er/personality you are using as an instrument to do your work in the World
- Thus comes a developing sense of 'personal will' which can now be used to secure that which is thought about and desired
- With personal will comes 'self' determination and volition
- The Afrikan Root Race consciousness was exercising the ability
- To choose whether to remain exquisitely attuned and act in accord with
- Divine Will, Law, and Plan or
- To act out of accord in exercising personal will, man-made law and plan
- This is the ability to plan and chart one's own course based upon the degree and measure of what you now 'know' or 'think you know' the 'self' to be
- This is the Heru - sphere 6, of your Spiritual Faculty
- Instead of being under the grace, guidance and Divine Moor-ing of Divine Will and Mind - Higher Ego or Higher Manas
- You began learning the painful process of
- Directing your own personal will
- A will that would serve the now increasingly *limited and limiting sense/sight* of
- The One True Self

This brings us to the next -

Chapter 18
The 7 Planes of Consciousness

What are the 7 Planes of Consciousness?

> **Metaphysical Key To:**
> The Number 7
> The 7 Planes of Consciousness, 7 Division of The Solar Systemic Planes
> The Septenary/Heptanary Nature of Man and Woman and Creation

Let's briefly review the following Key(s) from A.C.T.S. 1. Ka Ab Ba Building The Lighted Temple
The Tree of Life is composed of 7 planes, numbered 1 - the highest, through 7 - the lowest and is pictured at right. (See *Treatise on Cosmic Fire*). Plane number 1 is the most Spiritualized. Plane number 7 is the most materialized. As man/woman makes his/her descent through the planes below, consciousness becomes more dense and materialized. Each of the 7 planes represents a 'World' in which a certain expanse in consciousness is taking place. We seemingly leave our Eternal Home and begin this journey down the Tree of Life. From the first and highest plane, we descend as if taking an elevator through the seven planes of consciousness. Traveling from the invisible to the visible realm we experience many impacts along the way. The idea of course, as we make our descent is *to remain* in Ausarian consciousness, All consciousness - The highest plane of consciousness, Ba - sphere 1. In a state of Ausarian consciousness we are in alignment with Divine Mind as we manifest our work in the World on the lowest plane of consciousness. We have the use of personal 'will' to choose to do otherwise.

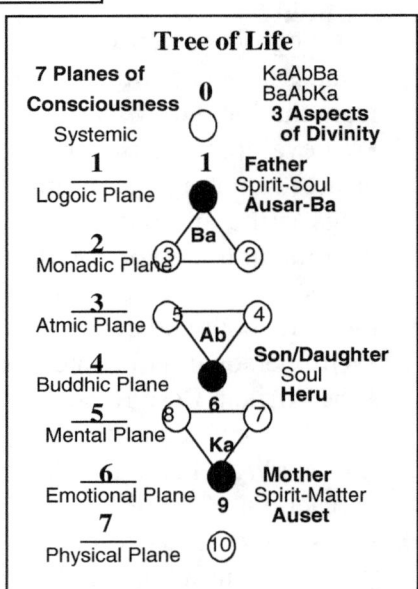

The Ancients were very familiar with the 7 planes or Arits of consciousness. This is pictured in the diagram at right from the Papyrus of Ani. Seen here are the 7 Hathors or celestial cow goddesses. Hathor is also known as Het-Heru - sphere 7. Each represents a plane in consciousness that must be ascended by the Bull of Heaven, Ausar, pictured at the bottom, who is you and me. Hathor glimpses the inner archetypal patterning of greater wholeness and beauty *upon each plane and* causes us - the Initiate - to aspire towards the divinely intended design. It is important to remember that even though we are looking at 7 discrete divisions in consciousness, the only separation is the one created by our own illusion of separative or broken consciousness. When we are using the Het-Heru/Hathor part of our Spiritual equipment at a

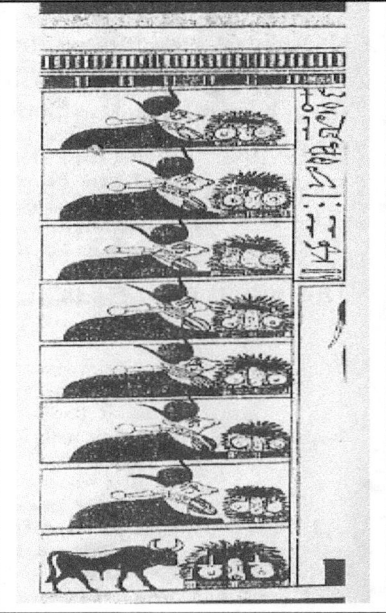

higher turn of the spiral or optimal level, we are magnetically attracting the higher ideal to be manifested in our lives.

It is in studying the planes and sub-planes of consciousness that the subtle qualities of the Deities and Soul Divisions are revealed. I give my deepest appreciation to Dr. Michael Robbins for his guidance here. The 7 Systemic Planes of Consciousness find relationship to the 7 divisions within the Tree of Life.

As man makes his descent to the more dense and materialized planes below he/she 'forgets' to identify *as/with* the fullness of the One True Self Identification as Ausar - sphere 1, and The Unlimited Access To All Potential that he/she *is*. The story of Ausarian resurrection that follows throughout this text is the story of understanding and transcending the fragmentation that occurs in consciousness as we make our descent from the Higher planes of consciousness to the lower planes. This brokeness in consciousness manifests in our outer World as the pain of separation from our One True God-Self. We grow 'down' and 'up' the Tree of Life by our descent and re-ascent of the 7 planes of consciousness. Through this re-ascent in consciousness the 7 are made 1. This process of At-One-ing is the Ausarianization of Consciousness. It is where we may 'get an eye full' or know the fullest, 'I'. **For more information see *A.C.T.S. 1. Ka Ab Ba Building The Lighted Temple* and refer to the aforementioned Key(s):**

Chapter 19
The Goose and the Golden Egg
The Second Significant Event Occurring in Consciousness During the Afrikan Root Race is Called the Separation of the Sexes.

Let's continue to dispel the word <u>Negroes</u>:

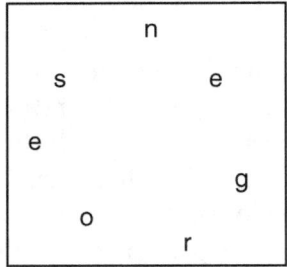

Derived Word List Continued:
eg(g)

Definition: Dictionary
<u>egg</u> - 1. A female gamete; an ovum. Also called egg cell. B. The round or oval female reproductive body of various animals, including birds, reptiles, amphibians, fishes, and insects, consisting usually of an embryo surrounded by nutrient material and a protective covering. C. The oval.

Meaning:
In the Afrikan Cosmology of Kamit the Egg is symbolic of the entire Psycho/Spiritual Journey in Unfolding Consciousness. It represents a time-space continuum. The culmination of the Egg is to sound the fullness of the Vibration of the One True Self as Ba or Ausar Ba. For more information see ***A.C.T.S. 1. Ka Ab Ba Building The Lighted Temple***
and refer to Key(s):

> **Metaphysical Key To:**
> Cosmogony and Cosmogenisis
> **Universal Ba** *To*
> **Individualized Ba** Man and Woman

For now it is important to understand that:
1. For the Kamitians this Egg is symbolized by many forms and called by many names. Some of which include: Ba, Universal Ba, Individual Ba, The World Egg, World Soul, Khepera, The Goose, The Golden Egg, Geb, Ausar, Heru, Ra, The Eye of Ra upon the waters of Nun, etc.
2. A few of the Metu Neter (hieroglyphic) symbols used to refer to the World Egg are pictured on the next page and from left to right and include:
    a. The scarab beetle, Khepera, which contains the Eggs or to-be Sun-Sons/Daughters to be born into manifestation

b. The bird (more specifically, the bearded man headed hawk) symbolizing the Soul or Ba
c. The Kamitic deity Ptah fashioning the Egg of the World upon the Potter's Wheel, which he works with his foot. (See Budge)
d. The Goose or Golden Egg. This is also the geometric figure of the sphere or circle

a.

b.

c.

d.
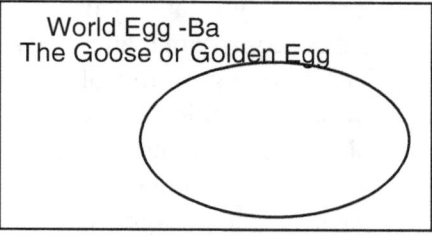

The Most Primal 'N' Word is Nu or Nun
What is Nu (Nun) and the arising of the Cosmic Egg?

According to E.A. Wallis Budge, *The Gods of The Egyptians, V.I*, p. 295-303. (Papyrus of Nes-Amsu) "The Book of Knowing the Evolutions of Ra, and of Overthrowing Apepi."

I came into being from primeval matter, and I appeared under the form of multitudes of things from the beginning. Nothing existed at that time, and it was I who made whatsoever was made. I was alone, and there was no other being who worked with me in that place. I made all the forms under which I appeared by means (or, out of) the god-soul which I raised up out of Nu, out of a state of ineptness (or, out of the inert mass).

I found there (i.e., in Nu) no place wherein I could stand. I worked a spell on my heart, and I laid a foundation before me, and I made whatsoever was made. I was alone. I laid a foundation in (or, by) my heart, and I made the other things which came into being, and the things of Khepera which were made were manifold, and their offspring came into existence from the things to which they gave birth. It was I who emitted Shu, and it was I who emitted Tefnut, and from being one god (or, the one god) I became three, that is to say, the two other gods who came into being on this earth came from myself, and Shu and Tefnut were raised up from out of Nu wherein they had been.

We see from the above that it is within the - waters of space - called – Nu or Nun by the Kamitians, that the INFINITE, BOUNDLESS ALL, SPIRIT/MATTER, takes within the limitless unconditioned substance of ITSELF to see ITSELF reflected in form. As you will recall the creative process from, *A.C.T.S. 1. Ka Ab Ba Building The Lighted Temple*, in understanding of Cosmogony and Cosmogenisis we understand that:
1. Within the INFINITE, BOUNDLESS ALL, AMEN there is a *Stirring*. Within this INFINITE, BOUNDLESS, BLACKNESS, DARKNESS OF SPIRIT, The ABSOLUTE ALL AND ALL

The Ausarianization of Consciousness Tablet Series 2 – A.C.T.S. 2
Metaphysical Keys To the Tree of Life & Oracle Keys to Dispelling Illusion
The Psycho/Spiritual Journey of Unfolding Consciousness

Stirs within the limitless unconditioned substance of ITSELF. This Spirit/Matter is called – Nu (N) by the Kamitians.* It is the waters of space.

2. There is an arising of the Great Breath and the fires of Ra. As the fires of Ra thrills across the primordial waters of Nu(N) the twin creative forces, called Shu & Tefnut by the Kamitians, are set to work.

3. These are the children of Ra. They are the centrifugal and centripetal twin forces at work in nature producing air, heat, light (Shu) and moisture (Tefnut). Together they engage in an infolding and unfolding, play and display between themselves, like the yin and yang symbol. Through their interweaving dance, Spirit emanates outward to pervade ITSELF in matter.

4. The circumgyration of the fires of Ra upon the waters raises a 'mound' within Nu. As the fire circles, flames leap and seek to pierce the mound or 'egg,' just as the male sperm seeks to penetrate the female ovum.

5. At last, one solitary spark leaps high above all other flames. It takes aim, makes its descent and shooting forth as a solitary Ray of the ABSOLUTE this fire penetrates and impregnates the primordial, mother/matter Nun.

6. From this stirring within AMEN, THE ALL sphere 0 - in the Tree of Life, there is a raying forth of Light and the One issues forth as Creator – sphere 1, Ba.

7. The One egg, now fecundated (fertilized) becomes the One Universal Ba or Cosmic Egg. The One Universal Ba is humbly pictured in the diagram, at right, as no image can adequately capture the divine movement. The One Universal Ba is also called the World Egg and the World Soul.

8. The dance of the twin forces of Shu and Tefnut enables the coming into manifestation of myriad Life-forms. From this egg which is the Universal Ba all spheres arise. Thus Super Galaxies, Galaxies, Constellations, Suns, Planets, Man and tiniest Atom come into created being. Therefore Ba is tiniest Atom, Ba is ultimately Universe, and Ba is everything in between. This is pictured in the diagram at right.

Let's appreciate the limitation in any diagram representing the evolutionary advancement in consciousness. In these representations, innumerable entities on every rung of the evolutionary ladder of conscious Spiritual development are left out. Nevertheless, the idea is to see the same *'essential'* Ba at every level of its immersion. This is expressed accordingly: E.A. Wallis Budge. *The Gods of the Egyptians, V.II*, p. 299.

> The mythological and religious texts contain indications that the Egyptians believed in what may be described as a "World-Soul," which they called Ba; its symbol was a bearded man-headed hawk…

---

* See Budge, *Prt Em Hru. (The Egyptian Book of the Dead).*

This symbol of Ba is again pictured at right.

What is Khepera?

In addition to letters (Neteru) the Kamitians used picture images or ideagraphs from nature all around them to communicate ideas which is, when combined, the language called MTU NTR. The Kamitians used the symbol Khepera, which powerfully expresses this divine creative process. Khepera is a scarab beetle that lays eggs, then rolls them up in dung and pushes them along in a ball. Another image of Khepera is pictured at right. The One Universal Ba is symbolized by the Scarab beetle Khepera. Within the One Universal Ba there is the particularization into the many. This is symbolized by the numerous eggs within the beetle Khepera which are the myriad to-be created forms, to-be birthed forth.

What was the Separation of the Sexes?

This brings us to the next -

Metaphysical Key To:
The Separation of the Sexes
The Afrikan 3rd Root Race consciousness is called the Egg-born.

Accordingly: *Secret Doctrine, V.ll*, p. 197.

> Almost sexless, in its early beginnings, it [the Third Race] became bisexual or androgynous; very gradually of course...But it is evident that the units of the Third Race humanity began to separate in their pre-natal shells, or eggs, and to issue of them as distinct male and female babes, ages after the appearance of its early progenitors.

The Afrikan 3rd Root Race consciousness is called the Egg-born. (See Barborka. *The Divine Plan*, p. 288.) It is in the 3rd Root Race that the separation of sexes occurred. From being previously a-sexual and hermaphrodite, humanity 'evolved' to become what it is now. A distinct man - bearing sperm, and a distinct woman - bearing eggs, who through sexual intercourse give birth to live young. The Afrikan 3rd Root Race becomes the egg born. *(Secret Doctrine V. ll*, p. 132, 198).

This division of the sexes is expressed as narrative of the Kamitic second *Book of Tehuti* called, the *Divine Pymander*, and is given accordingly: Alvin Boyd Kuhn. *The Lost Light*, p. 467 - 8.

> Being hermaphroditic, he is governed by powers both male and female. Air and water, the account runs, drew down from fire and Aether their subtle powers, and so nature produced bodies in the shape of men. **Thereupon the bond of all things was loosed by the will of God, and the males were cut apart from the females.** And straightway God ordered the creatures to increase and multiply, and bade them know themselves to be immortal, the cause of death being the too ardent love of body. **He that knew himself to be a mixture of high spirit with lowly body advanced to "superstantial good." But he that through erroneous love was enamored of body, abode wandering in darkness, sensible suffering the things of death.**

The Ausarianization of Consciousness Tablet Series 2 – A.C.T.S. 2
Metaphysical Keys To the Tree of Life & Oracle Keys to Dispelling Illusion
The Psycho/Spiritual Journey of Unfolding Consciousness

#8. Oracle Metaphysical Dis-Spelling Key: Meaning. See the relationship and oracle or story of the Neteru – Put word list together to tell a story.

Meaning:
Since all derives from the Black race, the Negro woman is Khepera on her scale of manifestation. Within her body are the **eggs** of the Races in the human family.

★*Afrikans/Negroes* - *The Black Woman is Khepera, bearing the eggs of the Races.*
★*Afrikans/Negroes* - Egg, The Golden Egg.

We will continue to deepen our understanding of the 'egg' as - **Our Story Continues...**

It is through Heru, which is the 4th plane in the Tree of Life that you come to relate the 3 Higher planes of consciousness (1-3, above) – the Higher Ego and Higher Manas with the 3 lower planes (5-7, below) – the lower ego and lower Manas. Heru is that aspect of your Spiritual Faculty where you are linking the Higher Spiritual nature with the lower material nature - both within you. We will see that this relating by the Heru aspect in you is how you find your way back Home after you have made your descent down the Tree of Life. This is expressed accordingly by: Gerald Massey. *Ancient Egypt. The Light of The World*, p. 892.

In his birth he says, "I am the babe" born as the connecting link betwixt earth and heaven, and as the one who does not die the second death (ch.42). **He issues from the disc or from the egg. He is pursued by the Herrut-reptile, but, as he says, his egg remains unpierced by the destroyer.**

This is derived from the Ritual Text of the *Prt Em Hru* which is further expressed accordingly: E.A. Wallis Budge. *The Egyptian Book of The Dead*, p. 356.

> I come forth and advance and my name is unknown. I am yesterday, and my name is 'Seer of millions of years.' I travel, I travel along the path of Heru the Judge. I am the lord of eternity; I feel and I have power to perceive. I am the lord of the red crown. I am the Sun's eye, yea, **I am in my egg, in my egg.** It is granted unto me to live therewith. **I am in the Sun's eye**, when it closeth, and I live by the strength thereof. I come forth and I shine; I enter in and I come to life. **I am in the Sun's eye, my seat is on my throne, and I sit thereon with the eye.** I am Heru who pass through millions of years. I have governed my throne and I rule it by the words of my mouth; and whether [I] speak or whether [I] keep silence, I keep the balance even. Verily my forms are changed. I am the god Unen, from season unto season;
> what is mine is with me. **I am the only One born of an only One.**

Secrets of Race & Consciousness Afrikan Cosmology of Kamit
with The Spiritual Meaning of The 'N' Word(s)
Neggur - The Goose Goddess who laid the Sun Egg, the Cosmic Egg

Revealed in Ka Ab Ba *(Kabala)* The Tree Of Life   **M**etaphysical **M**ysteries **M**eaning

★*Afrikans/Negroes* - "I am the babe" born as the connecting link betwixt earth and heaven, and as the one who does not die the second death *(ch.42)*.
★*Afrikans/Negroes* - *His egg remains unpierced by the destroyer.*
★*Afrikans/Negroes* - *I am the only One born of an only One.*
★*Afrikans/Negroes* - *I come forth and advance and my name is unknown*
★*Afrikans/Negroes* - *The name that proceeds the name that is unknown.*
★*Afrikans/Negroes* -. *I am Heru who pass through millions of years.*

As Heru we may all affirm: *I am the only One born of an only One.* This is Biblically expressed as the 'Only begotten Son.' Father-Spirit has a conscious experience of Mother-Matter. Ab Soul is the conscious experience of the divine marriage between the Father and Mother. As Heru, the relating aspect of Ab Soul, the *seeming* duality between Spirit-Matter with its myriad objective forms in play and display as Ba and Ka are seen as ONE.

We can see in these three diagrams moving from left to right that:

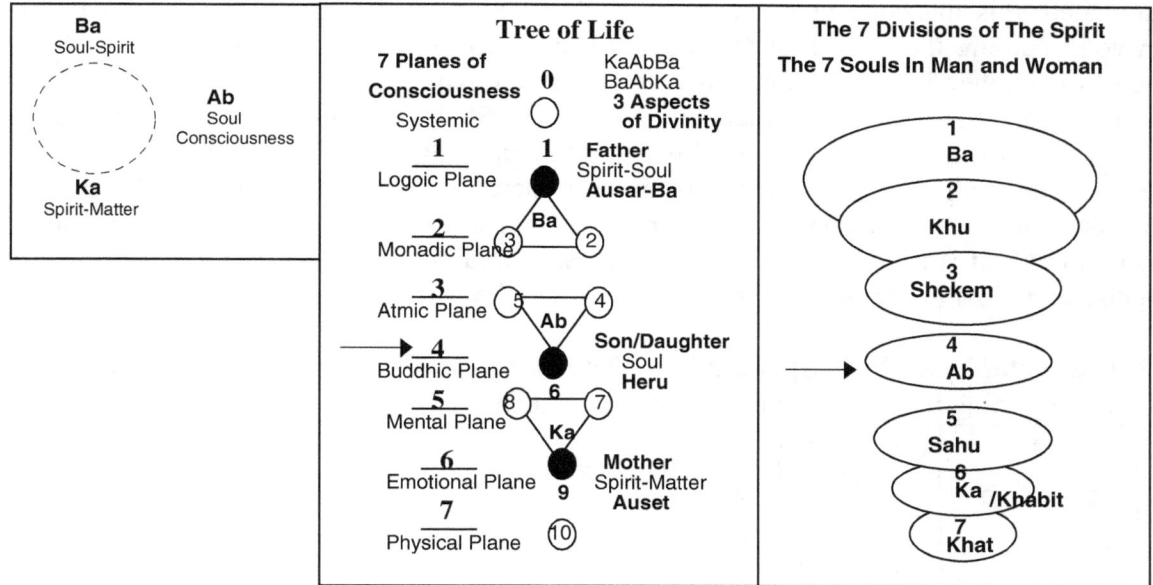

1. The Arising of the 1 and the 3 in the Divine Trinity
2. The 7 Planes of Consciousness
3. Heru (sphere 6) is located upon the 4th plane of consciousness in the Tree of Life (see arrow)
4. The Ab Triangle is the middle or 2nd triangle in the Tree of Life
5. The Ab Triangle is comprised of spheres 4, 5 and 6 in the Tree of Life
6. Heru as part of the Ab Triangle is the 2nd Aspect of Divinity in the Divine Trinity
7. The 4th division of Spirit or Soul is Ab
8. The 7 divisions of the Spirit, which are the 7 Souls.

Little else will be said here regarding the separation of the sexes except the obvious - which is the yearning that man and woman have to re-unite with the 'other side' of themselves persists till this day. This incessant yearning has contributed to the so called, 'mating dance' physical birth or reproduction and the 'battle '*between* the sexes' - all of which are 'seemingly' played out upon the physical plane. Even though you have precipitated out upon the physical plane in a predominantly male or female body, both male and female energies are resident within you. These are the positive (+) and receptive (-) or opposite poles.

Uniting the opposites is ultimately the Spiritual mating dance and battle *within* upon the long road of Ausarian resurrection. This battle within is waged between:

a. Spirit and Matter
b. Soul and personality/Ka-erect-er
c. That which is divine and that which is human in man and woman.

The ultimate marriage is not an external one occurring between man and woman. The ultimate marriage is the divine marriage within between Ausar and Auset as Spirit-Matter. When consummated, this marriage gives birth to the Son/Daughter as Heru or Karest/Christ Principle within you. You are the *becoming One* as you grow into full Soul conscious Sunship. It is a re-uniting of the Higher Self and lower self within. You are King Menes (Narmer) who is uniting the North and the South of Kamit. To meet and marry ones Soulmate* in the course of your journey is just an outer reflection of an inner Spiritual union happening within. Any disruption of the two-one-ness of the primal couple in consciousness is merely illusion. The seeming 'Two that have become One' as man and woman on the physical plane gives reflection of God on Earth. To reconstruct the Self is to move beyond the appearance and know the Self as One, and to know the Self as the *same* Self *everywhere present*. Let's dispell the word <u>marriage:</u>

 # 1. Oracle Metaphysical Dis-Spelling Key: Put letters of word or words together in a circle, like a serpent putting its tail in its mouth. Coming full Circle.

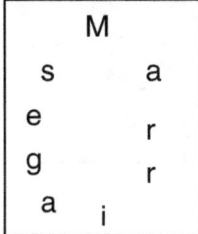 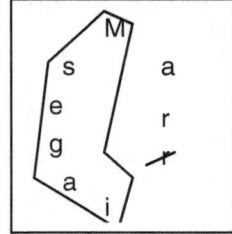

#2. Oracle Metaphysical Dis-Spelling Key: Read letters, putting together words, going forwards, backwards and in zig-zag patterns.
#3. Oracle Metaphysical Dis-Spelling Key: You may crossover in order to use a letter more than once. Place re-used letter in parenthesis ( ).
#4. Oracle Metaphysical Dis-Spelling Key: You may add a letter to complete a word. Place added letter in parenthesis ( ).
#5. Oracle Metaphysical Dis-Spelling Key: Letter substitution-you may substitute a letter. Place substituted letter in parenthesis ( ).
#6. Oracle Metaphysical Dis-Spelling Key: Make a list of derived words.

---
*See On The Way To Finding Your Soulmate. By Dr. Terri Nelson.

#12. Oracle Metaphysical Dispelling Key: Take out duplication of letters so that each letter appears only once.

Derived Word List:
Ra Images -

#8. Oracle Metaphysical Dis-Spelling Key: Meaning. See the relationship and oracle or story of the Neteru – Put word list together to tell a story.
Meaning:
Ra Images are the many ways the Sun Ra as Son/Daughter sees ITSELF in the other while still poised within the Ultimate Marriage of/as the One.

★*Afrikans/Negroes - Ra Images, The Marriage of Father/Spirit and Mother/Matter.*
★*Afrikans/Negroes - Ra Images are the many ways the Sun Ra as Son/Daughter sees ITSELF in the other while still poised within the Ultimate Marriage of/as the One.*

Let's continue to dispel the word <u>Negroes:</u>

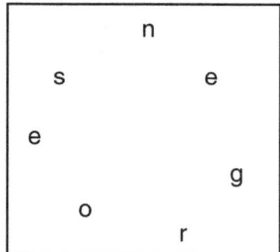

Derived Word List Continued:
Neg.

#7. Oracle Metaphysical Dis-Spelling Key: Look up definition (dictionary, glossary, reference texts, etc.)
Definition: In continuing to dispell the word Negroes the next key meanings come directly from the Kamitic language accordingly: E.A. Wallis Budge. *An Egyptian Hieroglyphic Dictionary,* p. 398

<u>Neg</u> – A bull, the four horned bull, god of heaven, to cackle.
    Meaning: Bull, Cow, symbols of generativity, virility and fertility.
<u>Negan</u> – Bull, ox.
<u>Negau</u> – The door keeper of the 4th Pylon.
<u>Negengen</u> – To destroy or break in pieces. (We will further dispel this word shortly).
<u>Negg</u>, <u>Negaga</u> - To cackle to quack.
<u>Nega</u> – cackler.
<u>Neggur</u> – the goose-goddess who laid the sun-egg.
    – <u>Gengen ur</u> – the Goose-god who laid the Cosmic Egg, Ibid: p. 472.
<u>Negagat</u> – Pendent of the breasts of a woman.

In the Kamitic tradition, the Divine Goose or "Great Cackler," laid the Cosmic Egg. This is pictured in the diagram at right. We will dispell the word cackler shortly.

#8. Oracle Metaphysical Dis-Spelling Key: Meaning. See the relationship and oracle or story of the Neteru - Put word list together to tell a story.

Meaning:
Here from Budge we have the word neggur accordingly: - the goose-god who laid the cosmic Egg.

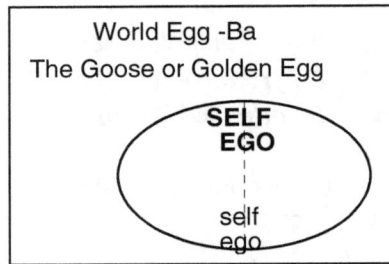

Let's dispel the word neggur:
#11. Oracle Metaphysical Dis-Spelling Key: What does the word sound like? Say the word out loud and then silently in a meditative state.

Derived Sounds Like List:
neggur sounds like negre, niger or nigger

Meaning:
Are we starting to see that the word Negur has older origin in its meaning than the 'negative' 16th century one so familiar to the so called 'modern World'?

★*Afrikans/Negroes* - *Neggur* -The goose-goddess who laid the sun-egg
★*Afrikans/Negroes* - The bull, the four horned bull, god of heaven, the cackler

Derived Word List Continued:
Go(o)se - Is derived from the Kamitic word neggur itself. See above.
Go Se(e) - Just as it sounds. To *Go* and *See*.
Seer -The wise, knower.
Neg eros - The bull of life.
Org see - To see from the original beginning.
R(i)ng see o - The ring of that which is seen full circle.
One r(i)sen G - The One risen G - od.
Snore (ing) G - The God - *unstirred*.
Seros, Neros - The God of the Sun and Moon Cycles of time.

Chapter 20
Negroes, Goose and The Game of Hide and Go Seek
AMEN Ra The Beautiful Goose

What is the meaning of the goose in the Kamitic Spiritual tradition?
Let's continue to the dispel the word <u>goose</u>:

#7. Oracle Metaphysical Dis-Spelling Key: Look up definition (dictionary, glossary, reference texts, etc.)
Definition: Accordingly: E.A. Wallis Budge. *The Gods of The Egyptians, V. l*, p. 374 - 375.
<u>Go(o)se</u> - "The Goose, or at least one species of it, was sacred to Amen-Ra, a fact which is hard to explain [read here: Hard for those who do not understand Our Story]. In a drawing given by Signor Lanzone we have a vase of flowers resting upon the ends of two pylon-shaped buildings, and on each of these stands a goose with its shadow, behind it, or by its side; the five lines of the text above read, **"Amen-Ra, the beautiful Goose,"** and **"the beautiful Goose of Amen-Ra."** In another scene which is likewise reproduced by Lanzone, is depicted a goose with its shadow standing on a building as before, and opposite to it is seated Amen-Ra; before the god and the goose is a table of offerings. The words above the god read, "Amen-Ra, the hearer of entreaty," and those over the goose are "the beautiful Goose, greatly beloved," In the earliest time the goose or rather gander, was associated with Seb [read here: Geb] or, the erpat, of the gods, who is called in the Book of the Dead **"the Great Cackler"**.

The Deity Geb (Seb, Keb) is pictured at right. He is the God of the Earth and he has the symbol of the Goose, who is sacred to him, on his head.

And Continuing:

The goose was a favourite article of food in Egypt, and was greatly in request for offerings in the temples; according to Herodotus (ii.37) a portion of the daily food of the priests consisted of goose flesh. The goose is said to have been sacred to Isis [read here: Auset], and the centre of the great trade in the bird was (chenoboscium or Chenoboscia), i.e., the "Goose pen," a town in Upper Egypt, which was situated in the nome Diospolites, and was quite near to the marshes wherein large numbers of geese were fattened systematically."

#8. Oracle Metaphysical Dis-Spelling Key: Meaning. See the relationship and oracle or story of the Neteru – Put word list together to tell a story.
Meaning:
When we say, 'Amen-Ra the beautiful Goose' - this is an At-one-ing identification which is stating - *I am that I am.* When we say, 'the beautiful Goose of Amen-Ra', there is the arising of subject and object. An awareness that has arisen in consciousness. We ask, Which Self am I? In the diagram at right we

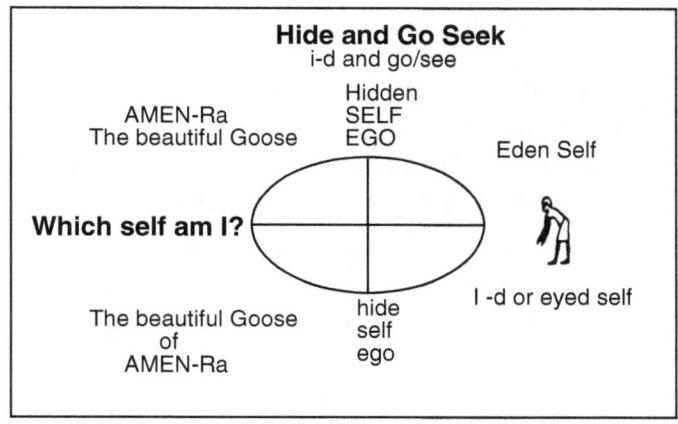

see the Hidden SELF - 'Amen-Ra the beautiful Goose.'

Let's dispel the word <u>hidden</u>:

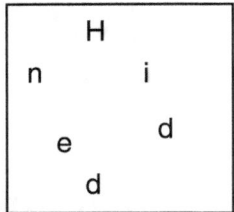

Derived Word List:
<u>Eden</u>
<u>Id</u>

Meaning:
Above the horizontal line or horizon we see the Hidden Self in the garden of Eden before it *goes out to see the* Self reflected in the 'seeming other self. Below the horizontal line we see the hide self - 'the beautiful Goose of Amen-Ra.', the self that 'seemingly' goes out. Likwise, if we dispell the word <u>hide</u> it reveals the word I-de. It is the I, eyed self, I-d-entity or I.D. It is the individuality we come to think we are.

1. The interiorly focused SELF - remains resident in the Higher World, the Higher Ego (Ba, Ab) *while* operating in the lower World through the use of mental, emotional and physical Soul bodies.
2. The exteriorly focused self - 'forgets' it residence in the Higher. This self is now hiding under bush, after bush or skin after skin of material form. Such hiding blots out or obscures the Light of the Soul, Ba.

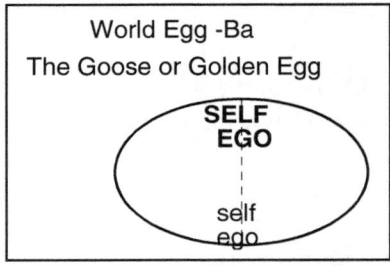

You can see in the diagram at right how the goose egg as a symbol of the skull also represents the left and right hemispheres of the brain. This is expressed accordingly: E. A. Wallis Budge. *The Gods of The Egyptians, V.I* p.109.

> The skull of this Pepi is that of the divine Goose; he cometh-forth and raiseth himself up in heaven.

We will dispell the word <u>Erpat</u> shortly.
Let's dispell the word <u>Cackler</u>:
 # 1. Oracle Metaphysical Dis-Spelling Key: Put letters of word or words together in a circle, like a serpent putting its tail in its mouth. Coming full Circle.

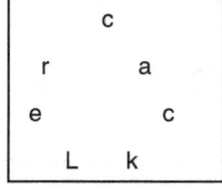 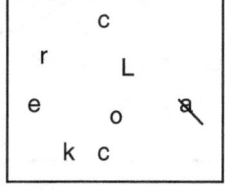

#11. Oracle Metaphysical Dis-Spelling Key: What does the word sound like? Say the word out loud and then silently in a meditative state.

Derived Sounds Like Word List:
Cl(o)cker - Letter 'o' substitutes for letter 'a.' What does the word Cackler sound like? Cackler sounds like clocker.

#8. Oracle Metaphysical Dis-Spelling Key: Meaning. See the relationship and oracle or story of the Neteru – Put word list together to tell a stor

Meaning:
The goose is the clocker. It starts the time and keeps time.

Dispelling of the word 'Negroes' brings us to the basic game in unfolding consciousness and Ausarian Resurrection. It is a game you know well called 'Hide and Go Seek.'

Let's review how the Game of *Hide and Go Seek* played

Players: In the Game of Hide and Go Seek you are the One True Self who 'seemingly' projects a 'self'- which is the same One Self - that then goes and hides. As you go hide the same one self under a bush and *forget* the One True Self that you are - your Soul Light becomes dimmed.•

Object of the Game:
1. The *self* goes out to hide while the *Self* remains at Ba(se) and counts or *cackles*, thus keeping time.
2. The Cackler is the clocker. The self moves out in a ring-pass-not of activity or circle defined by space and time. The clocker counts off, 1, 2, 3, 4, 5 and so on, up to some finite number. When that number is reached the Self goes out to find the self.
3. Meanwhile the self is also looking to find the Self, and make its return back Home to Ba(se). If the Self spots the self and reaches Ba(se) *first,* it shouts, 'I got your goose'. If the self can get back to Home Ba(se) first, it then shouts, 'I got my goose'.
4. What have we 'got' in playing this game? We are re-uniting the EGO with the ego, which falsely came to believe itself as separate. We get our Egg, our Ego, our Negroes back together again.

#2. Oracle Metaphysical Dis-Spelling Key: Read letters, putting together words, going forwards, backwards and in zig-zag patterns.
#3. Oracle Metaphysical Dis-Spelling Key: You may crossover in order to use a letter more than once. Place re-used letter in parenthesis ( ).
#4. Oracle Metaphysical Dis-Spelling Key: You may add a letter to complete a word. Place added letter in parenthesis ( ).
#5. Oracle Metaphysical Dis-Spelling Key: Letter substitution-you may substitute a letter. Place substituted letter in parenthesis ( ).

• We should take note that post 911 our greatest Light as a humanity may be hidden under a Bush (president) – at a time most perilous and most propitious, a time for greater darkness or greater illumination.

#6. Oracle Metaphysical Dis-Spelling Key: Make a list of derived words. Try to make the longest continuous unbroken word or string of words.

Secret Meaning of the Word Cracker

Let's dispel the word cracker:

Derived Word List Continued:

Crack EL - El is a name for God. Crack EL is fragmented consciousness of God or Broken God consciousness.

Cracke(r) - Does this give insight into why Europeans/Whites find it so insulting to be called 'crackers' by 'Negroes'? On some deep psycho-spiritual level, whites are seen as having cracked the egg, leading to part-I-cularization in consciousness? Cracker is part-o-cular or part seeing. It is the fragmentation of the I or eye that sees. It is apart - i - ed.

Meaning:
Again, a prayer is made that Ausar may,
> 'be saved from the attack made against him "at the crossing." (ch.135). This indicates that assault on his young divinity is made as soon as he crosses the line on the west in his descent. He is then **"the youngling in the egg"** and subject to the Herut attack. Here the dragon lay in wait to devour the young child'.

And Likewise

Expressed accordingly:

> My nest is not seen, **and I have not broken [read here: cracked] my egg.** I am lord of millions of years. I have made my nest in the uttermost parts of heaven. I have come down unto the earth of Seb [read here: Geb, Keb]

Let's now revisit and further dispel the word Negengen as previously described.

#7. Oracle Metaphysical Dis-Spelling Key: Look up definition (dictionary, glossary, reference texts, etc.)
Definition: E.A. Wallis Budge. *An Egyptian Hieroglyphic Dictionary,* p. 398.
Negengen - to destroy or break in pieces.

#8. Oracle Metaphysical Dis-Spelling Key: Meaning. See the relationship and oracle or story of the Neteru – Put word list together to tell a story.
Meaning:
In dispelling the word Ne-gen gen we see that if we reverse the double 'gen gen' to 'neg neg, then essentially it is to neg neg 2 times or to 're-neg'. Let's dispel the word reneg or renege.

Definition: Thesaurus, Dictionary.
Renege - To go back on, break your word, break a promise. 1. To fail to carry out a promise or commitment. See renegade.

Meaning Continued:
To renege is to fail to come back to the consciousness of the fullness of the One True Self you have always been from the beginingless beginning. It is to be renegade from your

stationing in your eternal home while/as you do you work in the outer World. You renege on your full identity or I.D. You are negengen.

To review from *A.C.T.S. 1. Ka Ab Ba Building The Lighted Temple* we learned about the downspiral in material consciousness in this time cycle of Planetary history. This is expressed accordingly: Vera Stanley Adler. *Initiation of The World,* p.140:

> Civilization moved westward once more. Those branches of the Aryan sub-races who were to perform the great feat of taking the deepest, most blinding dip into matter, there to wrestle for its mastery on its own level (without the aid of spiritual insight) were being collected together in the ordained lands-France, Germany, Britain and many of their neighbors. It is now time for the lowest depths of the material World to be sounded, and having been mastered fairly, upon its own level, to be raised and fused with the highest possible spiritual level.*

Remember the childhood jingle Humpty Dumpty?
The following nursery rhyme reflects the brokeness, separation and part-i-cularization in consciousness operative within man and woman and between the human family on our Planet today. It is the result of the descent down the Tree of Life and becoming forgetful of our Image and Likeness of God - symbolized by Ausar - The One True Self - sphere 1.

"Humpty Dumpty
Sat on a wall
Humpty Dumpty
Had a Great Fall
All the King's horses and all the King's men
Couldn't put Humpty together again"

What is the Metaphysical Meaning of the Game Hide and Go Seek?
- The *Hidden Self* is the Eternal that we are and have always been from the beginningless beginning.
- The *hide self* is what we have hidden under coats of skin or a bush.
- These coats of skin are the physical, emotional and mental Soul bodies.
- We hide under flesh in the physical body.
- We hide under glamour of emotions such as: fear, desire, loss, anger, greed, etc
- We hide under our thoughtforms, all the thinking about thing-ness in our minds.
- Where is the true Self to be found under all of this game playing that deludes and diminishes us into a lesser sense?
- It is a game that has us thinking the Self is separated, isolated, from the One True Self.
- How could this be when IT *is* the same One True Self which is in all Selves?
- The Self that is seeking, and the Self that is sought, *are One.*

---

* In her book, *The Initiation of The World*, p.140, Vera Stanley Adler is describing a smaller Kali Yuga cycle (4,320, 43,200) within the greater Kali Yuga of 432,000 . Nevertheless her description for the smaller cycle is aptly reflected in the larger cycle.

- You just had to *go-see or goose* for yourself.
- We go hide then we must seek the self that we have hidden.
- As the One Self urges the other 'seeming self(s)' to return, the hiding self is stimulated to return and touch goose - Aha!

The Egg of Earth Humanity Individual and Collective Consciousness

From the arising of these Twin Forces we see the company of the Gods emerge. In the following Cosmic genealogy we see Gods/Goddesses Shu and Tefnut give birth to Geb and Nut who in turn, give birth to the Gods/Goddesses:

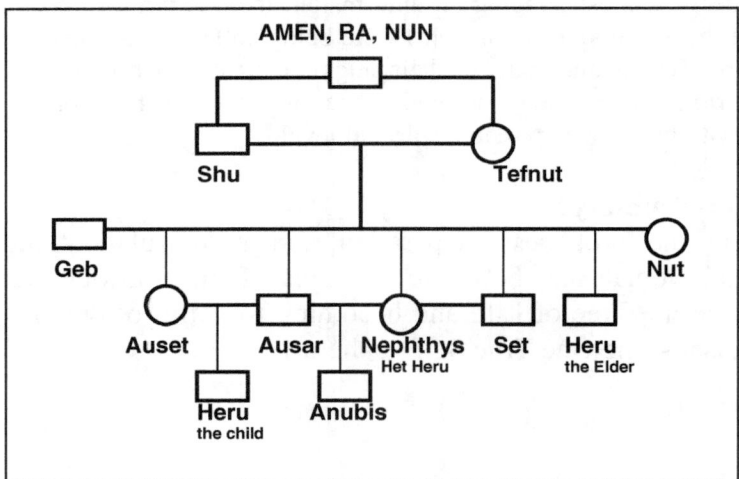

Let's take for closer examination the words, 'In the earliest time the goose or rather gander, was associated with Geb (Seb, Keb), the erpat, of the gods'. The goose was a sacred animal to Geb, as such he was sometimes called "The Great Cackler" As the God of earth, the earth formed his body and was called the "house of Geb." Accordingly: E. A. Wallace Budge. The *Gods of The Egyptians*. V. 2. 94 -99.

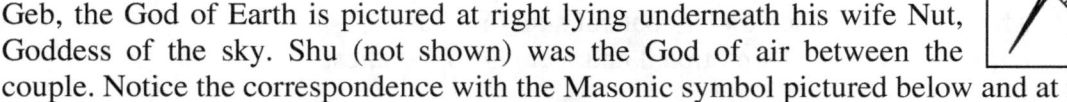

Geb, the God of Earth is pictured at right lying underneath his wife Nut, Goddess of the sky. Shu (not shown) was the God of air between the couple. Notice the correspondence with the Masonic symbol pictured below and at right.

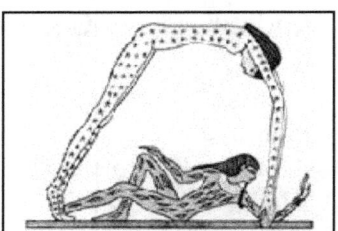

In Kamit Cosmology, Geb and Nut produced the Great Egg from which the Sun-god sprang. Again pictured at right, we see the Golden Goose on the head of Geb. The Goose/Gander - like Khepera, like the Black Man/Woman, like the Neg (Bull/Cow) - is a symbol of fertility, virility and generativity. The goose eggs, symbolize the birth to humanity, or more accurately, the individual and collective consciousness of humanity. Geb is one of the company of the gods who watch the weighing of the heart of the deceased in the Judgment Hall of Ausar. He provides

the righteous with the necessary words of power to enable them to make their escape from the earth wherein their bodies were laid, but the wicked were held fast by Geb (Seb, Keb). Geb would hold imprisoned the souls of the wicked, that they might not ascend to heaven. Are we starting to see the importance of a 'word(s)' in our Spiritual and Psycholological Journey of Unfolding Consciousness?

Secrets of Race & Consciousness Afrikan Cosmology of Kamit
with The Spiritual Meaning of The 'N' Word(s)
Neggur - The Goose Goddess who laid the Sun Egg, the Cosmic Egg

Revealed in Ka Ab Ba *(Kabala)* The Tree Of Life   Metaphysical Mysteries Meaning

Let's take for closer examination and dispell the words, Nut and Geb using the next -

> **Metaphysical Keys to:**
> **Oracle Metaphysical Dis-Spelling Keys**

#15. Oracle Metaphysical Dis-Spelling Key: You may combine two or more words as one word.
Derived Word List:
Nutgeb

Let's continue to dispell the word Nutgeb:
 # 1. Oracle Metaphysical Dis-Spelling Key: Put letters of word or words together in a circle, like a serpent putting its tail in its mouth. Coming full Circle.

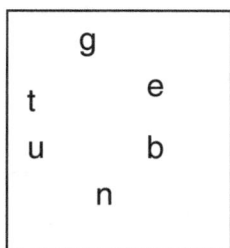 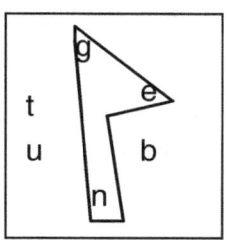

#2. Oracle Metaphysical Dis-Spelling Key: Read letters, putting together words, going forwards, backwards and in zig-zag patterns.
#6. Oracle Metaphysical Dis-Spelling Key: Make a list of derived words. Try to make the longest continuous unbroken word or string of words.

Derived Word List Continued:
Genbut

#7. Oracle Metaphysical Dis-Spelling Key: Look up definition (dictionary, glossary, reference texts, etc.)
Definition: Accordingly: E.A. Wallis Budge. *An Egyptian Hieroglyphic Dictionary.v.ll.* p. 809.
Genbut - A man with woolly hair. A people of Punt.

Geb, Seb and Keb are given as names for the Earth God. Let's dispel the word Seb:

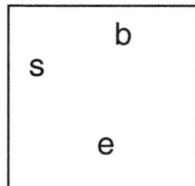 

Derived word list:
Bes

The Ausarianization of Consciousness Tablet Series 2 – A.C.T.S. 2
Metaphysical Keys To the Tree of Life & Oracle Keys to Dispelling Illusion
The Psycho/Spiritual Journey of Unfolding Consciousness

Definition: Bes, pictured at right, was a fertility god who personified the earth itself. He was not a god of Egyptian origin. Bes was described as 'Coming from the Divine Land' and 'Lord of Punt'. He is associated with pregnancy, childbirth, protection, music, merriment and war. He is linked with the goddesses, Hathor (Het-Heru), Ta-urt, and wife Beset – the divine mothers.

#8. Oracle Metaphysical Dis-Spelling Key: Meaning. See the relationship and oracle or story of the Neteru - Put word list together to tell a story.
Meaning: Bes - is miscalled pigmy, dwarf, or bushman because of his short stature and is related to the Twa and San Bushmen who are a class of our Ancestral Progenitors.

Pictured at right we see the combined triple deities of Nut, Geb and Shu.
Let's dispel the words Nut, Geb and Shu:
#15. Oracle Metaphysical Dis-Spelling Key: You may combine two or more words as one word.

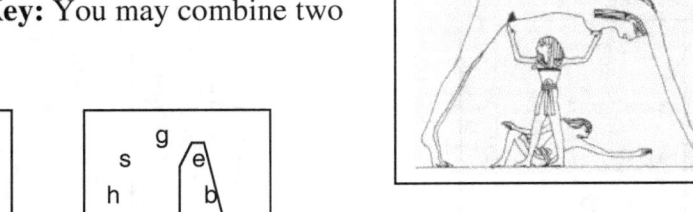

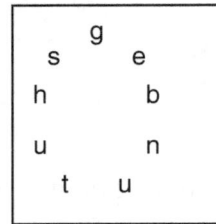 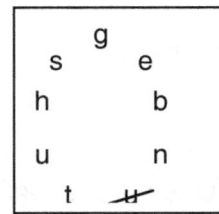 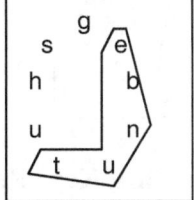

 # 1. Oracle Metaphysical Dis-Spelling Key: Put letters of word or words together in a circle, like a serpent putting its tail in its mouth. Coming full Circle.
#2. Oracle Metaphysical Dis-Spelling Key: Read letters, putting together words, going forwards, backwards and in zig-zag patterns.
#5. Oracle Metaphysical Dis-Spelling Key: Letter substitution-you may substitute a letter. Place substituted letter in parenthesis ( ).
#6. Oracle Metaphysical Dis-Spelling Key: Make a list of derived words. Try to make the longest continuous unbroken word or string of words.
#7. Oracle Metaphysical Dis-Spelling Key: Look up definition (dictionary, glossary, reference texts, etc.)
#8. Oracle Metaphysical Dis-Spelling Key: Meaning. See the relationship and oracle or story of the Neteru - Put word list together to tell a story.
#9. Oracle Metaphysical Dis-Spelling Key: Take each letter one at a time or in combination with one or more letters and derive its meaning.
#12. Oracle Metaphysical Dispelling Key: Take out duplication of letters so that each letter appears only once.

Derived Word List:
B GET SUN
SHENUT G B
Nehesu

NutBe/NutBa/Bentu/B(a)ntu

#8. Oracle Metaphysical Dis-Spelling Key: Meaning. See the relationship and oracle or story of the Neteru - Put word list together to tell a story.

Meaning:
B GET SUN - be gotten Sun/Son
SHENUT G B - outgoing footsteps 'b' of the Shenit or Shinning G-od. Recall the word, Shenit and Shine, dispelled previously, p. 62 - 64, 94.
Recall the words, *'I am the only One born of an only One'*, p.101, from the *Prt Em Hru* and the words, *'Only begotten Son'*, Biblically expressed.
Nehesu –Negroes.
NutBe/NutBa/Bentu/B(a)ntu – Ba means Soul. The Souls of Nut, Nubians.
Accordingly: Dr Kimbwandende Kia Bunseki Fu-Kiau. Bantu means Sacred human beings.

In the Kikongo language Dr Kimbwandende Kia Bunseki Fu-Kiau teaches the mantra,
    Mono I nginga ninga
    I am a seed of a seed.

The seed has correspondence with the Sun and the Sun has correspondence with the Cosmic Egg or Universe. All have correspondence with the eye or the All Seeing Eye of Ra. All have correspondence with the Ego, individual and collective consciousness of humanity. See, *Ka Ab Ba Building The Lighted Temple* for more on the Cosmology and Cosmogenesis of the Cosmic Egg.

- When the eye of Ra, the Sun God
- Arises upon the waters of Nun
- It sees
- In the game of seeing ITSELF
- It see(d)s the seeming multiple selfs
- Each seed is - a self sighting of the One
- And the Same Self everywhere (seen)

Let's dispel the words Nut, Seb and Shu:
#15. Oracle Metaphysical Dis-Spelling Key: You may combine two or more words as one word.

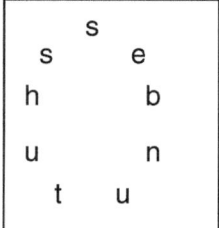 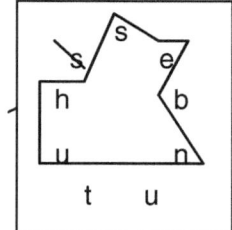

Derived Word List:
Nesu – b(i)t, Neshu –b(it), Nesu – but

#8. Oracle Metaphysical Dis-Spelling Key: Meaning. See the relationship and oracle or story of the Neteru - Put word list together to tell a story.
Meaning:
Nesu – b(i)t, Neshu –b(it), Nesu – but - the title for King of Upper and Lower Kamit/Egypt.
Accordingly: Hilary Wilson. *Understanding Hieroglyphic*. p. 54 -55.

Let's dispel the words Nut, Keb, Shu:
#15. Oracle Metaphysical Dis-Spelling Key: You may combine two or more words as one word.

#11. Oracle Metaphysical Dis-Spelling Key: What does the word sound like? Say the word out loud and then silently in a meditative state.
Derived Word List:
Kebsenut - Sounds like – Kebsenuef
 Meaning: - God of the West, one of the four Children of Heru, the symbol of the Falcon/Hawk, Soul, Sun

As stated earlier, in the earliest time the goose or rather gander, was associated with Seb, the erpat, of the gods, who is called in the Book of the Dead **"the Great Cackler"**.

Let's dispell erpat:

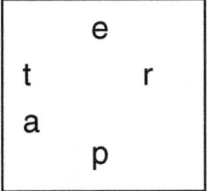

Derived Word List:
Part
(S)epar(a)t(e)
Trap
Tear
Reap T -Reap from the creations of the mother.
Rape T - Rape the creations of the mother.
Prate
  Definition: Thesaurus:
  Prate - Talk, babble, chat, cackle.

Era - specific time period.
  Definition:
  Era - Number; they were without number; numberless

Taper
> **Definition:**
> Taper - To delimit, diminish, lesson

Ap(p)ear
> **Definition:**
> To become visible. To come into existence. To seem likely.

Meaning:
The Goose who begins to cackle, talk and keep time. Thus begins the 'seeming' divisioning of the fullness of the total sound boundaried by the Egg into lesser sounds or cackles, which now delimit space and time, or - era. Creating room for era, which is a period of time, paradoxically creates room for a period of error. It marks a period of trial and testing the way of descent and re-ascent. To babble is to make *ba/by*, *Ba* or *Ba el* sounds - not quite the whole sound of Ba. Thus the appearance of all the seeming selves.

Derived Word List Continued:

Apt
> **Definition:** 1. We have the following meaning for Apt accordingly: E.A. Wallis Budge. *Hieroglyphic Glossary V. l*, p. 5, 119, 414.
>
> **Apt** - **To flutter, to alight as a bird. Goose, duck; part of a ship; green goose.**
> App - To journey, to traverse.
> Aper - A boat equipped with everything necessary and a crew; mantle, garment; a kind of goose; the egg of the aper goose.
> Ap - A verb of motion, to travel, to go, to go in, to go out; to fly, the winged disk, the summer solstice.
> Aperit - A name of the Eye of Horus [read here: Heru]

Apt
> **Definition:** Here we find a quote from Albert Churchward. *Signs and Symbols of Primordial Man*, p. 124, giving more meaning to the word 'Apt' accordingly:
> Apt - "Thus the Elder Horus, who was the child of the Great Mother Apt, was the child of his mother who was born but not begotten…."

Aperture
> **Definition:** *Dictionary*.
> Aperture - A usually adjustable opening in an optical instrument, such as a camera or a telescope that limits the amount of light passing through a lens or onto a mirror.

Meaning:
To see through an aperture is to get a 'bird's eye view.' A narrowing or expanding view by the eye. A device that delimits so that you can see in part.

Chapter 21
N-G-R – The Goose-Goddess who laid the Cosmic Sun Egg
N-G-R   The 'N' Word For God
The R-e-n-e-g-i-n-g King   The R-e-i-n-i-n-g King   The R-e-ne-g-a-d-e King

As stated earlier, the name for the 'divne words/speech of the Gods' is variously spelled and some of the forms are as follows: Mtu Ntr, Mdw Ntr, Medu Neter, Mdw Netcher, Metu Neter, Medew Netjer, Mdw, Net-ger and so on. Like the word Metu Neter, in the language itself, various vowels are added, substituted, and/or subtracted before or after the primal consonants used to make up a word and convey its meaning. The vowels lend themselves to facility in pronunciation.

The words Neter, Netcher, Netjer, Ntr, or Net-ger mean God, Divine, or qualities of Divinity. It is easy to see how the word for God could be pronounced N-G-R. Subsequently, the words Negroes, Nigers, Niggers, Nigeria, etc. evolve as vowels are added/substituted/subtracted before or after these primal consonants. We can likewise see from the previous chapter how Neter, Netcher, Netjer, Ntr, Net-ger or **'N-G-R'** may move from a positive, life promoting and unifying vibration to a vibration that is destructive, disintegrating and life negating when sounded.

Let's dispel the word '**N-G-R' or N-G-R-I'** :
#9. Oracle Metaphysical Dis-Spelling Key: Take each letter one at a time or in combination with one or more letters and derive its meaning.
Derived letter or Neter list:
N – out of the waters of Nun, Fount of all possibilities
G – the mouth of the Universal God opens, whose breath
R – gives rise to the fire of Ra, causing the arising of the ALL seeing Eye of Ra
I – the eye that sees

You will recall the from chapter 4 the following Metaphysical Laws -

Metaphysical Law Key To: The Law of Vibration	**Metaphysical Key To:** Involutionary and Evolutionary Cycles The Spiritualization and Materialization in Consciousness

We can see how **'N-G-R'** , **N-G-R-I,** or **N-G-R-E** may move from a positive life promoting vibration to a vibration that is destructive and life negating in our Afrikan Cosmology of the Goose-goddess who laid the Cosmic Egg. Words may be seen as having a Positive, Neutral or Negative vibration and meaning in Metu Neter and English, depending on intent, invocation and circumstance. This is demonstrated in the word list that follows:

Secrets of Race & Consciousness Afrikan Cosmology of Kamit
with The Spiritual Meaning of The 'N' Word(s)
Neggur - The Goose Goddess who laid the Sun Egg, the Cosmic Egg

Revealed in Ka Ab Ba *(Kabala)* The Tree Of Life   **M**etaphysical **M**ysteries **M**eaning

Mtu Ntr		English		Other
E.A. Wallis Budge. An Egyptian Hieroglyphic Dictionary.V. 1 & ll		*The American Heritage Dictionary of The English Language*		
Neggur - the goose-goddess who laid the sun-egg	Negengen - to destroy, to break in pieces	Negus, Negoos - (King, title Ethiopian Emperors)	Denigrate	*We find some powerful uses of the N word in the Kikongo language. A short list of Kikongo words and their meaning is given accordingly: Dr Kimbwandende Kia Bunseki Fu-Kiau*
Gengen ur - the Goose-god who laid the Cosmic Egg	Neg,nega - to strike, to smite, to cut off, to cut open, to hew, to slay to crush	Negress	Degenerate	
Neter, Netcher, Netjer, Ntr, Net-ger, N-G-R - God, Divine, or qualities of Divinity		Negro	Niggardly	
		Green – negre,	Nigger	**Kikongo**
		Meaning:	Ignorant	Nginga - Seed
	Neg, nega - to lack, to want, to be short of, to be few in number	Afrikans/Negroes are to the human kingdom what vegetables are to the vegetable kingdom - we blanket the earth, giving life and vitality. *Dr Nteri*	Indigent	Mwene Kongo - King
Negau - bull, ox, cow (symbols of fertility/generativity)			English	NGIENA - I AM
	Negeb - to break, to be destroyed, to come to an end		Genuflect	Ngolo - Energy, power, electricity
Neg - bull, bull of bulls	Negebgeb - to break		Genocide	Zinga - Living
Neg - the four horned bull god of heaven	Negeb - a water god		Gentrifica-tion	Ngindu - Psyche
	Negemgem - to conspire against, to hatch a plot	Engender	Negative	Me Mpungu - God Almighty
Negau - the doorkeeper of the 4th Pylon		Negotiate	Neglect	Kinenga - balance
	Negen - to cut, to slay	Generous	Negation	Nganga - Masters
Neg - to cackle		Gene	Negro	Ku Kanga –school of initiation
Negg - to cackle to quack	Negeh - to be weak, inactive	Generativity	Renege	N'king-umia-nzingila - Principles of life/living
Negaga - to cackle, to quack		Genital	Gun	Kalunga - One-who-is-complete-by-self, the all-in-all
Nega - cackler		Genius	Gang	
Negneg - ur - no meaning listed		Integrity	Hung	Yungual - to burn up
Negaga - ur - no meaning listed		Intelligence		
		Integer		
Negit - one of the eight weeping goddesses		Ignite		
		Negative		
Negagat - pendent of the breasts of a woman		Integrate		
		Gynecology		
Negait - semen, essence		Ing (all action, to be, to do)		
		Engineer		
		Dignity		
		Energy		
		English		
		Enlighten		
		King		
		Q(g)ueen		
		Generation		
		Granite (see		

The Ausarianization of Consciousness Tablet Series 2 – A.C.T.S. 2
Metaphysical Keys To the Tree of Life & Oracle Keys to Dispelling Illusion
The Psycho/Spiritual Journey of Unfolding Consciousness

Negnit - a goddess (solar?) who befriended the dead Neges - to overflow Ngesges - to be heaped up full with something, to overflow, overloaded, overflowing		statues in Kamit, made of) Genuflect Genuine Nzinga –Queen of Angola Gang Genii Magnify Hung (hekau, mantra)		
Gengen ur - the Goose-god who laid the Cosmic Egg Gengen - t - a seed or plant used in medicine Gengenu - records, archives, annals Gen - reed, plant, water plants Genur - a god who presides over offerings Gen urit - goddess of offerings Genn - to be gentle or gracious Gen - petitioner, to beseech Gen-t - heap, abundance Genu - a kind of bird, crane Genbut - a man with wooly hair Gemh - sight, glance, look Gemh - to see, to look, to perceive Gen-t - memorial, record, archive, memorandum	Gen - to cry out, to beg. Gen - to be weak, helpless, limp Genn - to be weak, helpless, to be paralysed or spellbound Genn - weaknesses, defects, troubles Genf - to revile to abuse Genmu- servants, vassals Genkh - to work Genkha - to be subject to, to toil under orders Gemh - to weep, to mourn			Negus nagast – king Nigiste Nagast - queen, *Historical Dictionary of Ethiopia By David Hamilton Shinn, p. 220. (Ethiopia)* Huang – King *Columbia Encyclopedia, Sixth Edition Date: 2008 (China)* Yang di-Pertuan Negara - "He who is made Lord of the State - Malay royalty *(Malay)* Ngwenyama - King *royal title (Swazi)* Ghana - King title 'war chief' *History Corner, The Empire of (Ghana)* Gangga Negara - "a city on the Ganges", the name derived from Ganganagar Kingdom *(Sanskrit)* Gyname - This west African symbol means" None know the beginning or end of the world except for God.
Kring - Mantra, Hekau (Metu Neter, Sanskrit)				**Royal Names.** *ChinaroadLowchen.* Konge - King *(Danish)* Koning - King *(Dutch)* Konig - King *(German)* Konnungur - King *(Icelandic)* Kung - King *(Sweedish)*

The R-e-n-e-g-i-n-g King   The R-e-i-n-i-n-g King   The R-e-ne-g-a-d-e King

In our Afrikan Cosmology of the Goose-goddess who laid the Cosmic Sun Egg we see that –

• On a Higher Spiritual Vibration and turn of the spiral we move within/from a state of wholeness and intergrity of the Egg with the invocation of the Neter or name:

Neggur – The goose-goddess who laid the sun-egg or **Gengen ur** – the Goose-god who laid the Cosmic Sun Egg.

With so many references to the word 'King' even in this short list of words – let's recall again as previously expressed -

> In his birth he says, "I am the babe" born as the connecting link betwixt earth and heaven, and as the one who does not die the second death (ch.42). **He issues from the disc or from the egg. He is pursued by the Herrut-reptile, but, as he says, his egg remains unpierced by the destroyer.**

> I come forth and advance and my name is unknown. I am yesterday, and my name is 'Seer of millions of years.' I travel, I travel along the path of Heru the Judge. I am the lord of eternity; I feel and I have power to perceive. I am the lord of the **red crown**. I am the Sun's eye, yea, I am **in my egg, in my egg**. It is granted unto me to live therewith. **I am in the Sun's eye,** when it closeth, and I live by the strength thereof. I come forth and I **shine**; I enter in and I come to life. I am in the **Sun's eye**, my seat is on my throne, and I sit thereon with the eye. I am Heru who pass through millions of years. I have governed my throne and I rule it by the words of my mouth; and whether [I] speak or whether [I] keep silence, **I keep the balance even**. Verily my forms are changed. I am the god Unen, from season unto season; what is mine is with me. **I am the only One born of an only One.**

In this verse Heru, which is you and I, is the Sun's eye, Lord of the red crown, and King seated upon the throne which he/she rules as the only One born of an only One, as a Sun -Son/Daughter of God. See *A.C.T.S. 1. Ka Ab Ba Building The Lighted Temple* for a more complete understanding of Heru, the Ka rest (Christ) within you and the battle that is waged between Heru with his jealous brother Set for ascendency to the throne as ***King.***

Let's dispell the word **K-I-N-G** and **N-G-R-I'**:
#15. Oracle Metaphysical Dis-Spelling Key: You may combine two or more words as one word.
#12. Oracle Metaphysical Dispelling Key: Take out duplication of letters so that each letter appears only once. If we combine the words King with N-G-R-I we have -

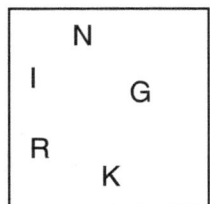

Derived word list:
N-G K-R-I'

Let's continue to dispel the word '**N-G K-R-I**':
#9. Oracle Metaphysical Dis-Spelling Key: Take each letter one at a time or in combination with one or more letters and derive its meaning.
Derived letter or Neter list:
N – out of the waters of Nun, Fount of all possibilities
G – the mouth of the Universal God opens, whose breath
R – gives rise to the fire of Ra, causing the arising of the ALL seeing Eye of Ra
I – the eye that sees
K – in all directions of space and time

Meaning: The **'N-G K-R-I'** is the Reinging King.

We will dispell the letter 'K' shortly. For now we can see that:
•On a Lower Material Vibration and turn of the spiral we move to a state where the Egg has been weakened, cracked, bound, and diminished with the invocation of the Neter or name:
Negengen – To destroy or break in pieces
Recall the word, **Negengen**, dispelled previously, p. 105, 109.
In dispelling the word Ne-gen gen we see that if we reverse the double 'gen gen' to 'neg neg, then essentially it is to neg neg 2 times or to're-neg'. Let's dispel the word <u>reneg or renege</u>.
Definition: Thesaurus, Dictionary.
<u>Renege</u> - To go back on, break your word, break a promise. 1. To fail to carry out a promise or commitment. See renegade.
Meaning Continued:
To renege is to fail to come back to the consciousness of the fullness of the One True Self you have always been from the begininglass beginning. It is to be renegade from your stationing in your eternal home while/as you do you work in the outer World. You renege on your full identity or I.D. You are negengen.

Meaning Continued:
The R-e-n-e-g-i-n-g King - this is how the reing-ing King, N-G-K-R-I is dethroned and becomes the renege-ing King, less than the fullness of the one True Self that he/she has always been from the begininglass beginning. He/she suffers a brokenness in consciousness of who they are as Sun/Son –Daughter God.

Again, a prayer is made that Ausar may,
> 'be saved from the attack made against him "at the crossing." (ch. 135). This indicates that assault on his young divinity is made **as soon as he crosses the line on the west** in his descent. He is then "the **youngling in the egg**" and subject to the Herut attack. Here the dragon lay in wait to devour the young child.

> My nest is not seen, and I have not broken [read here: cracked] my egg. I am lord of millions of years. I have made my nest in the uttermost parts of heaven. I have come down unto the earth of Seb [read here: Geb, Keb]'

Meaning Continued:

Secrets of Race & Consciousness Afrikan Cosmology of Kamit
with The Spiritual Meaning of The 'N' Word(s)
Neggur - The Goose Goddess who laid the Sun Egg, the Cosmic Egg

Revealed in Ka Ab Ba *(Kabala)* The Tree Of Life   **M**etaphysical **M**ysteries **M**eaning

The R-e-i-n-i-n-g King - the word N-G-K-R-I is to be sounded oracly and circularly as indicated by the diagrams at right. When done thus so, it renders the sound, sounded in the ancient hekau or mantra (word of power) **'K-r-i-n-g'**. This ancient mantra is invocative of power and corresponds with the deity Seker in the 3rd sphere of the Tree of Life (see *Ka Ab Ba Building The Lighted Temple*, Dr Terri Nelson, see Ancient Mantras). 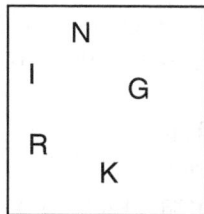 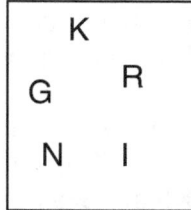 Remember, each letter is a Neter, a divine quality of God, and a living being. When combined and put in a circle they become a mouthpiece through which God speaks. So God is speaking through the 'N''G' 'K''R''I' or K' 'R' 'I' 'N' 'G'. It is about the intention during meditation that guides what is manifested in the use of this Metu Neter. More information will be revealed in future, *The Ausarianization of Consciousness Tablet Series – A.C.T.S.* For now it is important, especially for our youth of today, when sounding this word of power to do so by enunciating the 'N' first by putting the tongue at the roof of the mouth and sounding the rest of the word oracly and circulary as if one continuous sound as in the following:.

N-G K-R-I N-G K-R-I N-G K-R-I N-G K-R-I N-G K-R-I N-G K-R-I N-G K-R-I N-G K-R-I-N-G
Or souned with the just the power of the consonants
N-G- K-R N-G K-R N-G K-R N-G K-R N-G K-R N-G K-R N-G K-R N-G K-R N-G K-R- N-G K-R N-G K

What Does the Letter/Neter ' K ' Represent?
Not only did the lower vibration of, N-I-G-R and N-G-K-R-I begin to be used but the vibrational energy of the 'K' became distorted in our Afrikan Psyche with the terrorizing that took place in the name of this Neter under 'KKK' - the Klu Klux Klan. When the energies are invoked in this way they have become inverted and distorted.

The 'K' symbol pictured at right is one of the most powerful symbols in the Ancient Mysteries. When viewed one dimentionally, two K's are seen here turned back to back. However, you must move within your 1st eye and see this symbol as K's that are rotating, within the sphere, which is the Golden Sun God Egg. If you imagine yourself sitting within this symbol and *spinning* around in all directions like the Jack(s) you perhaps played with as a child - you witness/become the revolving face(s) of the ONE GOD - WHO now sees in all directions. It is a symbol of advanced humanity who is now able to see the 'seeming' other brother's/brothers' or sister's/sisters' point of view. Ж is the Sema or Smai Tawi symbol of unification that combines the Meter Neter sema which means union with the symbols for the two lands of Kamit - Papyrus for the North and Lotus flower for the South. In the first Smai Tawi symbol pictured at right, Deities Heru and Set find unity, balance, poise and equanimity within Universal Law.

The **Ж or АЖЕ** Neter symbol is likewise the Null, or zero point '0' from which we move from the unmanifest to the manifest. It is the point of arising and moving out it into matter and the point where matter is abstracted back into Spirit. The Smai Tawi symbol is the ancient flooding of the Nile or Hapi River during the Season

of Aket. Deities Hapi are pictured at right making up this same symbol. This flooding has correspondence with the arising of the Universal Waters or Life Force, which brings renewal and regeneration. When we practice Shækem RA AЖ E we open ourselves to be as channels for this life giving energy, just as the Nile itself is a life giving channel, flooding its restorative waters.

This same symbol, pictured at right is seen carved on the thrones of the Kings of Ancient Kamit. Pictured at right we see King Khafre Seated.(Giza; Fourth Dynasty, reign of Khafre (ca. 2520–2494 B.C.E.). Graywacke; H. 47 1/4 in. (120 cm). Egyptian Museum, Cairo (CG 15).

How do we derive this symbol in the Cosmic Egg?
As indicated in, **A.C.T.S. 1. Ka Ab Ba Building The Lighted Temple in the following review:** Recall our Cosmic Egg from previous chapters pictured at right. This is the symbol of the World Egg which then becomes divided as follows:

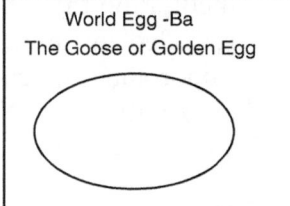
World Egg -Ba
The Goose or Golden Egg

1. The vertical line on the cross of **Spirit-Matter** forming a left and right half of the circle

2. The horizontal line on the cross of **Manifestation** forming an upper and lower circle

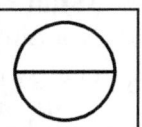

3. Arising at the center and intersecting each axis and forming a crossroad again we have•

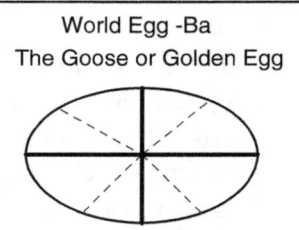
World Egg -Ba
The Goose or Golden Egg

What Do The V's's Represent?
The lines forming the 'V' of the 'K' represent the outgoing footsteps in the Spiritual and Psychological Journey of Unfolding Consciousness in time and space along the involutional and evolutional arc pictured at left. In the Afrikan Cosmology of Kamit these outgoing foot steps are symbolized as the foot steps of the Goose, pictured at right, the Goose God, the *Neggur, the Ego*.

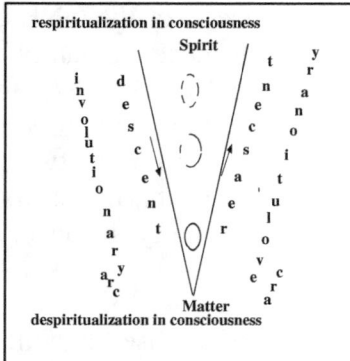
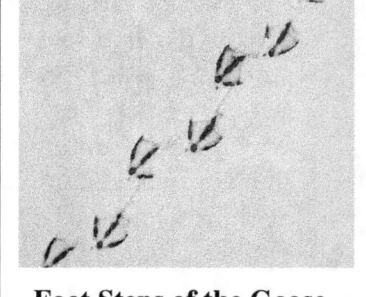
Foot Steps of the Goose

•We have been too spooked up to put three K's or KKK together

---

• See Dikengo symbol in the Kikongo Cosmology.

- Let alone be in free spin in our consciousness like a Jack.
- We will not restore our sight until we release our fear of KKK
- Tremendous inversion and distortion has been done to keep us from our Ancient wisdom and what the divine Neteru (letters and numbers) have to reveal

As we made our footsteps out of Afrika we populated the world. As such, the Metu Neter journeyed as a language out of Afrika also. As the Metu Neter journeyed out of Afrika it became garbled, confused and distorted by its distillation through the English language. As such the higher expression of the N word(s) moved from Metu Neter, divine speech, and became distillated through the English language, a lower expression of the N word(s). The resultant concentrated pollutant has contributed to the deep psychological scarification that we experience as Afrikan and Afrikan Diaspora.

How is this so? Words have a vibration. Words may vibrate at a higher Spiritual level, a more refined level. When Metu Neter was vibrating at this higher Spiritual, refined level this contributed to our greatness as an Afrikan people. Likewise, words may vibrate at a lower, coarse, dense and material level. As the Metu Neter went out into English, - 'words' - were negatively potenized to contribute to our demise as a people.

In furthering understanding of the Law of Vibration we turn to Metaphysical Key given in *A.C.T.S. 1. Ka Ab Ba Building The Lighted Temple*

Metaphysical Key To:
Right of Ascent and Descent of Spirit

1. Spirit has the right to make its deepest descent into matter without abstraction (withdrawal from form) and likewise
2. Spirit has the right to make its greatest ascent (while) in matter (form) without abstraction
3. It is the Law of Vibration in action

We stand as witnesses to a Spiritual law. If we could just bear to see and realize that it has been expressing itself before our very eyes.

What does this mean?
Man is both divine and human. Man has even appeared animal like and inhuman. It is the Law of Vibration in action. An example will serve to illustrate. Our example takes us aboard a slave ship where we may look at the condition of both slave and captain upon the slave ship. To see the demonstration of the law that Spirit reaches its lowest descent into matter without abstraction – we view first the condition of the slave.

The slave lay with shackled hands and feet for weeks now in the darkened hull of the slave ship. His muscles are abraded down to bone which is now exposed. His wounds are raw and infested. Death and human despair are all around him. The stench of vomit, human waste and rotting corpses assaults his senses. Appalled as we may be by this sight, we see that from behind the eyes of this man is *Spirit* – and that – Spirit has the right to find its way into the lowliest material condition without abstraction or death of the form of this man. Even though he cries out to death for release from his agony and suffering, he is living through these conditions.

Next –

We likewise view the captain above on deck the slave ship. The sun is upon the captain's face. Yet he is obsessed and consumed by thoughts of greed and lust. He murders with little or no provocation anyone who thwarts his mission, whether slave or crewman. He passes long days on the ship with the sport of slave torture and humiliation. At night he comforts himself with the degradation and rape of slave women. Again we see in this man also that *Spirit* has the right of descent into matter without abstraction. Death does not come just because Spirit indwells in the vilest of mental, emotional and physical conditions. Even though in gloating arrogance he taunts death itself, he is living through these conditions.

The Ages of Light followed by the Ages of Dark must be seen as impersonal as the light of day that is followed by the dark cover of night. These cycles contribute to the rise and the fall of great civilizations in the ongoing Spiritual journey of man and woman. The optimal, supernal heights are followed by the most debased cycles of debauchery. This is a hard saying. In man's inhumanity to man there has been great injustice. In combining Metaphysical Keys in the following overlays we see the Law of Vibration revealed in the Tree of Life:

Metaphysical Key To:
The Overlay of The Law of Vibration and
The Respiritualization and Despiritualization cycle
Within The Tree of Life

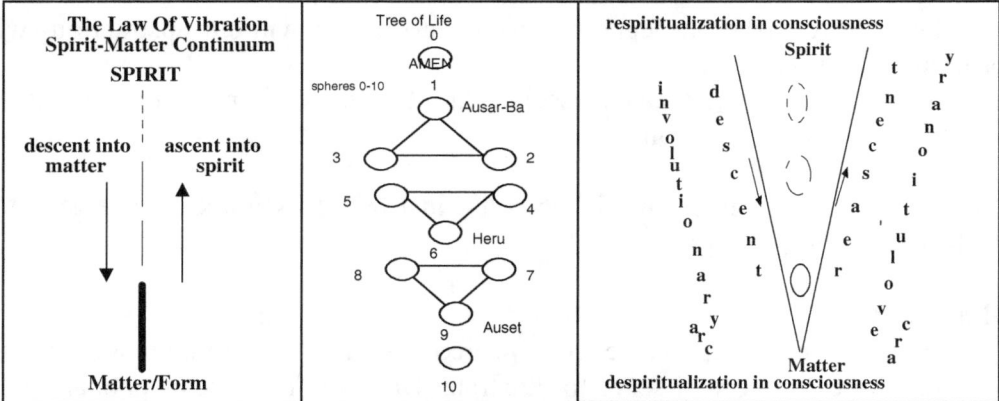

- So, as we have stood as witnesses to the low in the descent
- So we will stand in witness to the greatness of re-ascent.

Marcus Garvey expresses this according to: Dr. Tony Martin, *The Ideological and Organizational Struggles of Marcus Garvey.*

> Garveyism decreed that the attainment of its ultimate goals was inevitable, the goals in this case being the resurgence of the Black Race: "In the cycle of things he lost his position, but the same cycle will take him back to where he was once.

- We will walk once again upon the Earth as Gods
- When Spirit asserts its right to its highest ascent in woman and man
- After much rehearsal in the 7 planes of consciousness along its descent down
- Through the planes of the Tree of Life
- Thus does each Prodigal Sun – Son/Daughter
- Ultimately return Home
- Having gained the entire
- Conscious experience of Spirit
- At every level of its immersion into matter and
- Matter in its re-ascent into pure Spirit
- Every vile and glorious station
- Back to Omniscient consciousness, Ausarian Consciousness
- The Spiritual Journey is from God to God
- As you bring your consciousness back
- Into the awareness of the All
- The Amen in The Tree of Life
- You are set back to Ground '0'
- This re-absorption takes place through meditation
- And living in accord
- With the Universal Laws of Maat
- Man finds himself once again
- Polarized in the ONE
- The first sphere of the Tree of Life
- A King upon the thrown
- As the One of Ausar Ba
- You are able to draw from The Fount Of All Possibility
- All that is needed to work co-creatively
- In the great Divine Plan.
- This Soul awareness attunes you to the source
- Of Omnipotence, Omnipresence, and Omniscience

In Meditation Deep, affirm:
- I Have Not Been Negengen As An Afrikan
- I Have Not Been Reneging, Going Back On, Breaking My Word, Breaking My Promise, Nor Failing To Carry Out My Promise, My Commitment
- I Have Not Been Negengen, Renegade, Failing To Come Back To The Consciousness Of The Fullness Of The One True Self That I Have Always Been From The Beginingless Beginning.
- I Have Not Been Negengen, Renegade From My Stationing In My Eternal Home While/As I do My Work In The Outer World.
- I Have Not Negengen Causing Us To suffer A Brokenness In Consciousness Of Who We Are As Sun-Sons/Daughters Of GOD
- I Have Not Been Reneging On My Full Identity Or I.D, Causing My Continued Dethroning As King/Queen.

The Ausarianization of Consciousness Tablet Series 2 – A.C.T.S. 2
Metaphysical Keys To the Tree of Life & Oracle Keys to Dispelling Illusion
The Psycho/Spiritual Journey of Unfolding Consciousness

• I Re-Gain Acendency To The Throne Within By Holding The Forces In-Balance
• I AM The Re-ing King, ' N-G K-R-I' On My Throne, The Fullness Of The One True Self That I AM And Have Always Been From The Beginingless Beginning

Sound the following Hekau oracly and circularly with the highest vibratory intention:

```
    N
 I
       G
 R
    K
```

'N-G K-R-I- N-G K-R-I- N-G K-R-I- N-G K-R-I-N-G K-R-I-N-G K-R-I-N-G-K-R-I-N-G- K-R-I'

Or souned with the just the power of the consonants
'N-G-K-R-N-G-K-R-N-G-K-R-N-G-K-R-N-G K-R-N-G K-R-N-G-K-R-N-G-K-R'
Sounds like: N-G-G-R or N-E-G-G-U-R

Let's Dispell the word <u>Green</u>:
Derived word list:
<u>Negre</u>

Meaning:
Afrikans/Negroes are to the human kingdom what vegetables are to the vegetable kingdom –
We blanket the earth, giving life, fertility, virility, vitality while harnessing the energy of/as the Sun – Son/Daughter.

Chant the hekau:
N-G K-R-I N-G K-R-I N-G K-R-I N-G K-R-I N-G K-R-I N-G K-R-I N-G K-R-I
Circurlarly and Oracaly, visualizing the color Green while doing healing work so that you may be as One with/as Ausar, pictured at right, the Green God of Life and Fertility.

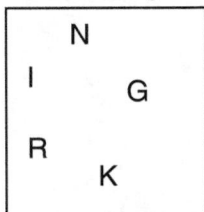

Chapter 22
Secret and Sacred Meaning of Ham, Hamsa and Kam
Bird of Life, The Man Swan

Let's continue to dispell the word <u>Goose</u>:
The Goose is equated with the Egyptian Bennu, the bird of return that typified renewal and renovation. This is expressed in the following:

#7. Oracle Metaphysical Dis-Spelling Key: Look up definition (dictionary, glossary, reference texts, etc.)
Definition: Accordingly: Gerald Massey. *A Book of The Beginnings*, p. 109.
<u>Goose</u> - "The Bennu in Egypt was the symbol of Osiris [read here: Ausar] the risen god or soul of the deceased... Han means to return, as is the goose."

What is Han, Hamsa, Kam, or Kamsa?
Hamsa or Hans (Sans) is the name of the goose or the Man-Swan. It is the egg symbolizing the Afrikan 3rd Root Race. Let's take note of the word Hamsa or Ham or Kam which means Black.

#8. Oracle Metaphysical Dis-Spelling Key: Meaning. See the relationship and oracle or story of the Neteru – Put word list together to tell a story.
Meaning: To return as the goose, Hamsa, Kam is to return to Black – the source

Let's dispel the words <u>Man-Swan</u>.
#11. Oracle Metaphysical Dis-Spelling Key: What does the word sound like? Say the word out loud and then silently in a meditative state.

Derived Sounds Like List:
<u>Man Swan</u> - Sounds like, Man Sworn - One who has taken an oath to be Maa Kheru, True of Word as he/she makes outgoing steps in consciousness.

Definition/Meaning: Geoffrey Barborka, in referencing the Secret Doctrine, says the following about the goose or swan accordingly: *The Divine Plan*, p. 217.

> There is a profound meaning attaching to the original representation of the caduceus. Attention is first directed to the wings. A clue is presented in this sloka:
>
> "Bestride the Bird of Life, if thou wouldst know."
> The Bird of Life is equivalent to Kala-hansa, a term applied to Brahman, the Supreme Spirit. {Ethmologically, hansa means goose or swan; kala is usually translated melodious; but one meaning of the verbal root kal is to announce the time; hence the term may be rendered the Swan which announces a cycle of time. H.P. Blavatsky gives this meaning for Kalahansa: the Swan in or out of time. The significance of this phrase is as follows: the "Swan in time" stands for the period of a Manvantara: the "Swan out of time" for a Pralaya; the Bird of Life always remains, whether it be a period of activity, or a period of rest. This is borne out by the passage: "Aye, sweet is rest between the wings of that which is not born; nor dies, but is the AUM throughout eternal ages.

The Maha Manvantara is the breathing out of Universe for a cycle of activity. This is followed by period of rest called the Maha Pralaya when the great breath is withdrawn and the Universe is abstracted back within the FOUNT OF ALL POSSIBILTIY, AMEN, the Nun from which it arose. The Universe is called the Universal Ba by the Kamitians. **For more information see *A.C.T.S. 1. Ka Ab Ba Building The Lighted Temple* and refer to Key(s):**

> **Metaphysical Key To:**
> Cosmogony and Cosmogenisis
> **Universal Ba *To***
> **Individualized Ba** Man and Woman

For now it is important to understand that:
• We are Kam/Ham the Goose/Swan, out of time
• We are Kam/Ham the Goose/Swan in time
• We are Aum throughout eternal ages.

★*Afrikans/Negroes - Bird of Life, always remains, whether it be a period of activity, or a period of rest.*
★*Afrikans/Negroes - Kamsa, Ham, Man swan.*
★*Afrikans/Negroes - Man sworn to return back to the SOURCE, back to THE DARK, THE BLACK, THE DEEP.*

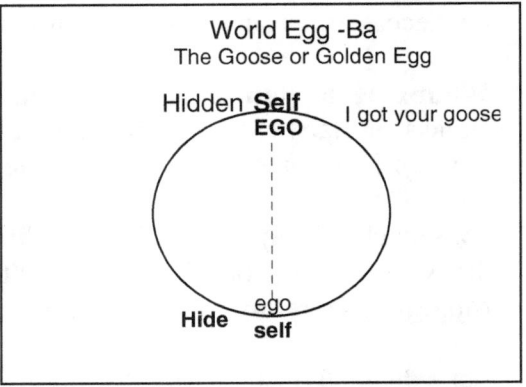

The double nature of Ka as the Spirit and Ka as the Approximating Ka is revealed in this passage. Ka, Kala, or Kahansa is 'the Bird of Life that always *remains* whether it is in a period of activity as an Approximating Ka or at rest as Spirit Ka. We will dispell the word <u>caduceus</u> in a moment. This is expressed accordingly: Alvin Boyd Kuhn. *The Lost Light*, p. 375.

> The goose portrayed on the head of Seb (Geb,Keb) in an Egyptian planisphere (according to Kircher) types the earth as "the goose that laid the golden egg daily." If this be but a photograph for the new-born daily sun of golden light, that sun in turn is the everlasting symbol of the rise of the golden egg of new divinity from out the confines of earth or the sea.. The god is the divine egg laid in humanity, for he is the heavenly fetus in the womb of the body. As he is destined to burgeon out, like the flower, into a burst of golden glory, its is by no means mere poetic fiction to call him the golden egg. And earth lays this golden nugget. The earth being our common mother, we have before us the Egyptian source of "Mother Goose," and the mysterious sagacity concealed in her catchy jingles.

• It is Earth - Planeary Earth Ba - that lays this golden nugget - the golden egg - being our common Mother, and
• It is the Black woman - Ausar Ba Woman - that lays this golden nugget - the golden egg of humanity - she being our common Mother.

And Continuing:

Ibid: p. 472.

> A prayer is made that the Osiris [Read here: Ausar] may be saved from the attack made against him "at the crossing." (ch. 135). This indicates that assault on his young divinity is made as soon as he crosses the line on the west in his descent. He is then "the youngling in the egg" and subject to the Herut attack. Here the dragon lay in wait to devour the young child.

If we dispel the word <u>Herut</u> we it reals the word <u>rut</u>. It is the rut that we get ourselves in that prevents our return stationing in the All consciousness.

And Continuing: The Tibetan. *Esoteric Astrology*, p. 86.

> In the zodiac of Denderah, the sign Cancer is represented by a beetle, called in Egypt [read here: Kamit], the scarab [read here; Khepera]. The word "scarab" means "only begotten"; it stands, therefore, for birth into incarnation, or, in relation to the aspirant, for the new birth. The month of June, in ancient Egypt was called "meore", which again means rebirth", and thus both the sign and the name hold steadily before us the thought of the taking of form and of coming in physical incarnation. In an ancient zodiac in India, dated about 400 B.C., the sign is represented again by a beetle.
>
> The Chinese called this sign "the red bird", for red is the symbol of desire, and the bird is the symbol of that flashing forth into incarnation and of appearance in time and space. The bird appears quite frequently in the zodiac and mythological stories, *Hamsa*, the bird of the Hindu tradition, "the bird out of time and space", stands equally for the manifestation of God and of man. Out of the darkness flashes the bird and flies across the horizon in the light of the day, disappearing again into the darkness. Our word, "goose", comes from the same Sanskrit root, through the Icelandic, and when we say, "What a goose you are", we are really making a most esoteric affirmation; we are saying to another human being: "You are, the bird out of time and space, you are the soul taking form; you are God in incarnation!"

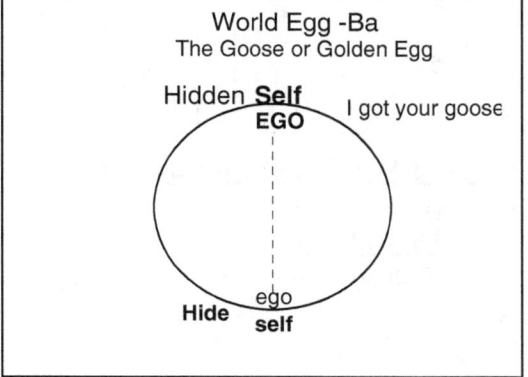

The words that the bird, 'stands equally for the manifestation of God and of man' are near and dear to my heart. They indicate the delicate balance within our Spiritual equipment which is both Human and Divine.

★*Afrikans/Negroes - Kamsa, Hamsa, Kam, Ham - manifestation of God and man.*

As Our Story continues we see that:
You are IT out on the loose
You are IT trying to touch Goose
You are IT having gone out on a roam
You are IT trying to find your way back HOME
You are IT, time is up - you renegade, out on the run
You are IT in your return, the 3 United and made One

Chapter 23
Afrikans/Negroes and The Secret and Sacred Meaning of The Caducceus

So we have seen that the Negroes, Ego, Man Swan, Man Sworn, or Goose 'goes out' and begins a cycle of time called the Manvantara by the Hindus. The Negroes or Egos are that which returns at the close of a cycle called a Pralaya then begins a period of rest. This is expressed accordingly: Geoffrey Barborka. *The Divine Plan*, p. 218.

> The tree of Life and Being, the Rod of the caducceus grows from and descends at every Beginning (every new manvantara) from the two dark wings of the Swan (Hansa –also read here: Hamsa) of Life. The two Serpents, the ever-living and its illusion (Spirit and matter) whose two heads grow from the one head between the wings, descends along the trunk, interrelated in close embrace. The two tails join on earth (the manifested Universe) into one and this is the great illusion, O Lanoo!

How are Afrikans/Negroes the symbol of the caduceus? What is the hidden or secret name?
Let's dispell the word <u>caducceus</u>:
#10. Oracle Metaphysical Dis-Spelling Key: Letter replacement. Here we have replaced the 'k' which had been substituted by the letter 'c.'

Derived Word List:
Kaducceus

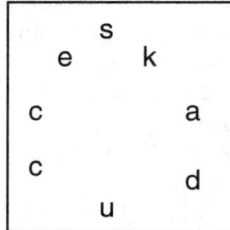 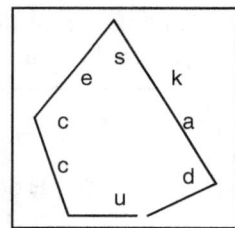

Derived Word List Continued:
Ka succeed
    Definition: Thesaurus.
       Succe(e)d – triumph, master, prevail, flourish, thrive, etc.
Ka
Seed

Meaning:
The Kaducceus is pictured at right.
The Spirit Ka - is the image and likeness of God.
The approximating Ka - is the degree to which your current self conscious awarenss is fully reflecting this image. Here the kaducces symbolizes all that is needed and divinely intended. When actualized it is the fullest measure of the divine image and likeness of God reflected in matter thus - 'Ka succeed.' It is how the Ka succeeds along its descent and re-ascent of the Tree of Life. At the lowest descent into material consciousness you do not

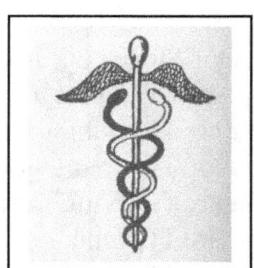

reflect the awareness that you are made in the fullness and likeness of God. As the approximating Ka suceeds up the Tree of Life in its reascent and identificaiton as/with Spirit Ka it more fully reflects and holds the identification with/as the One True Self – Ausar, sphere 1.

What is the Name or Neter of a Ka that succeeds.
★*Afrikans/Negroes - A Ka that succeeds is A-Free-Ka. A free Benuu. A Free Neggur. The Golden Goose. A free Soul. The seeker and the Sought are One.*

Did Kunta Kente in Roots appreciate the profound metaphysical meaning in the words he spoke when he said he wanted to be 'a free Nigger (Neggur)?

Chapter 24
What is This Line You Cross in Consciousness? Crossing the Line and Death

In the diagram at right we see the Golden Egg or Ba. We also see the Equinotical Line that has been drawn and denotes:
a. Division of the circle/egg in half
b. The horizon - which marks the Sun's passage by day and by night.

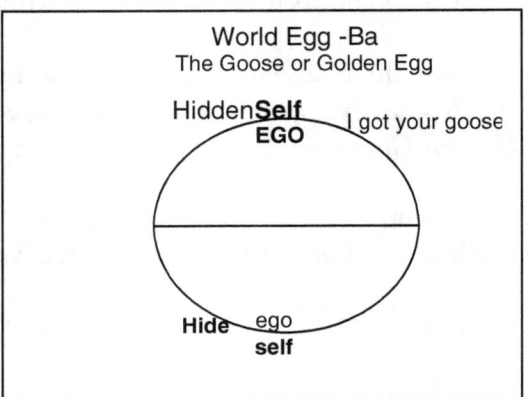

When you go out to 'hide' in your involutionary descent in consciousness you cross over the equinotical line. Thus you enter the more dense material realm. This is indicated by the dotted line in the next diagram below:

We recall the Spirit-matter continuum and the Law of Vibration: All is Spirit. Spirit is matter at its lowest level of vibration and Matter is Spirit at its highest level of vibration. This brings us to the next –

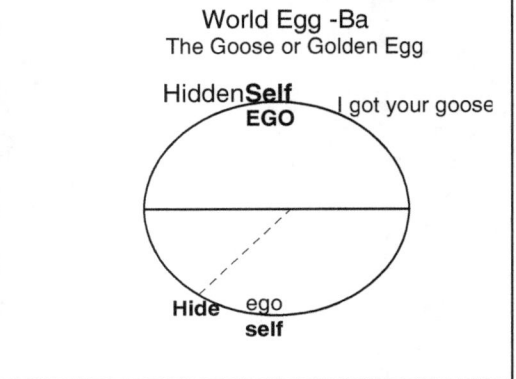

Meditation Key To:
Crossing over into Form/Manifestation
The precipitation into Form

Moving from left to right in the diagrams below, we see consciousness before it has crossed over the horizon to now make its descent along the Spirit-matter continuum into the more material consciousness.

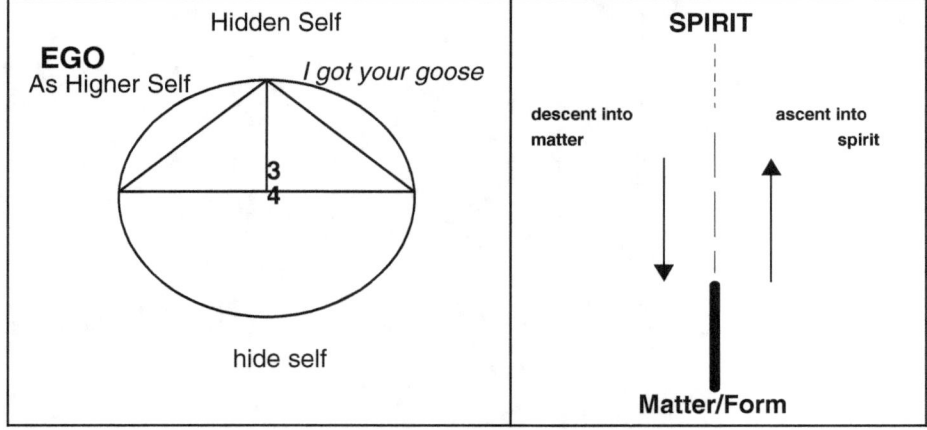

What is this line you cross in consciousness?
• The line is the 4th plane of consciousness in your Spiritual equipment

- It is the horizon where the Sun both rises and sets
- It is the balance point on the scales of justice Maat - sphere 4, in the Tree of Life
- It is the equinox where dark and light are held in balance.
- It is this line where we are 'seemingly' divided and made both Human and Divine
- It is the diaphragm in the human body.

If your awareness is below the horizon it is below the diaphragm and under the coats of skin which are called the physical, emotional, and mental Soul bodies. The Sakras (Chakras) below the diaphragm are the Base, the Sacral, and the Solar Plexus (see **A.C.T.S. 1. Ka Ab Ba Building The Lighted Temple**). It is the crossing over of Spirit into the material realm. If you forget your citizenship in the Higher realms, you become the particulate self, encapsulated under coats of skin. This is expressed accordingly: H. P. Blavatsky. *The Veil of Isis* [read here: - The Veil of Auset], V. 1, p. 2.

> As the cycle proceeded, man's eyes were more and more opened, until he came to know "good and evil" as well as the Elohim themselves. Having reached its summit, the cycle began to go downward. When the arc attained a certain point which brought it parallel with the fixed line of our terrestrial plane, the man was furnished by nature with "coats of skin," and the Lord God "clothed them.

The following analogy will serve to aid our understanding of the above quote:

If we put a tablespoon of sugar into a glass of water and stir it, the sugar dissolves and cannot be seen or detected in the water with the naked eye. If we repeat the process we have the same finding. However, if we continue the process of adding, then stirring in tablespoon after tablespoon of sugar to the water, we will reach a point of saturation and some measure of the particles of sugar will no longer stay in the solution. Anyone who has made lemonade or likes their coffee sweet knows this Metaphysical principle which is revealed in the diagram at right and aptly expressed in the following accordingly:

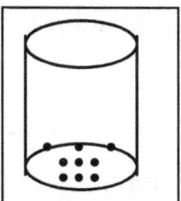

- Today in consciousness as a humanity
- We sit as one particulate after another
- In our limited, gran-ulated, encapsulated view of ourselves
- At the bottom of the glass
- We identify as the limited 'I' or ego that has to get 'somewhere'
- As one seeming, separate self encounters another seeming, separate self
- The lower fire - *fire by friction* - is at work
- In road rage with other particulates or separate selves
- We fend for this limited sense of 'self', along the way
- In rotary motion at the bottom of the glass we spin our wheels
- Violating the Laws of Right Relationship - Maat
- To access the higher fire of Ra - *Solar Fire and Electric fire*
- We must enter into Meditation - also called trance
- The process of Meditation is like taking the spoon
- And stirring all the particulatarizations, which is ourselves - *back into solution*

The Ausarianization of Consciousness Tablet Series 2 – A.C.T.S. 2
Metaphysical Keys To the Tree of Life & Oracle Keys to Dispelling Illusion
The Psycho/Spiritual Journey of Unfolding Consciousness

- This stirring is our access to the cohering power of Tehuti - sphere 2
- And fuller vibrational sounding of Seker - sphere 3
- When all particularzation is held seamlessly in solution
- And we *hold* within our 1st Eye
- We are at once able to witness the whole moving geometry in the Mind of God
- And know the *solution* to all life's challenges

How does the previous quote and analogy relate to consciousness?
The relationship is revealed as we move from left to right in the diagrams that follow:

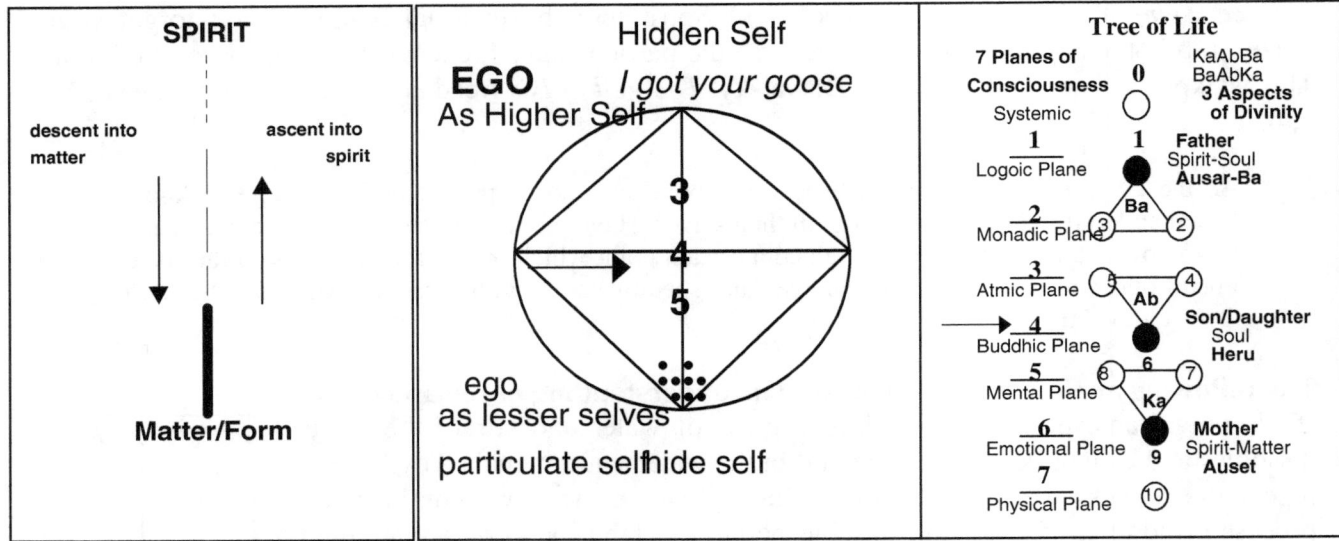

1. Of the seven planes of manifestation the Buddhic or Ab plane is the 4th
2. As the 4th plane it is halfway between - with 3 planes above and 3 planes below it
3. Planes 1, 2 and 3 above are most subtle and Spiritual.
4. Planes 5, 6, and 7 are more dense and material.
5. It is at the 4th plane that consciousness crosses over, moving from that which is *unitive* to that which is *particulate*
6. It is the place of 'seeming' division of Spirit and matter.
7. It represents demarcation of the Spirit-Matter continuum, shift from a higher to a lower vibration.
8. It is the invisible en route to becoming visible, the unmanifest enroute to becoming the manifest expression of God- in -Form.
9. It is the manifesting function of the Neter or Number 4. At the *crossing over* the unbroken seamless unity of God consciousness, Omniscient or Ausarian consciousness - is inner-sensed as divine ideation that starts to fall out of solution, touching the mental 5th plane as your thoughts, the emotional 6th plane as your emotions and the physical 7th plane as your physical sensations and appearances.
10. The problem comes in when you begin to identify as a particulate or lesser self who thinks he

11. or she is his thoughts, feelings or sensations.

Deeper understanding of this crossing over is expressed accordingly: Albert Churchward. *Origin and Evolution of the Human Race,* p. 140 - 141.

> This, in Africa, was the work of the Nilotic Negroes with Hero-Cult. They had divinized the old Mother Earth as Apt, who, in this phase, brought forth children. The Two divisions were fundamental and universal here amonst the Hero-Cult people as the two Tiruti; they had the two halves, North and South, divided by the Equinoctical line, the two Earths, upper and lower, the two houses of earth and heaven, etc. But there is always a distinction between the two classes of these Nilotic Negroes, the one with no Hero-Cult, with the old Earth Mother, and the other of Hero-Cult, who had divinized the old Earth Mother and divided her into the two different characters. This creation of man, or man and woman, was mystical in one sense, Totemic in another-in reality it was Evolution. This, however, explains the Semitic version of pre-Adamic and Adamic, which simply means pre-Totemic and Totemic.

This quote is pictured in the diagram at right. We choose to 'go out' in consciousness as whole beings or to leave our 'other half' at Home.

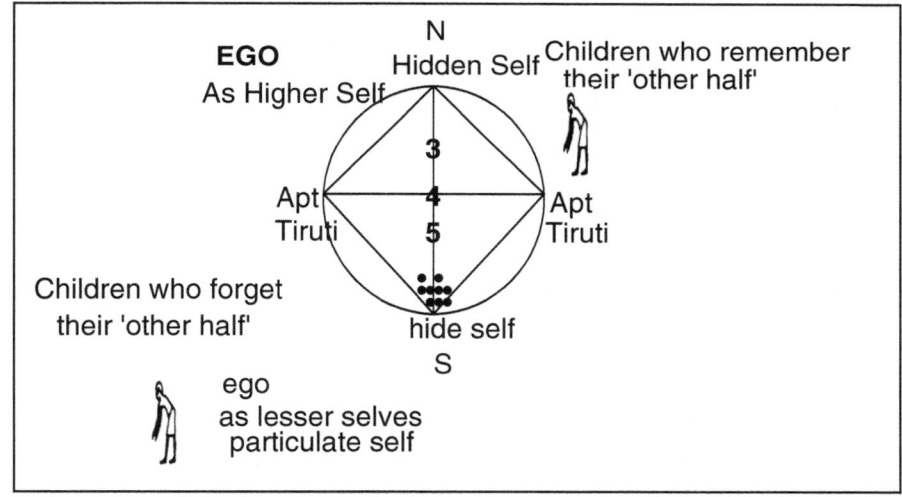

Let's dispell the word <u>totemic</u>:

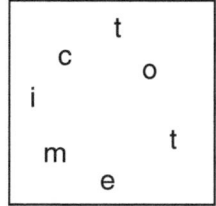 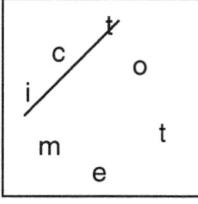 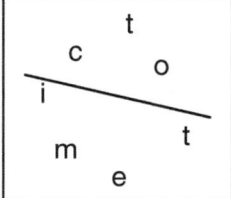

Derived Word List:
Time
Tic

Toc

Meaning:
The tic and the toc of time. The exteriorization of consciousness and self conscious participation in space and time. Thus, time-consciousness was begun.
• Within the Eternal now
• Before Time (Totemic)
• Before the Nigra (Negroes) cackles,
• Where Subject-Object are still at rest and seen as One
• No-thing is seen as outside the Self
• All is the Self, within the unbroken chain or consciousness of the Real G, Real God,
• Before the start of separative mind, subject and object, space and time.
• Within the 'ring-pass-not' or Chain of Consciousness of the ring-ing God
• The reigning God upon 7 planes of consciousness

Chapter 25
You are The Manes Who Comes to Know Death by Degrees

Who is the Manes?
You are the manes. As the manes who now knows 'death' you must bridge your way from the lower realms of consciousness back through to the Higher realms of consciousness. You are the Soul who has the power of Manes to create due to the ability to know and use the mind. This is expressed accordingly: *Rosicrucian Cosmo-Conception,* p. 283-284.

> Then his consciousness became focused in the physical World, although all things did not appear to his vision with clearly defined outlines until the latter part of the Atlantean Epoch [Read here: Negro-Semitic]. **Still he came by degrees to know death because of the break made in his consciousness** when it was shifted to the higher Worlds at death and back to the physical World at rebirth.

What is this 'death' made by the break in consciousness that man came to know by degrees?
Your descent down the Tree of Life is like the descent of the Sun as it sets in the sky on the horizon. As the Sun now makes it descent in the sky it rests at the equinox, teetering in the harmonious balance of equal day and equal night, before, crossing over where night now overcomes day. This is expressed accordingly: Alvin Boyd Kuhn. *The Lost Light,* p. 357.

> As the Sun in the sign of Leo we pass from the balance in the scales of Libra onto the sign of Scorpio. Accordingly: The allegorical function of the sign of Scorpio is most impressive. The god in his autumn descent into the body to make his hidden existence visible is stung into lethal sleep by the Scorpion – goddess. This is a most striking natural emblem of the swooning noted in connection with the downward march toward body. God caused a deep sleep to fall upon Adam when he was to be bifurcated into duality in earthly life.

The Kamitic Spiritual Tradition and writings teach much about the Psycho/Spiritual Journey and Ausarian Resurrection that is:
- The resurrection of immortal man
- Who has 'seemingly' become a mortal
- As he came to experience *a separated self*
- Who now knows *death*

Metaphysical Law Key:
The Law of Vibration

Our Story Continues...

Metaphysical Key To:
Involutionary and Evolutionary Cycles
The Spiritualization and Materialization in Consciousness

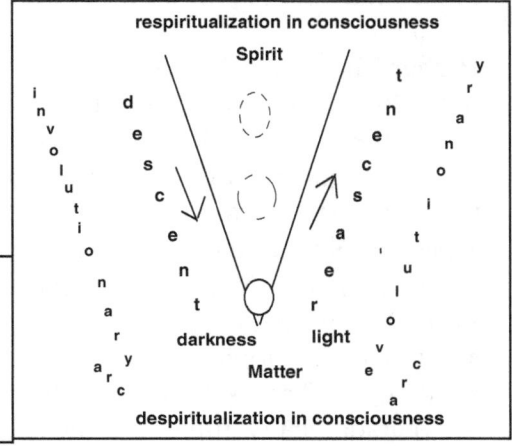

In aiding understanding of Cosmology and Cosmogenesis and the involutionary and evolutionary scheme, we note the following accordingly: Max Heindel. *Rosicrucian Cosmo-Conception*, p.185.

> From the point where the self-conscious individual Ego has come into being he must go on and expand his consciousness ...The period of time devoted to the attainment of self consciousness and to the building of the vehicles through which the spirit in man manifests is called "Involution." The subsequent period of existence, during which the Individual human being develops self-consciousness into divine omniscience, is called "Evolution.

Let's take for a closer examination here the statement: 'From the point where the self-conscious individual Ego has come into being he must go on and expand his consciousness ...' Here we see man and woman with the power of Ego which gives the power to choose. Man and woman in 'going out on their own' would deepen their descent to the lower planes of consciousness to know the 'self' at all levels of Spirit- in-form.

The previous diagram seeks to depict the 'involutionary cycle and evolutionary' cycle - which is the journey of Spirit in-form and its return journey in-form-lessness. The vertex in the 'V' illustrates how Spirit has made its deepest descent into matter. The left of the diagram depicts the involutionary arc or cycle, where unconscious man is in a period of divine accord and 'grace'. As the involutionary cycle proceeds he is becoming more self conscious. While still upon a higher arc in the earlier involutionary cycle, this growing consciousness is more Spiritualized. It is a consciousness that continues to build the *Divinely Intended Architectural Design* in accord with *Divine will, Divine Law, and Divine love*. Yet, as consciousness becomes despiritualized man may lose inner-sightedness and thus begins to build a World askew the divinely intended design.

As stated earlier, the different racial groups have responded differently to this event of individualization. Although occurring in the Afrikan 3rd Root Race this event of individualization would have its greater impact on the later Semitic 4th and Aryan/European 5th Root Races who would make their appearance on the Planet in a *later and descending* cycle of time.

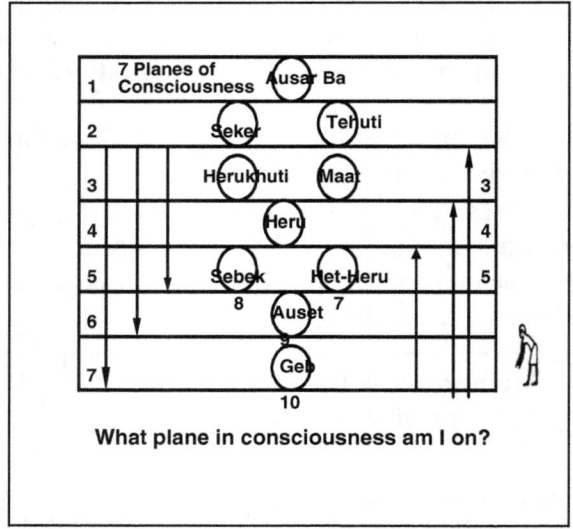

What plane in consciousness am I on?

Higher Manes and Middle Manes consciousness is polarized in the two higher triangles - the Ba and Ab of the Tree of Life. The next development in your Psycho/Spiritual Journey of Unfolding Consciousness was to become aware of the 3rd aspect or Ka• triangle which is the lower part of your equipment. You use this equipment or instrument to operate in the denser material World. With the awakening power to move the consciousness through the entire Spiritual instrument, along with developing use of personal will, you are making the conscious choice of which floor to reside upon. This is pictured in the previous diagram at right. Everything is happening all at once. Yet paradoxically time is what keeps everything from happening all at once. So how do we

---

• See KaAbBa Book 2 by Dr. Terri Nelson.

become aware as Self conscious humanity. This is expressed accordingly: Vera Stanley Adler. *The Initiations of The World,* p .36.

> The process of involution was now over as far as man was concerned. The 'fall' into matter was complete, the divine spark had descended and been buried within physical substance and the long struggle towards the light was about to begin.

Unlike the prior unity in your 'inner sightedness' your sense of a 'separated self' became more and more an 'I-dentity.' As I-dentity or ego (lower personal self) grew your sense of 'subject and object' came more into view. This is 'I 'd-entity', eye'd - entity or the ego that 'eyes' or sees itself and others as 'entity' This was the birth of separative and self reflective consciousness, a consciousness that would come into fuller expression during our present materialization cycle. Interior sightedness through the use of the 1st eye becomes less active and your two exteriorly focused physical eyes become more active. Inner sense which is an 'innocence' is the ability to see and glimpse the Puzzle Box Cover of the divinely intended design for manifestation. Inner-sense *dispelled* is innocence. Both 'innersense and innocence' are diminished with each passing cycle as man and woman became more and more 'outwardly and worldly' focused.

What is now glimpsed outwardly comes from the two outer physical eyes and senses. Without the aid of the 1st eye, what is now experienced can only be 'known' and 'seen' in part or part-'ocular'-ization. Thus, the 'eyed-entity' that man and woman think they see and know as 'self' or 'other' can only be a part or particularization of the whole - *THAT IT IS*.

So where in your Spiritual equipment is this ability still registered and accessible?
This brings us to the next -

Metaphysical Key To:
Ka Ab Ba and
The 3 primary Egoic states of Consciousness

The 3 primary Egoic States in Consciousness may be observed as follows:
1. Consciousness may remain unitive
2. Consciousness can become dualized and reconciliative/combative
3. Consciousness may become separative or particularized into many parts.

Chapter 26
3 Primary Egoic States of Consciousness Ka Ab Ba
Division into the 3 - The Nature of the Trinity at work in Man and Woman

How we perceive the 'outer World' depends upon which of these 3 primary Egoic states we find ourselves identified with. The qualities each expresses is shown in the following diagram:

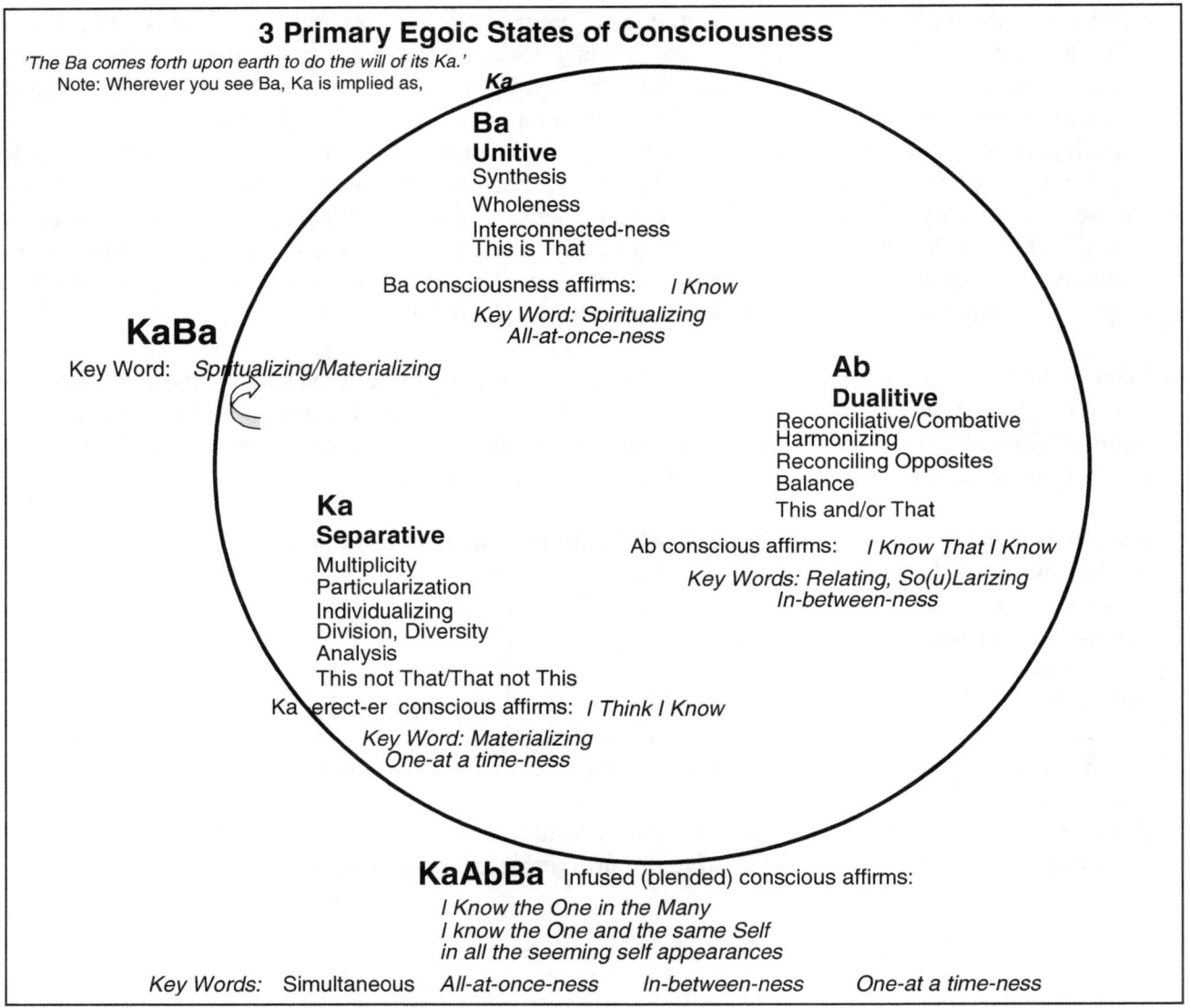

As you may recall from the fields of Psychology and Psychoanalysis, Sigmund Freud is said to have coined the terms *Superego, Ego and Id* to describe on a more narrow scale the process of unfolding consciousness. This brings us to the next -

> **Metaphysical Key To:**
> Ka Ab Ba and European Psychoanalysis

He was considered founder of psychological and psychoanalytic techniques used by counseling professionals (See Robert Bocock. *Freud and Modern Society*). As we have seen in ***A.C.T.S. 1. Ka Ab Ba Building The Lighted Temple*** the terms Id, Ego and SuperEgo are derived from the Ancient Wisdom sources of our Black Ancestors and are called KaAbBa.. The term SuperEgo connotes the Highest Soul Consciousness Ba and is our 1st Aspect of Divinity. The term Ego connotes Ab Soul Consciousness, the 2nd Aspect of Divinity. It is the governing agency within that is relating the two of SuperEgo and ID, or the Divine and Human. The term ID connotes the Ka Soul Consciousness and is our 3rd Aspect of Divinity.

This is expressed in the following which is testimony that other folks have known the 'stuff' of our Ancient Wisdom and called it something else, as seen in the table below:

Afrikan/Kamitic Term		Europeanized/Psychoanalytic Term
Ka	3rd Aspect of Divinity	ID (Id)
Ab	2nd Aspect of Divinity	Ego
Ba	1st Aspect of Divinity	SuperEgo

I find Freud's choice of the word 'Id', which is the Ka 3rd aspect triangle, of interest.
Let's dispell the word <u>Id</u>:
#9. Oracle Metaphysical Dis-Spelling Key: Take each letter one at a time or in combination with one or more letters and derive its meaning.

Derived letter or Neter list:
I D

#8. Oracle Metaphysical Dis-Spelling Key: Meaning. See the relationship and oracle or story of the Neteru – Put word list together to tell a story.
Meaning:
If we dispell this word we see that:
1. It is the word 'eyed' or what is seen.

2. It is also the word (or acronym) 'ID', or what we 'I'Dentify as the self (temporarily) on the way to full Identification in our SuperEgo function as Ausar Ba. This is a World in which we are asked for our ID as proof of *who* we are or who we say we are. We need an ID to get through the door in certain outer plane establishments (organizations, clubs, bars, schools, etc). In other words we 'Ka-rd' people in order to seemingly know who they are.
3. ID is also ID - entity, or the 'eyed entity'. Because we have eyed this entity we come to believe what our eye sees. After all, 'It is in the eye of the beholder'.
4. The so called Freudian terms, SuperEgo, Ego and ID (or Id) are just substitutions of the Kamitic terms Ba, Ab and Ka respectively.

5. Essentially your ID should *read* that you are the SuperEgo. If it does not, then this reflects that you are off into the lower ego, calling yourself something less than who you really are. It is about growing up from:
a. The collapsing of the lower ego - lower case 'e', a state of blurred vision or blindness into
b. The expanding of Higher Ego - capital 'E', a state of Full Eyesightedness which is
c. The restoration of the eye of Heru -

Let's dispel the word <u>Freud</u> if you have not done so mentally already:

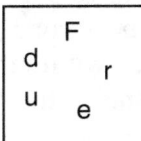

<u>Fraud</u> - It spells Fr(a)ud for a Planetary Humanity to possess a consciousness that has been made bereft or stripped of the contribution of the Afrikan Race people.
<u>Feudal</u> -

Meaning:
My research (see *A.C.T.S 1, KaAbBa - Building The Lighted Temple*) in the Psycho-Spiritual practices which are of Afrikan/Egyptian origin reveal that the terms Id, Ego and SuperEgo comprise a recent, renamed and condensed version found in these Ancient Wisdom sources and is named instead, *KaAbBa*. Racism sees Blacks as inferior and as a Race that has no 'relevant' prior history, source or plan applicable for Psychological well being and salvation other than that offered/imposed by Western Psychology or 'modern religion'. The tincture of Racism that pervades the Educational field, likewise pervades the Mental health field, contributing to disparities in wellness by its inherent pattern of denying and/or further removing Black/African descended people from *their* source of Psycho-Spiritual connection.

We must raise the question: What impact does the absence of African-centered approaches, ideation, constructs, and models have on efforts to promote wellness, wholeness and mental health in people of African descent? How can life promoting and meaningful interface with traditional settings (Mental Health, Education, etc.) continue if negation of African-centered inclusion continues? The book, Ka *Ab Ba Building The Lighted Temple* demonstrates that the Kamitians possessed a highly enlightened and elaborate Psychological/Spiritual system for shaping the highest character and moral development. Their practices reveal a holistic approach to wellness with self-transformational guidance assisting them in managing the daily affairs of life while knowing the immortality of the Soul and the divinity within. The Psycho/Spiritual Journey of Unfolding Consciousness was well understood by an Afrikan/Kamitic Ancestry.

This brings us to the next –

Secrets of Race & Consciousness Afrikan Cosmology of Kamit
with The Spiritual Meaning of The 'N' Word(s)
Neggur - The Goose Goddess who laid the Sun Egg, the Cosmic Egg

Revealed in Ka Ab Ba *(Kabala)* The Tree Of Life — Metaphysical Mysteries Meaning

Metaphysical Key To:
The Law of Correspondence
"As above, so below; as below, so above."

Just as –
Your passageway through doors on the outer physical plane depends on your ID Ka-rd, which will gain or block your admission into schools, businesses, clubs, organizations, government agencies, bank accounts, etc.

So too –
Your passageway through doors on the inner Spiritual plane depends on your ID Ka-rd, which will gain or block your admission if it does not reflect the *full conscious measure* of who we are. This brings us to the next -

Metaphysical Key To:
The Overlay of The 3 Primary Qualities of Consciousness/Mind.

By overlaying the diagram at right, the 3 primary Egoic states of consciousness are revealed within the Tree of Life which are described as: Unitive, Dual (Relating), and Separative-Discriminating. To review the 3 primary states of consciousness refer to Chapter 2 of this text and the following -

Metaphysical Key To:
Ka Ab Ba and Movement Within
The 3 primary Egoic states of Consciousness

Tree of Life
spheres 0-10
- Unitive
- Dual - Relating
- Separative - Discriminating

Brief review of the higher and lower spiral in these 3 primary states of consciousness is given as follows:

*Ka*Ba - Unitive Consciousness
On a higher turn of the spiral: You are the Drawer from the Fount of All Possibility with Unlimited Access to All Potential. Polarized within your Ausarian consciousness - your One I-dentity, you are above the rising and falling states which create duality in awareness and lead to pleasure and pain. You are continually imbued with inner Peace - *Hotep*. You are the Eternal Witness and Knower who 'goes out' into manifestation *while* remaining upon your heavenly throne. You 'return' to reside upon your own High plane of consciousness while 'going out to' establish the Kingdom of Heaven on the Earthly plane. It is from the heavenly heights of Ausarian consciousness that you stand resurrected and able to solve all of life's problems.

On a lower turn of the spiral: You are the exiled God who 'seemingly goes out' and walks the Earth trying to remember your divinity, Godliness, heavenly Home and the SELF as Life eternal. When you are not bringing your awareness to the Ausar Ba part of your Spiritual equipment you experience disconnection from All Power, All Wisdom, All Pervading

Presence. This is the diminished state of conscious livingness of/as God - actualizing in the physical World (Geb).

Ab - Dualtive Consciousness
On a higher turn of the spiral: Dualtive consciousness is reconciliative and able to sit with the opposites, the contending forces of dark and light, day and night, and thereby bring harmony into creation through skillful mediation of sometimes dissonant, sometimes consonant energies. You hold the balance as that which is higher or above as referenced with that which is lower or below.
On the lower turn of the spiral: Dualtive consciousness is combative and falls out of balance. It chooses the outer appearance of things without reference to the backdrop of the seamless unity of the One. Humanity begins its seeming battle with the contending forces from both within and without. Brother opposes brother, Sister opposes sister and the scales of Maat tip from assertion to aggression and Might rules over Right. The battle ensues and all manner of dissonance, upheaval, and warring prevails. Once we cross over the line on the West in our descent in consciousness we are subject to the 'Herut attack' of thinking we are the particulate self. What *a rut* we get the Self in!

Ka Ka-erect-er - Separative/Particulate Consciousness
On a higher turn of the spiral: As Ausar you are unlimited access to the Fount of All Possibility. Therefore you may precipitate all manner of creative potential. If your work is in accord with the divinely intended design then you Build the Lighted Temple that God may indwell in you and upon Earth. It is in the 'garment(s)' donned by Spirit that we see the reflection of God revealed. Separative/Particulate consciousness is the 'display' and our 'play' with 'Other-ness' and 'Thing-ness'. Thus do we become GOD conscious of the One True Self *everywhere*. All the seeming 'pieces' are cohering together through the power of love and wisdom and the underlying unity of the grand design is revealed. Separative/Particulate consciousness has likewise lead us to have great technological 'advances'. There is no shortage of inventions and gadgetry that may be precipitated out onto the physical plane for our usage, enjoyment and so called 'advantage'.
On a lower turn of the spiral:
Separative/Particulate consciousness dissolves the cohering power of love and instead sees divine ideation/wisdom in the mind of God (called the Khus by the Kamitians) as separate. In a World where sight of the interconnecting webwork and interdependence between all kingdoms of life of is not seen and upheld - man has killed, enslaved one another, destroyed and polluted the environment and violated his own nature, health and well being - Geb - sphere 10. Individualism reigns. Man and woman see themselves as a self separated from all other 'selves' and humanity is *hard at work* trying to make all the pieces fit back together again. But if we develop reverence for thingness and it becomes our God then Thing-ness takes us more and more into boundaried material conditioning and further away from the boundless unconditioning of Spirit.

The 7 Psycho-Spiritual Types in Unfolding Consciousness

This is suggestive of developing a new Typology of Consciousness which would examine the propensity for operating along particular lines or operating in a more blended consciousness admixture or Blended Konsciousness Admixture - **BKA** -capacity. For more information on see ***A.C.T.S. 1. Ka Ab Ba Building The Lighted Temple*** and refer to Key(s): What is BKA?

> **Metaphysical Key To**:
> Number 1 and 2
> **Ka**Ba **Unity/Two-Oneness Ka and Ba/Duality Or Diad**
> Out of the '0', Zero –
> Whenever:
>   There is the arising of the 1 as unity Ba (Monad)
>   There is the arising of the 2 of Duality – BaKa or KaBa (Diad)

For now it is important to understand that:
Developing a Typology of Race and Consciousness brings us to the next –

> **Metaphysical Key To**:
> 7 Psycho-Spiritual Types in Consciousness

The following Typology of 7 distinct Types is revealed in the Psycho/Spiritual Journey of Unfolding Consciousness and *The Ausarianization of Consciousness Tablet Series* and are indicated in chart on the next page:

The Ausarianization of Consciousness Tablet Series 2 – A.C.T.S. 2
Metaphysical Keys To the Tree of Life & Oracle Keys to Dispelling Illusion
The Psycho/Spiritual Journey of Unfolding Consciousness

7 Psycho-Spiritual Types in Consciousness

3 Primary Egoic States of Consciousness			
	Unitive Wholeness Synthesis Innerconnectedness *I Know* This is That	Duality - Harmonizing Reconciling Opposites Balance *I Know That I Know* This and/or That	Separative Multiplicity Particularization Division, Diversity Analysis *I Think I Know* This not That/That not This
Type 3	X		
Type 4		X	
Type 5			X
Type 3-4	X	X	
Type 3-5	X		X
Type 4-5		X	X
Type 3-4-5	X	X	X

Chapter 27
The Crossing Over in Consciousness and The Experience of Death Continued
Higher Manes – Middle Manes – Lower Manes

As the 3-4-5 Higher, Middle and Lower Manes in consciousness we are in turning point and must return or face doom.

Our Story Continues…
Let's return now to the theme of death and take for closer examination here the following words from an earlier quote, '…the latter part of the Atlantean Epoch [read here: Afrikan-Semitic or Middle Manes Root Race - consciousness]. Still he came by degrees to know death because of the break made in his consciousness when it was shifted to the Higher Worlds at death and back to the physical World at rebirth.'

At this point we see that the Dual/Reconciliative conscious now experiences *'death'* as a break is made in his continuity of consciousness. The 'unbroken consciousness' of the Early Manes and Middle Manes consciousness is no longer a continuously, sustainable and stabilized state of awareness for man and woman. Separative consciousness must now juxtapose the duality of the Higher and lower nature in man and woman. It is the battle within between the contending forces of what is commonly called good and evil, righteousness and unrighteousness or Divine and Human.

What is this line you cross in consciousness?
The answer to this is found within the following accordingly: The Tibetan. *Treatise on Cosmic Fire*, p. 1102.

> This separation [read here: break in consciousness] is brought about through the initial activity of the Ego [read here: Heru - sphere 6] who produces the first of those forms which he intends to use during the cycle of incarnation, through the bringing together of these energies through self-engendered impulse [read here: the will]. He, for purposes of development, identifies himself with that form, and thus temporarily separates himself off from his own real Self. [read here: Ausar - sphere 1]] Through the veil of mental matter [read here:: manes] he first knows separation, and undergoes his first experiences of the three Worlds [read here: physical, emotional and mental planes of consciousness]. This deals with separation from the highest aspect… Thus it can be truly said that the "mind slays
> the Real" and serves as the "great Deluder" of the Self in the one case, and as the "great Separator…

This brings us to the next –

> **Meditation Key To:**
> Higher Manes, Middle Manes, and Lower Manes

The Ausarianization of Consciousness Tablet Series 2 – A.C.T.S. 2
Metaphysical Keys To the Tree of Life & Oracle Keys to Dispelling Illusion
The Psycho/Spiritual Journey of Unfolding Consciousness

Moving from left to right this is expressed in the following diagrams:

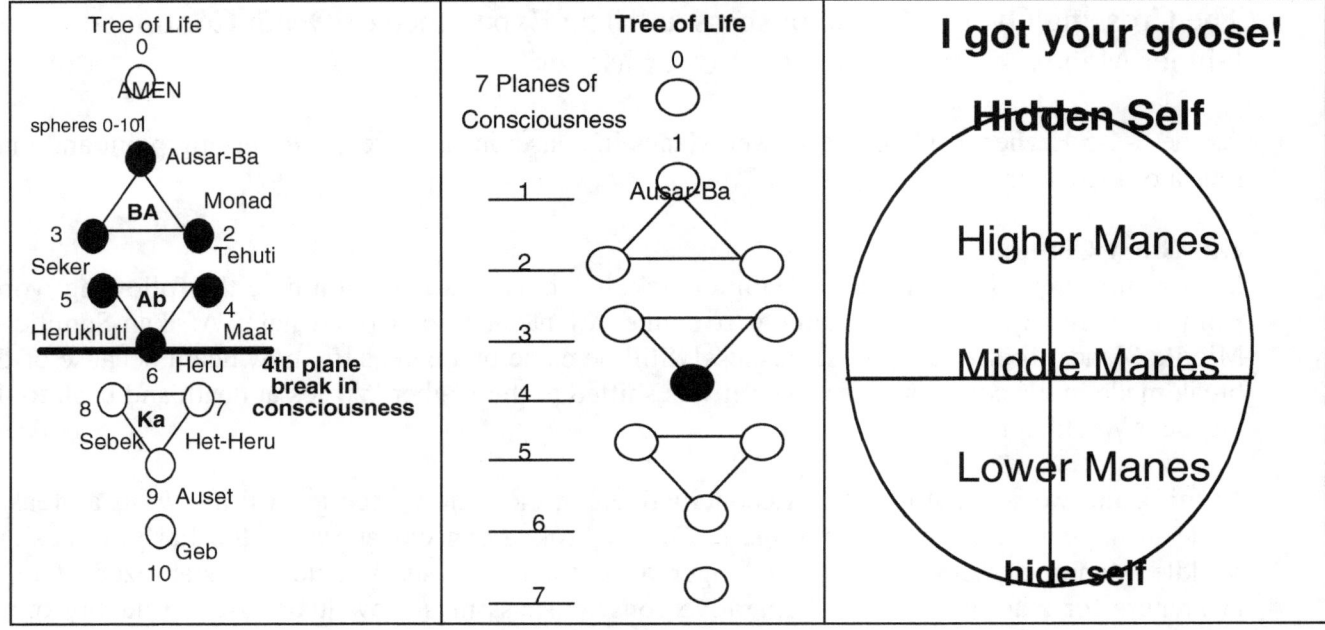

Chapter 28
The Secret and Sacred Meaning of Semitic and Aryan Consciousness

Just as this text has been unveiling the hidden meaning in the word Negroes, so too must their be the unveiling of the words Semitic and Aryan. As we proceed we are reminded of the earlier -

> **Metaphysical Key To:**
> Read from the angle of consciousness and not just from the angle of the physical form Each Root Race is manifesting through.

Let's dispell the word <u>Semitic</u>: Continue to use, **Oracle Metaphysical Dis-Spelling Keys** as previously described.

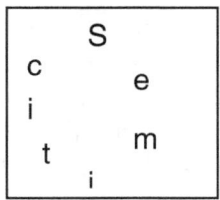

Derived Word List:
Tic
Time
Semi -

> **Definition:**
> <u>Semi</u> -1. Half; semicircle. 2. Partial. 3. Resembling or having some of the characteristics of.

Meaning:
Dispelling the word Semitic reveals the Neteru 'Semi' and 'Tic'. We see that it contains the word Semi which is half day and half night, half light and half dark. Again, it is the 4th plane of consciousness that demarcates the 3 Higher floors (planes) from the lower floors. You are the Semi-tic consciousness who is moving back and forth trying to keep the balance and reconcile opposites. As the seeker who goes out and forgets their 'mooring' in the All Conscious, you become unbalanced. The harmonious relationship of the divine marriage between Spirit-matter within you is no longer held. You have caused them to be separated and divorced. It is important to ask yourself the following:
1. Am I desiring the finite things of the material World to the point where I as Ausar relinquish my access to the Infinite Fount of All Possibility?
2. As I have intercourse (have sex to procreate) exteriorly with physical bodies in order to reproduce myself do I forget to have intercourse interiorly with Spiritual ideation - the divine Khus - in order to remember the divine design and participate in co-creative reproduction of One True SELF as God King dwelling in/on Earth?

Let's dispell the word <u>divorce:</u>

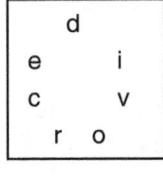 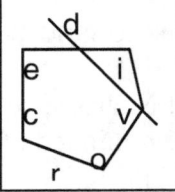

Derived word list:
Divided Voice r
Deceiver i
Dec(e)iv(e) r o - To deceive the fires of Ra - full circle (o).

Meaning:
To be of divided voice (sound). Two voices instead of one demonstrating the ability to talk out of both sides of your mouth, to babble/Babel, and to no longer be of one tongue. To have forked tongue. To operate out of the deceiving eye of double vision, to deceive the fires of Ra in double dealing. On a higher turn of the spiral earlier Semitic 4th Root Race consciousness is holding the two arms of the scales in balance without tipping in either direction and becoming unbalanced. In the later 4th and 5th Aryan/European Root Races consciousness would tip and the scales and would become unbalanced.

Let's dispel the word <u>Aryan:</u>

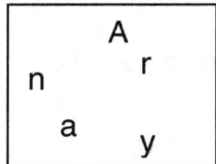

Derived Word List:
A n(u) Ray
Awry-an

>**Definition** - Skewed, off beam, off center, out of kilter, twisted. 1. In a position that is turned or twisted toward one side; askew. 2. Away from the correct course; amiss.

Meaning:
Dispelling the word Aryan reveals the Neteru of An(u) Ray and A(w)ry.
<u>An(u) Ray</u> is a Ray of the ABSOLUTE. It is A Ray arising from the stirring within the Nu. It is Ra, a Sun - Son/Daughter of God. If we look at the Neter or letter 'Y' we see that it is the 3 seeing eyes.

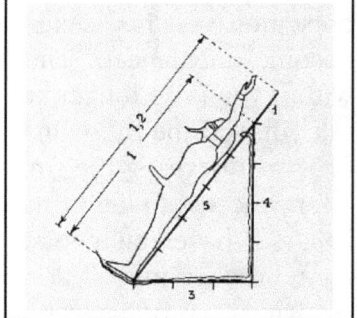

It is the 2 physical eyes and the middle or 1st eye that sees in all directions. It is the grounding of dual/double vision on Earth in physical form to express the Two-Oneness of Spirit/Matter.

Secrets of Race & Consciousness Afrikan Cosmology of Kamit
with The Spiritual Meaning of The 'N' Word(s)
Neggur - The Goose Goddess who laid the Sun Egg, the Cosmic Egg

Revealed in Ka Ab Ba *(Kabala)* The Tree Of Life   Metaphysical Mysteries Meaning

<u>Awryan</u> - is one who has fallen short of being the fullest measure of the One True Self that we are and have always been from the beginningless beginning. It is to be be out of kilter. It is to build askew the divinely intended design.

One might ask does the 'going out' in consciousness by the 3rd Afrikan/Negro Root Race, the first human Race cause the development of the other coats of skin, i. e. the other Root Races. Would the Red, Yellow, and White Races have unfolded if we had 'stayed home' in consciousness. Do they in fact arise out of our 'willingness' to roam - as the prodigal son who leaves our Heavenly Home? And what happened to the biblical Joseph, the favored son after he was giving, "a coat of many colors" [read here: coats, skins of many colors]? He was sold into slavery, the depths of coarse material conditions but maintained poised in the dreamtime of his Ba or Higher Manas consciousness that he may know the inner arrangement and out-working of the divine plan.

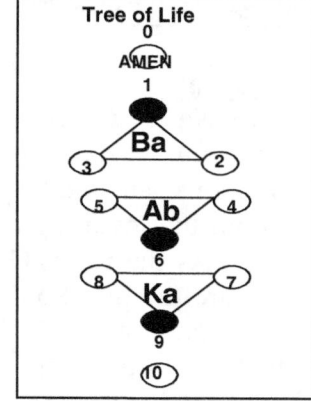

We return now to two earlier quotes: Alvin Boyd Kuhn. *The Lost Light*, p. 472.

> A prayer is made that the Osiris [Read here: Ausar] may be saved from the attack made against him "at the crossing." (ch.135). This indicates that assault on his young divinity is made as soon as he crosses the line on the west in his descent. He is then "the youngling in the egg" and subject to the Herut attack. Here the dragon lay in wait to devour the young child

And Like wise –

Accordingly: Max Heindel, *Rosicrucian Cosmo Conception*, p. 311 - 312.

> Races are but an evanescent feature of evolution…Races are simply steps in evolution which must be taken, otherwise there will be no progress for the spirits reborn in them.

★*Afrikans/Negroes - Anu Ra(y) of the ABSOLUTE - Unrefracted, Undivided, Undistorted, Undeflected, Undimished.*
★*Afrikans/Negroes – Semi or Dualitive Navigators of Time-Space, Day-Night, Dark-Light, Spirit-Matter, Life-Death, Boundlessness-Bounded, Infinite-Finite, Macrocosm-Microcosm.*

Let's continue to dispell the name <u>Negroes</u>:

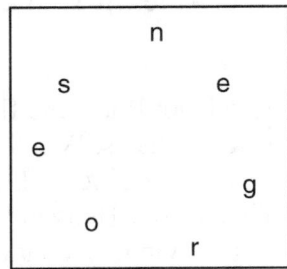 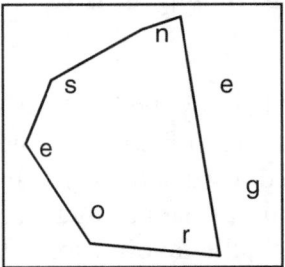

Derived Word List Continued:
Rosen G, R(i)sen G

Meaning:
The Neter G is for God. By identifying as your thoughts, emotions, and body you operating within the lesser ego or lesser God self. As the rosen G or risen God you are the Sun-Son/Daughter who has come over the horizon. You have collected your brokeness or parts and know wholeness. The Rosen or Risen God is seen in the diagram at right.

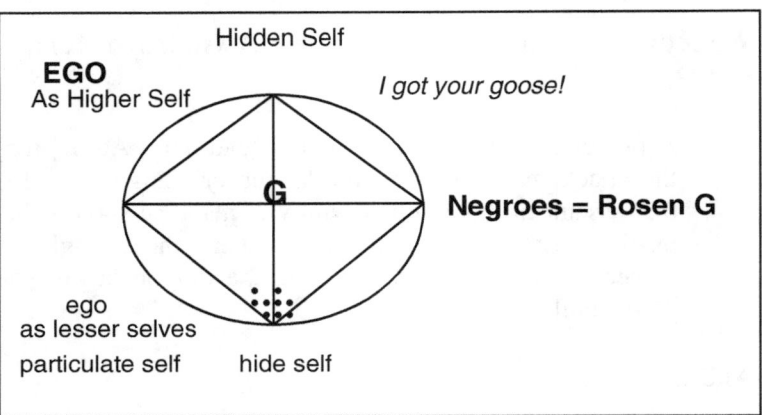

Derived Word List Continued:
Neros G, Neros God, NeGroes
Meaning:
We are told by the Ancient wisdom about the Neros or Naros cycle. The Neros cycle occurs approximately every 600 years when at the new moon in January a certain star configuration will repeat itself each cycle. God like and Great teachers who have come among us at these cyclically scheduled time periods, include: Akenaton 1300 B.C.E, Buddha 600 B.C.E., Jesus 29 A.C.E., Mohamet 600 (to name a few). The World has been watching since 1800 for the appearance of that one who will both bring and herald a greater increase of light into the World. As the Neros God the Negro is the Golden Egg or Ego that makes its descent down - then back up - the Tree of Life.

★*Afrikans/Negroes* - *The cyclically re-appearing Neros, God, who comes to remind humanity of its divinity within.*
★*Afrikans/Negroes* - Akenaton, Buddha, Jesus, Muhammed (to name a few).

How and in what form(s) has this World Teacher made his/her appearance in the 1800's?

The answer to this question and further detail on Neros cycle see Chapter entitled, Understanding Cycles of Time, *A.C.T.S 3*.

Later we become the Fattened Goose

Let's take for closer examination the words, 'geese were fattened systematically' from the previous quote. In understanding the Psycho/Spiritual Journey in Unfolding Consciousness:

Let's look at the following words that are associated with fattened goose.

Definition: Budge. *Hieroglyphic Glossary V. 1*, p. 386.

Tchetau - Fattened geese.

Tchett - To speak, to say word, speech, language, sayings proverbs, aphorisms. Saying of the Father; Speech of Negroland, Sudani language.

Thchet metu - To recite formulae.

Tchett - Star, the time of the culmination of a star (5-pointed).

Tchetchi - The "stablished one," or he of the Tchet pillar, i. e., Osiris.

Tchet - The sacred pillar or tree trunk which was worshipped in certain parts of the Delta in predynastic times, and with which the backbone of Osiris [read here: Ausar] was subsequently identified; the divine word, speech deified; to shine, light, brilliance, radiance.

Meaning:

We find the speech of Negroland means the word 'tchett.' The fattened geese sounds the fullness of the One True Self.

- A fattened goose is a Phat-ed, Pthat-ed or Ptah-ed goose who is returning Home and able to say 'I know that I know'
- He or she has gained the full self consciousness awareness at every level of immersion into matter
- He is Phat because he has followed the mandate of Ptah which is Seker - sphere 3, and the Planet Saturn in the Tree of Life
- He is becoming the fullest measure, moving through the 'rings' of Saturn and sounding the Fullness of the WORD, The One True Self

Let's continue to dispell the word Negroes

Derived Word List:

green

geo -

Definition:

geo - Earth; geocentric. 2. Geography; [Greek geo-from ge, earth].

Meaning:

Afrikans/Negroes are to the human kingdom what vegetables are to the vegetable kingdom - we blanket the earth, giving life and vitality.

Derived Word List Continued:

Se(e)

Son - Negroes are the arising of the son and the eye that sees.
No egress
No segre - No segregation

Definition:
Egress - 1. The act of coming or going out; emergence. 2. The right of going out. 3. A path or opening for going out; an exit. 4. Astronomy. The emergence of a celestial body from eclipse or occultation. [Latin egressus, from past participle of egredi, to go out].

Definition:
Segregate - 1. To separate or isolate from others or from a main body or group. 2. To impose the separation of (a race or class) from the rest of society. 3. Genetic. To undergo genetic segregation. [Latin segregare, segregat- :se-, apart; grex, greg-, flock].
Segregation - 1. The act or process of segregating or the condition of being segregated. 2. The policy and practice of imposing the social separation of races, as in schools, housing, and industry, especially so as to practice discrimination against people of color in a predominantly white society. 3. Genetics. The separation of paired alleles especially during meiosis, so that the members of each pair of alleles appear in different gametes.

Definition: This principle of non separativeness by Negroes is expressed accordingly:
The Tibetan: p. 96. *The Problem of Humanity*.
"If we can get some idea of the significance of these problems, materially and spiritually, and can gain some insight into the responsibilities involved, much of usefulness may be gained. In the case of the Jews, the sin of separateness is deeply inherent in the race itself, as well as among those among whom they live, but for the perpetuation of the separation the Jews are largely responsible; in the case of the Negro, the separative instinct derives from the white people; the Negro is struggling to end it and, therefore, the spiritual forces of the World are on the side of the Negro."

Meaning:
★*Afrikans/Negroes - The Negroes as 'egos' seemingly go out from the Egg. In their so called 'individuality' they see themselves as separate from the One. But this is an illusion. Negroes is nosegre - no separation.*
★*Afrikans/Negroes - Negroes is a state or condition of pre-separation or pre-segregation. There is no-thing 'apart' from the 'flock.'.*

Derived Word List Continued:
Gen – Beginning.
Genes -

Definition:
Genes - A hereditary unit that occupies a specific location on a chromosome and determines a particular characteristic in an organism. Genes exist in a number of different forms and can undergo mutation. [From Greek, genos, race, offspring].

Meaning:
★*Afrikans/Negroes - The repositories of genes or primordial gene-tic information. They are the time and (outgoing) motion. Therefore Negroes are eng/enderers of time and space.*

Derived Word List Continued:
Or(i)gn see - The origin of the Egos Racial bodies.
go ren – go name, ren means 'name' in Kamitic tradition.

Meaning:
★ Afrikans/Negroes -Become the Manes, the Namer and Knower of things.

Meaning:
· As we move in conscious from a state of Being
· Into the 'seeming' process of Becoming we are :
· The Seeker in the process of Seeking the Sought
· The Knower in the process of knowing the Known

★ Afrikans/Negroes - Going out = The fall
★ Afrikans/Negroes - Return = Resurrection

This going out represents the 'fall' into materiality. It is the human mind becoming attached to the appearance of the objective World. The human consciousness becomes caught in the lower ego instead of remaining polarized in the Higher Ego or All Self. Instead of the consciousness of the One Eg(o), it is a consciousness particulated into the many eg(o)s. From Egg to eggs.

Chapter 29
Have All Races Gone Out? Have All Races Gone Out to the Same Degree in the Materialization in Consciousness and Precipitating Outcomes on the Physical Plane?

Just as the Negroes or Black Race displays a whole array of colors of skin (Black, brown, red, yellow, white) eye colors (black brown, hazel, blue), hair textures (tightly coiled (peppercorn or whoolly, frizzy, curly, straight) there is likewise a whole array in unfolding consciousness. There are those who have gone out and not forgotten to return. Those in a process of return. Those who are yet to return. (See chapter on, 7 Psycho-Spiritual Types in Consciousness).

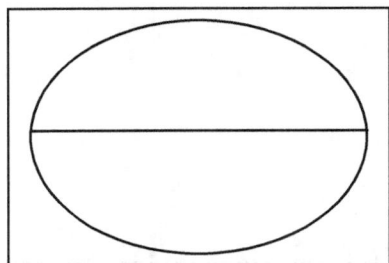 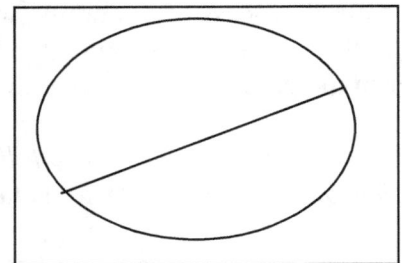

That not all Gooses or Egos have gone out and forgotten to return is captured by African tribal people. This is expressed about the 3rd Root Race Aborigines in the following accordingly: Robert Lawlor. Voice *of The First Day. Awakening In The Aboriginal Dreamtime,* p. 74.

> For the Aborigines there is no fall; paradise is the earth in its pristine beauty. All that is earthly is a reflection or externalization of the events of Dreamtime. There is no part of this existence that needs to be transcended, repressed, or gone beyond. There are many falls in the Dreamtime, the falls and vicissitudes of the Creative Ancestor, not of humans. The Dreamtime is re-enacted in its entirety, with all the anger, rage, warfare, lust, cruel and beautiful, grandiose and impoverished. Developing these destructive and constructive potentials in ritual does not spill them out into the external World, to exhaust themselves and the earth in endless cycles of actualization.

This dynamic in consciousness is so vividly demonstrated in the documentary Shaka Zulu. Prior battles between tribes were enacted through ritual display were hostilities, anger, and rage were enacted. The destructive and constructive potentials in ritual did not spill out into the external World in an endless cycle of actualization which exhausts the Earth's resources and soaks her in blood. The documentary takes upon place a backdrop when the Aryan/European Race has been externalizing destructive potentials in outwardly conquering Africa for nearly three thousand years. Shaka Zulu teaches his army to move out of the Dreamtime or Unitive consciousness to meet those who are acting from a particulate consciousness. The following is intended to give example of this shift and is expressed accordingly: *Encyclopedia Britannica.*

> After serving six years with brilliance as a warrior of the Mtetwa Empire Shaka was sent in 1816 to take over the Zulu, as which, at this time, probably numbered fewer than 1,500,

> occupying an area on the White Umfolozi River. They were among the smallest of the more than 800 Eastern Nguni–Bantu clans, but from the day of Shaka's arrival they commenced their march to greatness. Shaka ruled with an iron hand from the outset, meting out instant death for the slightest opposition.
>
> His first act was to reorganize the army. Like all the clans, the Zulu were armed with oxhide shields and spindly throwing spears. Battles were little more than brief and relatively bloodless clashes in which the outnumbered side prudently gave way before extensive casualties occurred.
>
> Shaka first rearmed his men with long-bladed, short-shafted stabbing assegais, which forced them to fight at close quarters. …Shaka fought for extermination, incorporating the remnants of the clans he smashed into the Zulu.

This ritualized consciousness that plays out the discordant energies and hostilities without spilling over *can be* externalized into movement of destruction and extermination. We have likewise seen much posturing and flexing around pushing the 'button' of Nuclear warfare - a warfare that if precipitated out of ritualized dreamtime has the capacity to devastate our Planet and all her kingdoms - human, animal, vegetable and mineral.

The question could be asked, how far do we *go out* into:
1. Precipitating weapons of mass destruction
2. Precipitating 'thing-ness' - more computers, gadgetry onto the physical plane which exhausts our Earth's resources and suffocates us in clutter, trash, chemical waste, poverty, etc.
3. Precipitating the tampering with DNA, life, e.g. cloning.

Instead let us ask, How do we make our return home?
Ausarian resurrection is the consciousness of the One and the many without *attachment* to the 'seeming' multiplicity into the many. One of many steps to be taken in our reconstruction is through the practice of meditation. This is well expressed in the following accordingly: Robert Lawlor. Voice of *The First Day. Awakening In The Aboriginal, p.* 362.

> The goal of meditation is to enhance the field of the individual or ego soul so that it acquires full independence from the physical body before death. Through constant exercise the spirit body of the individual ego soul [read here: individual Ba] is built up and transposed into a universal ego [read here: Universal Ba]. As the meditative practice matures, the individual becomes capable of living simultaneously in life and the afterlife. The advanced meditator achieves identity with the two extremes of existence, the undifferentiated universal continuum and the spiritual of the encapsulated individual World. After death this ability to live simultaneously in the individual and the universal is said to be retained.

- This is the simultaneous practice of 'going out' yet
- 'Staying Home' in consciousness
- Home is your true identification
- Not who you 'think' you become as you go out
- *Yet paradoxically*
- It is through the *going out* that you become aware of
- The full Self conscious Realized Being

- Of who you have always been
- From the begnningless beginning
- You hide within the 7 divisions of the Spirit and the 3 Aspects of Divinity
- Yet you come to Know the Self as 1

Chapter 30
The Secret and Sacred Meaning of the Word Nigger

If we now know more Metaphysically about what the Negroes are then what Metaphysically is the Nigger?
Before we can answer this question we must dispell another word.
Let's dispell the word <u>integer</u>:

Dictionary:
Integer – 1. A member of the set of positive whole numbers (1,2,3,…) negative whole numbers (-1,-2,-3,…) and zero (0). 2. A complete unit or entity. (Latin integer complete). Whole.

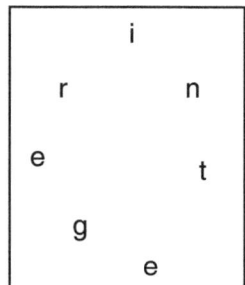

Derived Word List:
Ntr, Netri, - God
> **Definition:** E.A.. Wallis Budge. An Egyptian Hieroglyphic Dictionary. V. 1. p. 401.
> <u>Neter</u> - divine power, divine one, divine qualities of God. (Neteru –plural)

<u>Nig(g)er Nigre</u>
<u>Net</u>
<u>Re t (r)n i(n) g</u> - Returning
<u>Reign-(ing)-(nigger)</u>
<u>Entire G</u>
<u>Ring</u>
<u>Eg(g)</u>
<u>Ign(i)te re</u> - igniting the fire of Ra.
<u>Reg(r) t ing</u> - Regretting, not that we have gone out in consciousness, but that we have gone out and forgotten our heavenly abode.
<u>Integrity</u>
<u>Integr(a)(t)e</u>
<u>Regent</u>
<u>Neteri</u>

What is a Nig(g)er?
Let's dispel the word <u>Nigger</u>:
Meaning:

A Nig(g)er is an Integer that has lost its 'T.' A nigger is an integer that has lost its Ankh cross. The Ankh is the symbol of Life. We need the **'T'** cross in order to climb out of self imposed prison in which we have falsely encapsulated the Self.

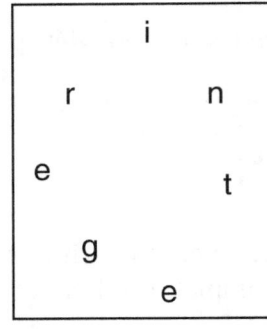 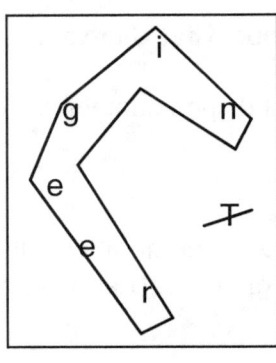 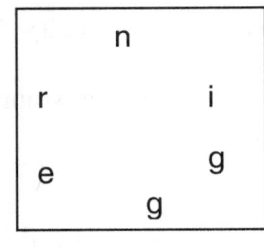

Derived Word List:
We have already dealt with: Egg, Gen(e), Ren, etc.
Ring - Sounding a note, vibration.
Reign(ing) - Ruling - (Nigger).
Ren - Kamitic word for 'name'.

.
Definition: Dictionary
Nigger - Offensive slang. 1. Used as a disparaging term for a Black person. *Neger,* black person, from French *negre,* from Spanish *negro.*

Meaning:
We must remember that we never really fell except in illusion. We are the Angels of heaven that we have always been. The diagram below illustrates the T – station, stops of initiation we must make in order to make our re-ascent. As the vertical line (Male positive energies) and the horizontal line (female receptive energies) intersect to form the cross bar T̲ we are relating Spirit and Matter.

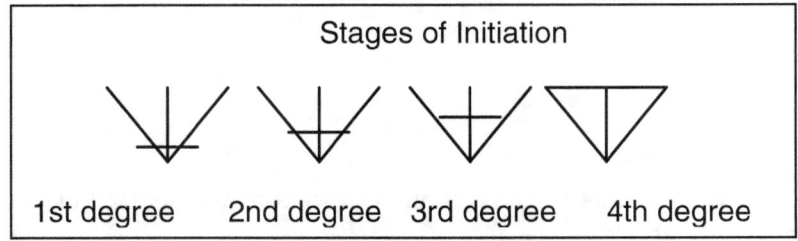

We likewise see here the Neter 'V'. (See ***A.C.T.S. 1. Ka Ab Ba Building The Lighted Temple*** on the vertex of the V and *Understanding What Time It Is*). You can see here the relationship between the V and T. Are you sitting watching TV. Are you an integer/(nigger) who is ignoring the cross, bowing down before the cross on two bended knees, 'gg' waiting to magically ascend the Tree of Life without the hard, arduous climb?. The cross is the ladder up the Tree of Life. Once upon a time you knew 'Life'. TV has put you to sleep. You have not surmounted the T - the Tau cross the breath of creator God. Do you mount the cross within yourself. Get up from sitting or prostrating yourself in front of the TV. Mount the cross of Ausarian resurrection. You have lost your head (mind). 'Get a head' back on your shoulders. Get a Life. The Ankh is the symbol for life and is pictured at right. You are a fallen angel on the wheel of birth and death, birth and death. How long before you mount the cross and come forth over the horizon as a Grand Master of your Life? To get a life is to get a head on your shoulders, the Ankh cross.

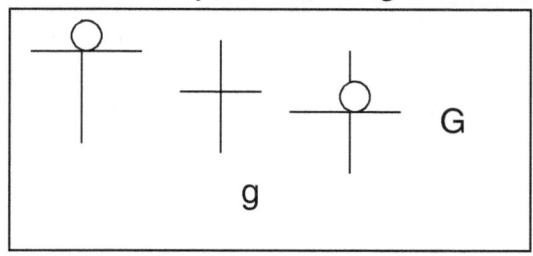
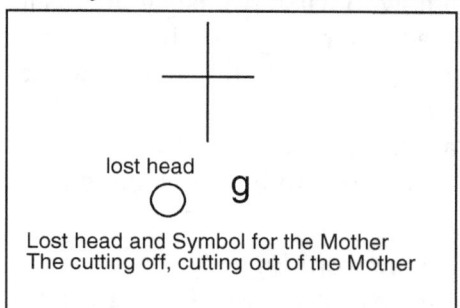

✶*Afrikans/Negroes* - The Divine Integer. The enumeration of the One and the Same Individuality everywhere.

What has happened to the Tau Cross, the Kamitic Ankh.?

We return to an earlier quote (See ***A.C.T.S. 1. Ka Ab Ba Building The Lighted Temple***) to derive further meaning on the Integer or Nigger that has lost its cross. This is expressed acccordingly: The Tibetan. *Cosmic Fire,* p. 748. From the Archives of the Lodge.

> From the nadir to the zenith, from eve unto the Day be with us, from the circle of manifestation to the centre of pralayic peace, is seen the enveloping blue, lost in the flame of achievement. Up from the pit of maya back to the portals of gold, forth from the gloom and darkness back to the splendour of day, rideth the Manifested One, the Avatar, bearing the shattered Cross. Naught can arrest His return, none can impede His Path, for He passeth along the upper way, bearing His people with Him.

Why is the cross – the Ankh - finally shattered?

It is served as a pole vault back into the heavens, the Spiritual realm, the Dreamtime of Unitive consciousness, wholeness. We need the Ankh when we make our descent down the Tree of Life. We need the Ankh when we make our re-ascent back up the Tree of Life.
•On the higher turn of the spiral we are the Neggur - in Dreamtime. The One who goes out, but does not forget to return. Who remains, At-One, whether in or out of time. The One at *rest* within the Golden Egg.
•On a lower turn of the spiral we are the Nigger when we have made our descent, lost our Ankh and can't find our way back up the Tree of Life. We have lost our 'life' and unlike, *Jack in the Beanstalk* - we have no way to climb back up to the treasures of Heaven.

Everytime we say the Neter or word Ankh we are making the sound of the Goose – *Honk. And what is happening in our deep psycho-spiritual sub-strata each time Negroes refer to whites as Honk-ies?*

Chapter 31
Secret and Sacred Meaning of the Word English
The Bridging Between the of Language of Metu Neter and English Continued

We return now to where we began in this text and the following is restated:
English is an outer language that is both spoken and written all over the World, thus it is giving architectural design and arrangement to the World and World affairs. However, it is just a distillate of all other languages that have preceded it. English would suggest itself as the last place to look for derivation on what are *Negroes*.' Nevertheless, someone said it well when they said, 'If you don't want someone to find something put it right under their nose.

Let's dispel the word <u>English</u>:
 # 1. Oracle Metaphysical Dis-Spelling Key: Put letters of word or words together in a circle, like a serpent putting its tail in its mouth. Coming full Circle.

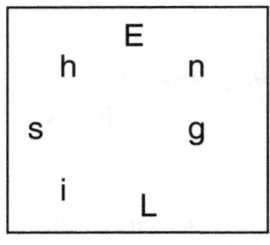 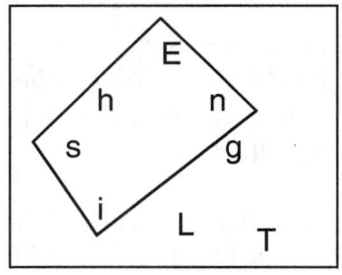

#2. Oracle Metaphysical Dis-Spelling Key: Read letters, putting together words, going forwards, backwards and in zig-zag patterns.
#3. Oracle Metaphysical Dis-Spelling Key: You may crossover in order to use a letter more than once. Place re-used letter in parenthesis ( ).
#4. Oracle Metaphysical Dis-Spelling Key: You may add a letter to complete a word. Place added letter in parenthesis ( ).
#5. Oracle Metaphysical Dis-Spelling Key: Letter substitution-you may substitute a letter. Place substituted letter in parenthesis ( ).
#6. Oracle Metaphysical Dis-Spelling Key: Make a list of derived words. Try to make the longest continuous unbroken word or string of words.
#14. Oracle Metaphysical Dis-Spelling Key: You may add the letter T which symbolizes the Ankh or Tau cross of Spirit and Matter.

<u>Derived Word List:</u>
<u>Neshi</u> - G 'L' You will recall that Nehesu/Nuhes/Nashi/Neshi/Nahsi are all Kamitic names for Negroes.

<u>Neg</u> - You will recall that Neg is the Kamitic name for a bull, the four horned bull, god of heaven, to cackle.
<u>Light</u> -

Secrets of Race & Consciousness Afrikan Cosmology of Kamit
with The Spiritual Meaning of The 'N' Word(s)
Neggur - The Goose Goddess who laid the Sun Egg, the Cosmic Egg

Revealed in Ka Ab Ba *(Kabala)* The Tree Of Life   M̲etaphysical M̲ysteries M̲eaning

<u>Shine G 'L', Shenit G 'L'</u> - The Shine (ing) G-od at all 4 angles 'L" or corners (of the Earth). Letter 'L' symbolizes the angles 4 'L's make up the 4 corners in the diagram.pictured at right.

#7. Oracle Metaphysical Dis-Spelling Key: Look up definition (dictionary, glossary, reference texts, etc.)

Derived Word List Continued:
<u>Hilt -</u>

> <u>Hilt -</u> To the limit; Completely ; Played a role to the Hilt (Middle English, from Old English.

<u>Sine -</u>

> **Definition:**

1. <u>Sine</u> - 1. Mathematics. In a right triangle, the ratio of the length of the side opposite an acute angle to the length of the hypotenuse 2. The ordinate of the endpoint of an arc of a unit circle centered at the origin of a Cartesian coordinate system, the arc being of length *x* and measured counterclockwise from the point (1, 0) if *x* is positive or clockwise if x is negative. [fold in a garment, from Latin, curve, fold]

#8. Oracle Metaphysical Dis-Spelling Key: Meaning. See the relationship and oracle or story of the Neteru - Put word list together to tell a story.

Meaning:
You will recall that the Neshi or Nehesu are Types of Negroes. They are the Shining Stars. The 5 pointed Star. This is called the *Amsu Heru* by the Kamitians. To become a 5 pointed STAR - Amsu Heru, is to measure up, become the <u>Sum</u> or the fullest measure of what you have always been from the beginningless beginning. As the collective consciousness in the human family we are the Sign (Sine) of Light or the Hilt of Sin. After having 'gone out' on the Psycho/Spiritual Journey of Unfolding Consciousness, every Soul must be brought 'back into the fold' of the Garment of God.

★*Afrikans/Negroes - As the collective consciousness in the human family we are the Sign (Sine) of Light or the Hilt of Sin. After having 'gone out' on the Psycho/Spiritual Journey of Unfolding Consciousness, every Soul must be brought 'back into the fold' of the Garment of God.*

Chapter 32
From Sage to Savage to Sage
Is Evolution A Myth?
Crossing the Line in Consciousness

When you go out to hide in your involutionary descent in consciousness you cross over the equinotical line. Thus you enter the more dense material realm. When you return in your evolutionary re-ascent in consciousness you cross back over the equinotical line. Thus you enter the more Spiritual realm. This is indicated in the 3 diagrams below. Man and woman have free will.

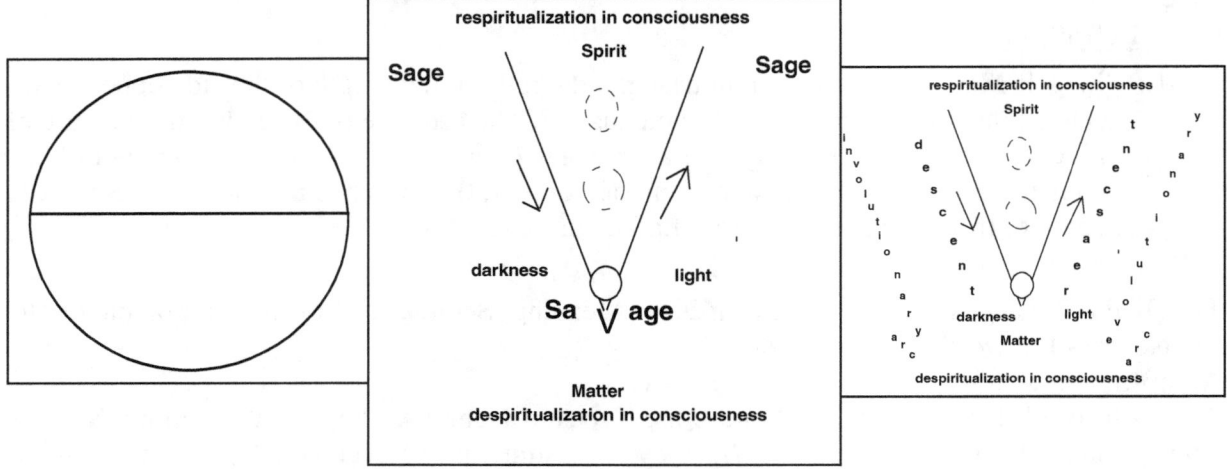

How is this accomplished?
To remain poised above the horizon in consciousness is to be *involved* within Higher Manas - Ausarian consciousness - *while simultaneously* moving the consciousness below the horizon to be *evolved* in manifesting part-i-cular aspects of the whole Kingdom of God on Earth - Geb sphere 10. You are the artist given free creative reign so that myriad possibilities may be expressed as you co-creative implement divine will and plan.

The so called 'World Super Powers' are in a 'Space race' in their desire to conquer other 'Worlds' beyond our Earth Globe. Yet, the only expandable boundary is in consciousness. How we understand who we are and our interconnection with every other being in creation is a window into our unfolding consciousness. The U. S. Space program has been named, The National Aeronautics and Space Administration, NASA. If we dispell the acronym NASA, the Neteru reveal that expansion into the waters of space (the Nu) is coming into fuller awareness of our NSA/A - NegroSemiticAryan-Admixture in Konsciousness. Karmically, we will not be allowed to bring our bad habits of unjust relationship to other 'Worlds' until - we 'do right'- here on Earth - before the presence of The Lord of the World - Ausar Ba, *The One in Whom We Live and Move and Have Our Being.*

Earth is our Planetary Home. We have got to get our 'local' Ba in order first. Ba means Soul. It is to come into the consciousness that all Souls or Bas are One. It is our first level of At-One-ing. Earth provides us with the rehearsal in At-One-ing that ultimately leads to our Self conscious At-One-ing all along the ladder of re-ascent with every entity in creation, up to and including the Universal Ba in total. Thus, this Earthly lesson is then transferable to other Star systems in Cosmos.

★*Afrikans/Negroes - To remain poised above the horizon in consciousness is to be involved within Higher Manas - Ausarian consciousness - while simultaneously moving the consciousness below the horizon to be evolved in manifesting part-i-cular aspects of the whole Kingdom of God on Earth - Geb sphere 10. You are the artist given free creative reign so that myriad possibilities may be expressed as you co-creative implement divine will and plan.*

Chapter 33
How are We Rounding the Corner in Our Collective Planetary Consciousness?

How might we rise as a Human Family and Together Make Earth Sacred Space?
How can we go and be At-One 'someplace' else when we can't be At-One at 'Home'?
We are foolish Earth children if we do not think we need one another to 'get' where we 'think' we are 'going'. In order to ascend into Unity consciousness you must come 'full circle' and claim your full lineage with your Ancient Ancestors of the early Root Races and your conscious connection with the Root Races as yet to make their appearance on our Earth Globe. This brings us to the next -

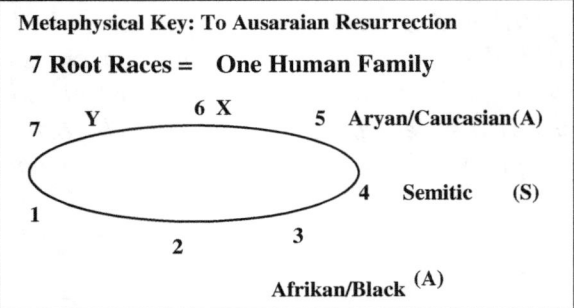

Metaphysical Key To:
Ausarian Resurrection
7 Root Races = One Human Family

This is pictured in the diagram at right in which all 7 Root Races are embraced. This consciousness in total is the collective experience of man and woman's pilgrimage. It is how we 'seemingly *leave* and *return* Home'. Each of the 7 Root Races plays its part in the long trod in gaining conscious re-membrance of the One True Self we have always been from the beginingless beginning. In the successively trodden footsteps required for the completed Psycho/Spiritual Journey - each Root Race is playing its part in revealing divinity in humanity.

Although diagrams have been used in this text to depict an involutionary and evolutionary unfolding in consciousness it is important for the reader to remember that everything is happening in the eternal *now*. Time is just man's feeble effort to keep everything from happening all at once. It is through time that we grasp the unfoldment of consciousness in each successive Root race and thereby are we made to see the following:

1. All 7 Root Races are but the One Human Family
2. The part each Root Race is playing upon the stage of our Divine and Human drama
3. As the Collective Consciousness of all 7 Root Races, we are 'the *One* Pilgrim' that both leaves and returns Home
4. As we are restored in Ausarian Consciousness, we hold the awareness that we are each *a part* and *together the whole* story of man and woman's journey - down and back- up the Tree of Life.
5. To try to wrap the mind around the concept of 7 Root Races that are in the process of unfolding *is* already a step in gathering the pieces of the broken body of Ausar. This is another concept that is symbolized by the mummy bandages of Ausar.

This is expressed accordingly: *The Secret Doctrine. V.ll,* p. 146 footnote:

> The mankind of the First Root-Race is the mankind of the second, third, fourth, fifth, etc. To the last of forms a cyclic and constant reincarnation of the Monads [read here: - Bas]

belonging to the Dhyan Chohans of our Planetary chain [read here: Ausar Ba, the Lord of the World].

You, along with the entire human family are engaged in the game of:
· I know
· I forget that I know
· I sleep
· I know not
· I re-awake and
· I think that I know
· Finally
· I remember and
· *I Know that I Know*

★*Afrikans/Negroes - As the Collective Consciousness of all 7 Root Races, we are 'the One Pilgrim' that both leaves and returns Home.*

And Likewise expressed accordingly: Geoffrey Barborka. *The Divine Plan*, p. 345.

> The Grand Cycle includes the progress of mankind from the appearance of primordial man of ethereal form. It runs through the inner cycles of his (man's) progress evolution from the ethereal down to the semi-ethereal and purely physical: down to the redemption of man from his coat of skin and matter, after which it continues running its course downward and then upward again, to meet at the culmination of a Round, when the manvantaric "Serpent swallows its tail' and seven minor cycles are passed. These are the great Glacial Cycles. (Secret Doctrine: 1, 642).

1. The **3-4-5, AfrikanSemiticAryan Konsciousness Admixture - ASA KA** is now the tip of the tongue.
2. This is depicted in the diagram as follows:

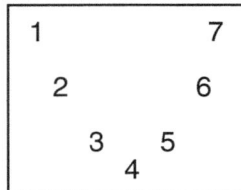 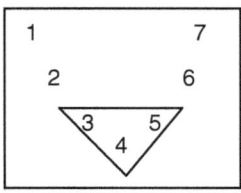

3. In our collective speech or word the questions becomes:
   a. What is rolling off the tip of our tongue about our Planetary achievement in human consciousness?
   b. What are we uttering as AfrikanSemiticAryan-Admixture in consciousness? Are these words of war and disharmony or words of peace and justice and right relationship?
4. Previously, we dispelled the word Earth which reveals the word <u>Heart</u>. 'Home' is where the Heart is. It is the 3-4-5 Planetary Konsciousness Admixture that is at

the core and the heart of the matter. Are we speaking from the Heart that has been made pure?

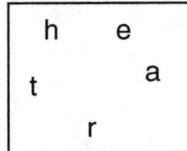 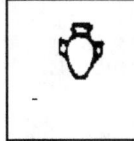

Chapter 34
The Wheel of Birth and Death
The Law of Reincarnation (Rebirth) &
The Law of Cause and Effect-Karma

Again in the discourse between Auset and Heru accordingly: *Virgin of the World.*

> O Heru, Then the Great God decreed that Love and Necessity should be the lords of life. Further, the lord of All said: 'Know, all of you who are set under My un-aging rule, that as longs as ye keep you free of sin, ye shall dwell in the fields of Heaven, but if some cause of blame for anything should attach itself to you, ye shall dwell in the place that Destiny allots condemned to mortal wombs.
>
> The Great God continued: 'If, then, the things imputed to your charge be slight, leaving the bond of fleshy frames subject to death, ye shall again embrace your origin in Heaven, and sigh no more; but if ye shall commit some greater sins, and with the end appointed of your frames be not advanced, no longer shall ye dwell in Heaven, nor even in the bodies of mankind, but shall continue after that to wander round in lives irrational.

Let's take this quote for closer examination and meaning. We see here that a period of divine grace is shown. Yet as man and woman exercise personal will and choice, he becomes an agent of *cause* as in the words "...but if some cause of blame for anything should attach itself to you...

What is the wheel of birth and death?
This is likewise the Law of Karma, the law of birth, death and reincarnation. **For more information see *A.C.T.S. 1. Ka Ab Ba Building The Lighted Temple* and refer to the following Key(s):**

> **Metaphysical Key To**:
> The Law of Reincarnation (Rebirth) &
> The Law of Cause and Effect -Karma
> *Overcoming Impediments # 4*
> Loss of the Laws to overcome death, fear of death and
> conscious accountability for actions. Loss of the (ability to have
> a Declaration of Innocence).

In briefest review, for now it is important to understand:
Accordingly in the *Kybalion*, p. 171 this Kamitic Law (named by the Greeks as Hermetic Law) is as follows:

> Every cause has its Effect; every Effect has its Cause; everything happens according to Law; Chance is but a name for Law not recognized; there are many planes of causation, but nothing escapes the Law.

In short, everything has a cause or chain of causes. Afrikan conscious people speak best to this law when they say, 'What goes around, comes around. Yet the loss of our real connection with this Ancient wisdom creates Impediment # 4.

In 325 A.D. the Council of Nicea rejected the idea of reincarnation and the transmigration of Souls and replaced it with the idea of a permanent heaven or hell for the individual Soul. And continuing in the discourse between Auset and Heru accordingly: *Virgin of the World.*

> Thus speaking, Heru mine, He gave to all the gift of breath, and thus continued: 'It is not without purpose or by chance I have laid down the law of your transforming, but as it will be for the worse if ye do something unseemly, so for the better, if ye shall will what's worthy of your birth.'

Let's take this quote for closer examination and meaning. The law of transforming is already given to humanity. This law is resident within your Spiritual Faculty, which is symbolized by the Tree of Life. But we may choose for many lifetimes to do what is 'unseemly' and yet we are better off, if we do what is 'worthy' of our birth. Karma 'attaches' itself and its accumulation must be addressed. Earth is a school in which men and women have much rehearsal and practice in demonstrating the Universal law of Right Relationship.

Chapter 35
The Scales of Maat The Weighing of the Heart
Standing Before The Lord Of The World

Heru is your inner government. It is that aspect of your Spiritual equipment that you have lost touch with as you came to live behind the separating veil of the physical, emotional and mental aspects of your equipment. Under this veil and spell of illusion, you begin to undergo the process of 'seeming death'. Only the process of initiation will help you to:
1. Pierce the veil and climb the rungs of the ladder or the branches of the Tree which is the Self, to the heights from which you have seemingly 'fallen
2. Dispell illusion and dissipate the power to wound

For more information see *A.C.T.S. 1. Ka Ab Ba Building The Lighted Temple* and refer to Key(s):

Metaphysical Key:
Sphere 4 Maat Meditation

For now it is important to understand:
There is no death. There is only the transmigration of the Soul from life into greater Life. Death is the seeming discontinuity of consciousness – a cutting into pieces of the ALL Consciousness. This is symbolized as the broken body of Ausar, cut into fourteen parts. At each 'death' the disciple appears again and again within the Hall of Amenta, that his heart may be weighed and thereby tested. Each time his heart has fallen short of being as light as the feather of Maat, he has to mount again the wheel of birth and death and fall back into the material realm. This cycle repeats itself as we undergo the Initiatory process. Higher states of consciousness are achieved -until the state of God Conscious is the stabilized Realization. The disciple, finally stands within the Hall of Amenta and is <u>*found*</u> *Maa Kheru.* Thus, you are justified as living in truth, morally and in total equilibrium with the laws of God.

What frees you from the wheel of birth and death is to conform your mental and desire nature into one-pointed aspiration to serve, working in accord with the Great Divine Plan and purpose. When the will is aligned with the divine purpose, the heart is made light, and purified. As full Self conscious identity grows, Son (Sun)ship is revealed until the radiant Sun blazes in full glory. Heru - sphere 6, is the Christ principle within you. Heru is the 'I' in, 'I arise and go to my Father's Home', Ausar - sphere 1. At last, Heru is the 'I' in, 'I and my Father - Ausar- are One This is the return to Ausarian Consciousness where the One True Self is Realized.

Today in your consciousness admixture you have had many incarnations upon the wheel of birth and death. Through the process of birth, death and rebirth the Soul has accumulated wisdom of many lifetimes. Man and woman are hard at play in the *Game of Manes* . Thus, Heru is the wisdom, Spiritual essence and guidance that you have been garnering in your long pilgrimage through from Afrikan to Semitic to Aryan consciousness.

Having acted from this fuller innersightedness within your Spiritual Faculty you stand within the Hall of Amenti and are found *Maa Kheru* - thus you are declared as justified in truth, living morally and in total equilibrium with the law of God - Universal laws that govern all relationships in God's created Universe. This is expressed accordingly: The Tibetan. *The Light of The Soul.* p.15.

> The mental body itself has five modifications or activities, and thus is a reflection, or correspondence of the fifth principle, as it manifests upon the fifth plane, the mental. The modifications are the lower shadow of manas (or mind in the microcosmic manifestation), and this mind is a reflection of mahat [read here: Maat] (the universal mind), or mind manifesting in the macrocosm. This is a great mystery but will reveal itself to the man who overcomes the five modifications of the lower mind, who through non-attachment to the lower, identifies himself with the higher, and who thus solves the mystery of the "Makara" and treads the Way of the Kumaras.

Here note that Maa Kheru and Makara are different Kamitc spelling for he or she who is found, *Justified.*

The Laws of Maat govern how karma is dispensed to man and woman for either choosing:
1. To build a World in accord and alignment with the divinely intended archetypal design for manifestation or
2. To build in violation of these Laws, thus building a World askew to the divinely intended design.

Maat - sphere 4, in the Tree of Life is the Kamitic deity whose symbols are the ostrich feather and the scales of justice. These are symbols of truth, righteousness, justice, World order, correctness, harmony and peace. These laws govern right relationships and guide man and woman in acting accordingly. They assure the right of every being to achieve its purpose of Self expression to the fullest while allowing others to achieve this same right of Self expression. The Maat faculty of man's spirit urges and guides him to live according to truth. The laws of Maat unifies the myriad relationships. They allow each entity its divine inheritance of full realization of the ONE TRUE SELF gradually conferred by Seker (sphere 3) in time and space allotments. The Kamitic Ancient Wisdom teaches much about the journey of the Soul and the Psycho/Spiritual Journey of Unfolding Consciousness.

The Judgment Scene is pictured on the following page.

Secrets of Race & Consciousness Afrikan Cosmology of Kamit
with The Spiritual Meaning of The 'N' Word(s)
Neggur - The Goose Goddess who laid the Sun Egg, the Cosmic Egg

Revealed in Ka Ab Ba *(Kabala)* The Tree Of Life   **M**etaphysical **M**ysteries **M**eaning

The Kamitic Spiritual Transmigration of the Soul is depicted above in the The Judgment Scene on this and the following page. The weighing of the heart ritual must be understood on 2 Levels. This brings us to the next -

Metaphysical Key:
1. The Weighing of the Individual Heart Man declared as Ma Kheru –
   Ausarianization of Individual Consciousness

2. The Weighing of the Planetary Heart of Collective Humanity
   Ausarianization of Planetary or Global Consciousness

Level 1
Weighing of The Individual Heart
The weighing of the heart is occurring for each individual man and woman. In the Judgment scene you enter within the Halls of Amenti (the Inner Plane) which is symbolized by the disciple Ani. You come before the scales and your heart is weighed against the feather of Maat. Heru (which is within you) leads you to stand before the Father, Ausar in the affirmation that, I and my Father are One. The presentation of a lesser self identification causes you to fall short of full identification as the One True Self.

Level 2.
Weighing of The Planetary Heart of Collective Humanity

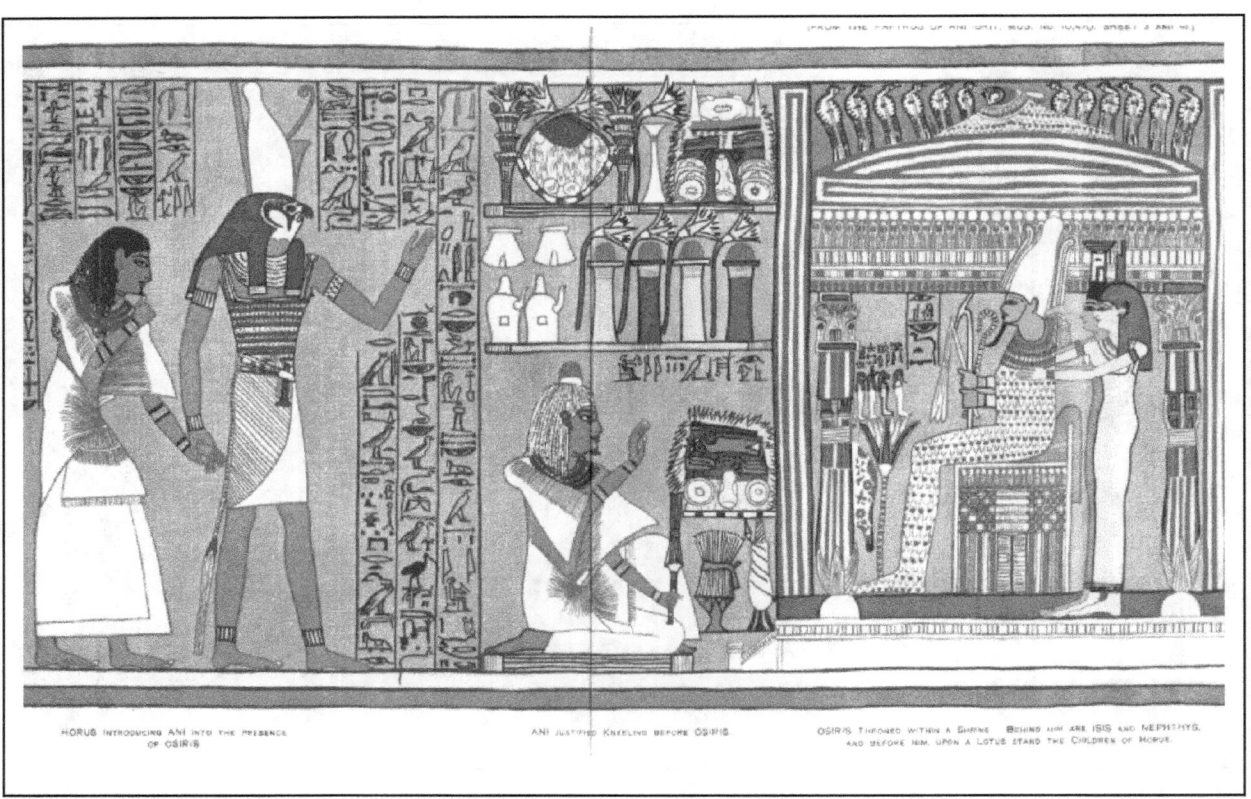

The weighing of the Planetary heart of collective humanity is likewise occurring. In the Judgment scene the whole of humanity enters within the Halls of Amenti (the Inner Plane). As a collective humanity we offer up to the Lord of the World our strides at just living and Godly service on Earth. Together, we constitute the body of Heru, also called the Body of Christ. This is Kamitically called the Karest. In mass formation, we constitute the Living God - Ausar. One by one, as individual men and women are found Maa Kheru, we join ranks to form a collective critical mass which changes the whole of the Planetary Mind and Consciousness. Standing before the Lord of the World, this inner group is at One with Divine, will, love and intelligence guiding our Earth's evolution. We are the Image and Likeness as a humanity of the Living God on Earth.

The Lord of the World is known by many Names (Ausar, God, Allah, Jehovah, The One in Whom We Live and Move and Have Our Being). Just as man and woman are working to bring personal will in accord with divine will on an individual level so is collective humanity working to come into alignment with Planetary Will, The Lord of the World - the One *in whom we live and move and have our Being.*

Appendix

Meditation Key To:
The Tree Of Life
The Big MAP

The Ausarianization of Consciousness Tablet Series 2 – A.C.T.S. 2
Metaphysical Keys To the Tree of Life & Oracle Keys to Dispelling Illusion
The Psycho/Spiritual Journey of Unfolding Consciousness

The Tree of Life — The big Map

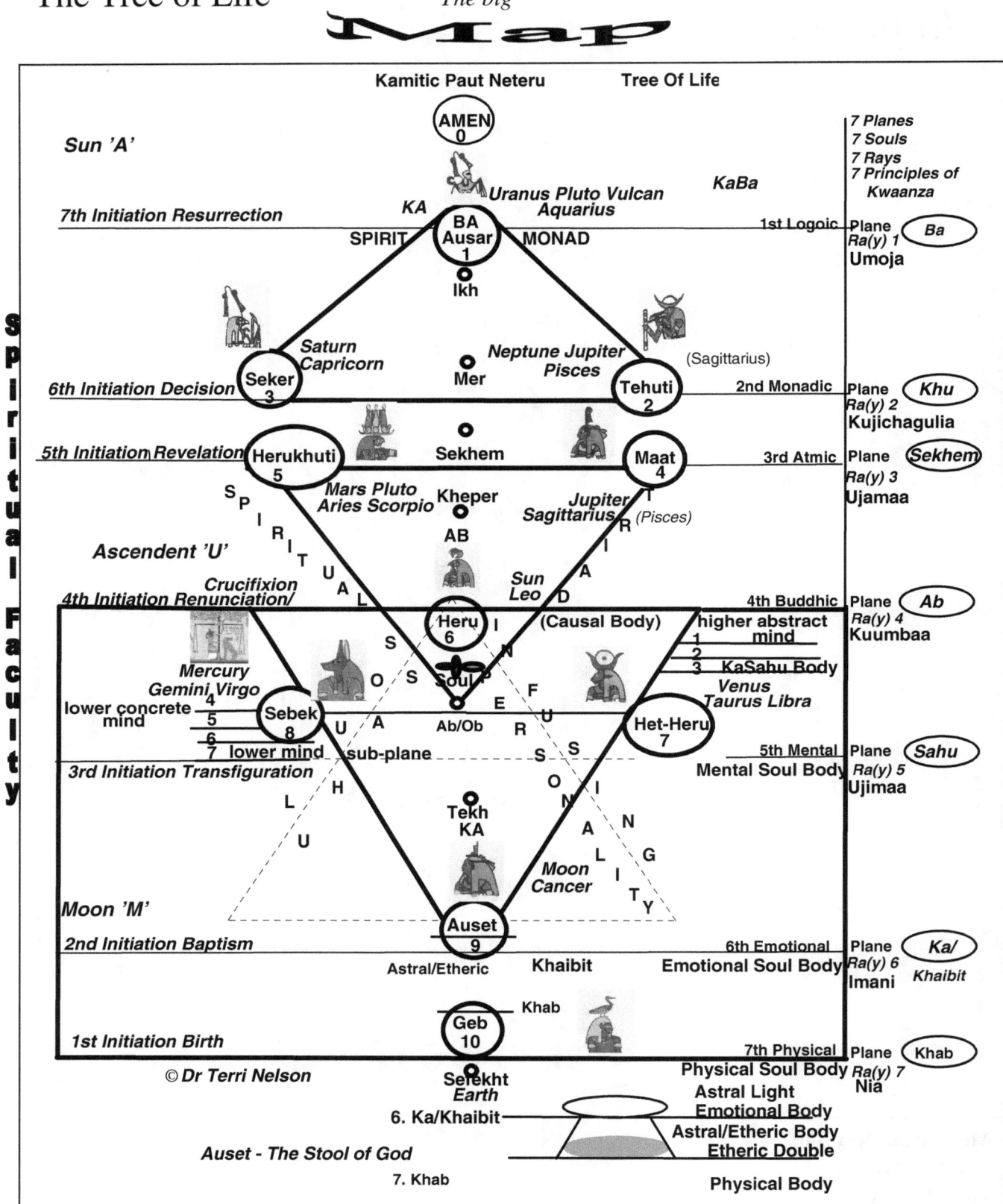

Oracle Metaphysical Dis-Spelling Keys

> **Metaphysical Keys to:**
> **Oracle Metaphysical Dis-Spelling Keys**

In using the Metaphysical Dis-Spelling Keys along with many other Metaphysical Keys to the Tree of Life we will attempt to break the 'spell of illusion' in our re-ascent up the Tree of Life.

 # 1. Oracle Metaphysical Dis-Spelling Key: Put letters of word or words together in a circle, like a serpent putting its tail in its mouth. Coming full Circle.

#2. Oracle Metaphysical Dis-Spelling Key: Read letters, putting together words, going forwards, backwards and in zig-zag patterns.

#3. Oracle Metaphysical Dis-Spelling Key: You may crossover in order to use a letter more than once. Place re-used letter in parenthesis ( ).

#4. Oracle Metaphysical Dis-Spelling Key: You may add a letter to complete a word. Place added letter in parenthesis ( ).

#5. Oracle Metaphysical Dis-Spelling Key: Letter substitution-you may substitute a letter. Place substituted letter in parenthesis ( ).

#6. Oracle Metaphysical Dis-Spelling Key: Make a list of derived words. Try to make the longest continuous unbroken word or string of words.

#7. Oracle Metaphysical Dis-Spelling Key: Look up definition (dictionary, glossary, reference texts, etc.)

#8. Oracle Metaphysical Dis-Spelling Key: Meaning. See the relationship and oracle or story of the Neteru - Put word list together to tell a story.

#9. Oracle Metaphysical Dis-Spelling Key: Take each letter one at a time or in combination with one or more letters and derive its meaning.

#10. Oracle Metaphysical Dis-Spelling Key: Letter replacement. Here we have replaced the 'k' which had been substituted by the letter 'c.'

#11. Oracle Metaphysical Dis-Spelling Key: What does the word sound like? Say the word out loud and then silently in a meditative state.

#12. Oracle Metaphysical Dispelling Key: Take out duplication of letters so that each letter appears only once.

#13. Oracle Metaphysical Dis-Spelling Key: You may abrade a letter so that it is changed to another letter as in 'h' to 'n'. Notice the loping off of the top of the 'h' to make 'n'.

> **Definition:** Dictionary
> Abrade - 1. To wear down or rub away by friction; erode. See synonyms at chafe. 2. To make weary through constant irritation; wear down spiritually. (Latin abradere, to scrape of: ab-, away.

#14. Oracle Metaphysical Dis-Spelling Key: You may add the letter T which symbolizes the Ankh or Tau cross of Spirit and Matter.

#15. Oracle Metaphysical Dis-Spelling Key: You may combine two or more words as one word.

The Story Of Ausar, Auset and Heru – The Divine Trinity

Metaphysical Key To:
The Story of
Ausar, Auset and Heru
The Divine Trinity

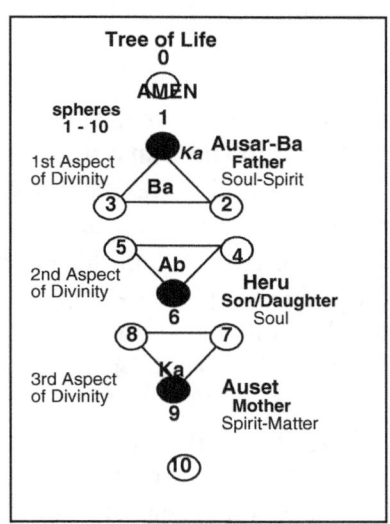

We now continue Our Story of: The Divine Trinity Ausar, Auset and Heru
A fuller version of the story is found in various texts. Excerpts from this story will be given as Our Story continues (See also, Budge, *The Book of Coming Forth by Day, Prt Em Hru,* (Egyptian Book of the Dead); *Osiris The Egyptian Religion of Resurrection;* Dr. Muata Ashby, *Ausarian Resurrection*). An abbreviated version is as follows:

Ausar is the divine King who ruled Kamit with his very abled wife Auset at his side. Ausar had established peace and harmony in the land of Kamit, which was governed under the Universal laws of Tehuti – sphere 2, and Maat – sphere 4. The Kamitic Laws of Tehuti are later referred to by the Greeks as the Hermetic Laws of Thoth, or Hermes Trismegistus (See also G.R.S Mead, *Thrice Greatest Hermes;* William Wynn Westcott, *Collectanea Hermetica;* Three Initiates, *Kyballion;* The Tibetan, *The 24 Tibetan Books)*. People lived in accord with divine will and purpose in building and maintaining a Kingdom. This brings us to the next

Metaphysical Key To:
Restoration of The 1st Eye
Overcoming impediment # 2
    Blindness

Their 1st eye was active and enabled them to see the divine architectural design for living in harmony with nature. There was no need for an external force within the Kingdom when all vibrated in accord with divine will and law. The people prospered and lived in peace known as Hotep. Ausar would travel to far off lands to establish God's kingdom. In his absence, his wife Auset was unwavering in her devotion to the divine rulership of Ausar.

All the while, their jealous brother Set was plotting to overthrow the Kingdom of Ausar. At last, Set found his opportunity which was occasioned by a banquet held for Ausar. Set, along with 72 of his confederates secretly plotted and devised a scheme in which they got the measurements of Ausar. They then had a royally jeweled sarcophagus made to his exact size. The coffin was just one of a myriad of sacred symbols used by the Kamitians to express the Psycho/Spiritual Journey of the Soul in the afterlife. These sacred symbols, the Ritual and all that was required for success in the journey in this life and the afterlife were central in their unfolding consciousness. So eagerly, guests at the banquet each took a turn at trying to fit the coffin - but without success.

Finally, Ausar's time to try it out for size had come. Naturally, since the coffin was specially designed for him, the King fit *exactly*. Immediately, the coffin was seized upon by Set and his evil doers who nailed it shut, cast it into the Nile – thereby drowning Ausar. At last, Ausar is slain by his jealous brother Set.

Upon learning about her husband's death, Auset wept violently and cut off a lock of her hair. She donned her mourning wear and began a long and ceaseless search for her beloved husband. Upon finding him she transformed herself into a swallow-hawk and caused the life force to be raised up from him, and by taking his seed into her body, she conceived their son, Heru. As you can see, this is the story of the *Immaculate Conception* which would later be incorporated into Christianity. She hid herself and the child. Later, Set came upon the body of Ausar. In an angry rage, he cut it into fourteen (14) pieces – one for each night of the waning Moon – and dispersed these about. Here we see the number 7 doubled into the number 14. The Number 7 reveals the Septenary of man/woman and Creation. This Metaphysical Key is later described.

When are we in Ausarian consciousness and what changed over time?
You are in Ausarian consciousness when you are King upon the throne in rulership of your Spiritual equipment. Thus, do you walk as God and Goddess upon Earth, and Heaven and Earth are made One. When Auset discovered what Set had done she again, with ceaseless devotion, went about re-gathering the broken body of her husband, burying and making a shrine to each piece as she went about her work. Later, Heru, the son of Ausar and Auset, eventually comes to maturity. A fierce battle ensues between Heru and Set in which Heru must avenge his Father's death and be restored as the rightful heir to the throne as King.

What is the brokenness of the body of Ausar?
1. The brokeness of the body of Ausar is a key, symbolizing the brokenness in man and woman's consciousness of the divinity within.
2. It is likewise a symbol of the brokenness, separation and part-I-cularization in consciousness of the divinity within the human family.
3. It is the result of the descent down the Tree of Life and the converging cycle(s) of time, which make up *The Perfect Storm,* in which we now live.

What causes the brokenness, separativeness and particularization in consciousness?
This separativeness, or particularization in consciousness occurs when we come to identify with selves that are less than the fullness of our True Identification as Ausar Ba – sphere 1. It is when we use the personal will to fashion a World that is based on a limited and limiting sense of a 'self' now seen in *part* and not in *wholeness*. We are the Tree of Life. It is our Spiritual Faculty both Divine and Human.

In Ausarian Resurrection, you are trying to put back together the broken consciousness within yourself and within the human family. In the involutionary descent, the process of 'death sets in' as man and woman exercise use of their personal will to freely choose right or wrong action. As man's consciousness develops he must also develop a 'conscience'. This is known as Ab by the Kamitians. It is the 2nd Aspect of Divinity and is symbolized by the human heart. This is Heru or the Karest/Christ principle within the 6th sphere in the Tree of Life. Conscience guides you to be and act in accord with the Universal Law of Right Relationship. Your obedience to these laws is what increases your Soul light and insures escape from death. Conscience is the internal Self

correction, which attunes you to the deific qualities or Neteru which keep you on course. You are connected with the qualities of deity through the:
1. The 11 spheres in the Tree of Life grouped within
2. The 3 primary triangles of KaAbBa or BaAbKa and channeling through the
3. The 7 Division into 7 Planes of Consciousness, 7 Divisions of Soul-Spirit – 7 Primordial Energies

The 7 Continents and The Super Continents
The Secret and Sacred Meaning of Pangea

Metaphysical Key To:
The 7 Continents and The Supercontinents
The Septenary Nature of Man and Creation
The Number 7

As an ancient people, we are former residents of the Earth's mantle before it broke or rifted into pieces of smaller land masses or Continents. We are told that some Continents have now even submerged at the bottom of the Pacific and Atlantic Oceans. The 7 separate Continents of today called; Africa, Australia, Antarctica, North America, South America, Asia, and Europe were one large land mass or Super Continent called Pangea, which then broke apart and was set adrift as 7 separate Continents at the beginning of the 4th Round approximately 250 million years ago. (See Plate tectonic maps and Continental drift animations by C. R. Scotese, PALEOMAP Project (www.scotese.com or Scotese, C. R., 2001. Atlas of Earth History, Volume 1, Paleogeography, PALEOMAP Project, Arlington, Texas, p. 52, for maps and dates).

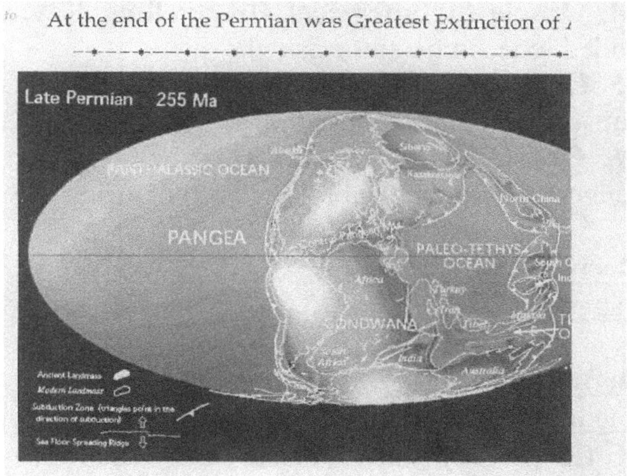

At the end of the Permian was Greatest Extinction of

Late Permian 255 Ma

Vast deserts covered western Pangea during the Permian as reptiles spread face of the supercontinent. 99% of all life perished during the extinction eve marked the end of the Paleozoic Era.

The Super Continent Pangea is pictured in the diagram at right. Earth is a great concourse for the Psycho/Spiritual Journey in Unfolding Human Consciousness. As a human Soul called Ba by the Kamitians we are in various stages of conscious unfoldment both as individuals and collectively as Earth Humanity.

The Secret and Sacred Meaning of Pangea.
Let's dispell the word <u>Pangea:</u>
#7. Oracle Metaphysical Dis-Spelling Key: Look up definition (dictionary, glossary, reference texts, etc.)

Definition:

The Ausarianization of Consciousness Tablet Series 2 – A.C.T.S. 2
Metaphysical Keys To the Tree of Life & Oracle Keys to Dispelling Illusion
The Psycho/Spiritual Journey of Unfolding Consciousness

Pangaea, Pangea - [n. the ancient super continent, comprising all the present continents joined together, which began to break up about 200 million years ago. See also: Laurasia, Gondwanaland [ETYMOLOGY: 20th Century: from Greek, literally: all-earth]. ETYMOLOGY: 14th Century: from Church Latin *paganus* civilian (hence, not a soldier of Christ), from Latin: countryman, villager, from *pagus* village]

 # 1. Oracle Metaphysical Dis-Spelling Key: Put letters of word or words together in a circle, like a serpent putting its tail in its mouth. Coming full Circle.

```
   P              P
 a   a          a   a
 e   n          e   n
   g              g
```

#2. Oracle Metaphysical Dis-Spelling Key: Read letters, putting together words, going forwards, backwards and in zig-zag patterns.
#3. Oracle Metaphysical Dis-Spelling Key: You may crossover in order to use a letter more than once. Place re-used letter in parenthesis ( ).
#4. Oracle Metaphysical Dis-Spelling Key: You may add a letter to complete a word. Place added letter in parenthesis ( ).
#5. Oracle Metaphysical Dis-Spelling Key: Letter substitution-you may substitute a letter. Place substituted letter in parenthesis ( ).
#6. Oracle Metaphysical Dis-Spelling Key: Make a list of derived words. Try to make the longest continuous unbroken word or string of words.

Derived Word List:
Pagan

Definition: *HyperDictionary.com*
Pagan - 1. [n] a person who does not acknowledge your God. 2. [adj] not acknowledging the God of Christianity and Judaism and Islam gentile, heathen, infidel, irreligious. See also: idol worshiper.

> Let's dispel the word religion:
> **Definition**: *WordReference.com dictionary*
> Religion - ETYMOLOGY: 12th Century: via Old French from Latin *religio* fear of the supernatural, piety, probably from *religare* to tie up, from re- + *ligare* to bind]

#8. Oracle Metaphysical Dis-Spelling Key: Meaning. See the relationship and oracle or story of the Neteru – Put word list together to tell a story.
Meaning:
To be irreligious is to be without a religion. We see here that the continent Pangea dispelled is the word Pagan. It is our Ancestors who lived in knowingness of wholeness or 'all Earth'. We dispelled the word Earth in *ACTS 1* to see that the word reveals Heart. Our movement from a consciousness of wholeness to brokeness corresponds with the breaking up of the Super Continent

into pieces or parts. Our broken consciousness reflects our broken hearts. When our heart and consciousness are broken so that we cannot act justly and lovingly, then we need religion to tie or bind us back together again. Those who are called Pagan, by the so called modern World, saw within the 1st eye, in unity and wholeness.

The Secret and Sacred Meaning of Continent
What should we make of hearing about Continents Pangea, Lemuria, Atlantis, Hyperboria, and so on? Are they to be understood allegorically or historically?
On the one hand -
It is wholly probable, if not absolutely certain, that these continents *did* exist. After all, what would be the big deal here? It has already been stated that the Earth's mantle was a large land mass that broke up into the now 7 'identifiable and currently named' land masses we call continents. We know whole Ancient civilizations are now underwater. Why not whole continents? Further, we know that the Earth and her inhabitants have been subject to various, cyclical cataclysms such as ice ages, floods, droughts, volcanic eruption, extinction of species (as in the dinosaurs) and Pole shifts. Such dramatic events have changed the face of the Earth and the species upon it.

On the other hand -
We are cautioned to not always make *literal* that which is in the realm of interacting forces. This is expressed in the following accordingly: Alvin Boyd Kuhn *The Lost Light*. p. 356:

> It is an axiom of occult and esoteric study that the World shall be alternately destroyed by fire and water. This has been accepted in a literal way, so that the legend is that the continent of Lemuria some millions of years ago was destroyed by fiery convulsions and the later continent of Atlantis submerged by water. If continents sink both fire and water must of necessity play a part in the development. It is true that living factual history, of men and of universes and planets, does in general carry out the outline of symbolism. Yet it may be suggested that perhaps in this instance it is possible that sheer typology became once more too directly historicized. As Horus and Sut [read here: Heru and Set] alternately vanquish each other in endless repetition, so fire and water eternally dominate in turn.

An analogy may best serve to give further explanation. It is reasonable to suggest that:
-Continents float upon the surface of the oceans.
just like
-Thoughts float upon the surface of the mind. (Thoughts make up the 'content' of the mind).
In time –
-Continents go 'beneath' the surface, when no longer needed as part of our immediate awareness.
just like
-Thoughts go 'beneath' the surface, when no longer needed as part of our immediate awareness.

However, *just because something goes below the surface or - is no longer 'upon the surface' of our great oceans or - 'upon our mind' - does not mean that it is 'gone'*. If Lemuria and Atlantia prove allegorical or mythological they may nevertheless serve as a bridge in the Psycho/Spiritual Journey of Unfolding Consciousness and thereby aid humanity.

Our Story Continues...
While all the debating *back and forth* goes on, nothing substantial changes in *Our Story* due to double speaks, or haggling between scientists and some of the 'custodians' of the Ancient Wisdom. These custodians are called by many names which includes – Esotericists, Masons, Spiritualist, etc. One may spend considerable time in debate about; who the 'Negroes' are, when did he appear and whether or not these Continents really existed. Yet, we must expand beyond just the 'debate' to find the Metaphysical Key or Keys that this information reveals *to our deep sub-consciousness*. The broader outlines reveal that:

1. The divine archetypal design is *inviolable, a*nd we see it at work in its enumeration of 7 Root Races that are unfolding in our 4th Earth Round Time Cycle.
2. *No matter what the date* of the Black man's appearance *millions* of years ago, *no matter upon what Continent* or land mass, *no matter what name* he is called by - it does not change the fact that the 3rd Negro/Black Root Race *precedes* the Semitic (Atlantian) and the Aryan Race (the most recent Root Race addition) in this human family unfolding in our Earth Story.
3. *No matter what the date, whether the 'records' have been misread or fudged, the Psycho/Spiritual Journey of Unfolding Consciousness whether 1.8 million years or 18 million years, it is the Negroes that began their outgoing footsteps into more material circumstance.*

The Secret and Sacred Meaning of Lemuria.
Could there be other meanings to the word Continent? Could there be other meanings to the word Lemuria?
Let's dispell the word <u>Continent:</u>
#11. Oracle Metaphysical Dis-Spelling Key: What does the word sound like? Say the word out loud and then silently in a meditative state.
#6. Oracle Metaphysical Dis-Spelling Key: Make a list of derived words.

<u>**Derived Word List:**</u>
<u>Cont(e)n(t)(m)ent</u> - We see that it reveals the word contentment.

#7. Oracle Metaphysical Dis-Spelling Key: Look up definition (dictionary, glossary, reference texts, etc.)
<u>Definition:</u> *Thesaurus.*
<u>Contentment</u> - Happiness, satisfaction, peace, ease, gratification, pleasure, comfort, serenity, content.

#8. Oracle Metaphysical Dis-Spelling Key: Meaning. See the relationship and oracle or story of the Neteru – Put word list together to tell a story.
<u>**Meaning:**</u>
The sinking of the continents Lemuria and Atlantis may be understood allegorically, which is from the angle of consciousness, as the *sinking or loss of contentment with the One True Self.*

The Secret and Sacred Meaning of Lemuria.
Let's dispell the word <u>Lemuria:</u>
#7. Oracle Metaphysical Dis-Spelling Key: Look up definition (dictionary, glossary, reference texts, etc.)
<u>Definition:</u>: Satguru Sivaya Subramuniyaswami. *Lemurian Scrolls*, p. 278.

Lemuria - "An Ancient continent described in the Lemurians Scrolls as the first continent on Earth to be inhabited by humans (Lemurians). Lemuria has been revealed by scripture and explained and made popular by numerous clairvoyants and mystics over the past hundred years as a highly advanced civilization with amazing technologies, maintaining the love of nature and appreciating its many gifts...Lemuria once formed a land mass that stretched from the Rocky Mountains in the United States west to South Africa. According to another source, it is an ancient continent thought to have formed a massive connection between India, Madagascar and South Africa. Still another theory places it in the South Pacific between North America and Australasia."

This Book reveals much and is a good reference. Although it contains much of the Ancient Wisdom it suffers the same fate as many other books. They are talking about Black-skinned people yet they represent these images in an Aryanized/European manner. *Incorrect.* After all, the Aryanized/Indian have been under the spell of the Caste system while they have been custodians of the Ancient Wisdom. The first humans make their appearance within the 3rd Root Black/Negro Race. This is the Race from which the other Racial hues - Brown, Red, Yellow and White - all emerge from.

#7. Oracle Metaphysical Dis-Spelling Key: Look up definition (dictionary, glossary, reference texts, etc.)
Definition Continued: H.P. Blavatsky. *Theosophical Glossary,* p. 187.
Lemuria - A modern term first used by some naturalists, and now adopted by Theosophist, to indicate a continent that according to the Secret Doctrine of the East, preceded Atlantis. Its Eastern name would not reveal much to European ears [read here: We are being told that the real name is not being revealed here].

 # 1. Oracle Metaphysical Dis-Spelling Key: Put letters of word or words together in a circle, like a serpent putting its tail in its mouth. Coming full Circle.
#2. Oracle Metaphysical Dis-Spelling Key: Read letters, putting together words, going forwards, backwards and in zig-zag patterns.
#3. Oracle Metaphysical Dis-Spelling Key: You may crossover in order to use a letter more than once. Place re-used letter in parenthesis ( ).
#4. Oracle Metaphysical Dis-Spelling Key: You may add a letter to complete a word. Place added letter in parenthesis ( ).
#5. Oracle Metaphysical Dis-Spelling Key: Letter substitution-you may substitute a letter. Place substituted letter in parenthesis ( ).
#6. Oracle Metaphysical Dis-Spelling Key: Make a list of derived words. Try to make the longest continuous unbroken word or string of words.

Derived Word List:
Ra Mur(a)l - Image of the Sun/Son. Ra is the Solar Deity or Sun to the Kamitians.
Mer, Mir - Mirror

Definition:
Mirror - Something that faithfully reflects or gives a true picture of something else. From Old French *mireor,* from *mirer,* From Latin *mirari.*

Derived Word List Continued:
Definition: Budge. *Hieroglyphic Glossary. V. l,* p. 307.
Mer - Like, as.
Mer - Lake; Any collection of water, lake, pool, cistern, reservoir, basin, canal, a particle of prohibition.
Merit - Copy, likeness.
Mer - A sea-going ship: inundation, flood, stream; libation tank; swampy land.
Merit - Celestial lake, heaven, sky.

Derived Word List Continued:
Rule Ma - Law of Maat, divine law. Maat is the Kamitic deity of right, just, and harmonious relationships.
Mira(c)Le, Miracle
ReaL Mu I - The Eye that arises within Mu or Nu/ the primal Mother/the waters of space/ and *sees*.
Laurel - Tree, evergreen, wreath, crown, honor.

#8. Oracle Metaphysical Dis-Spelling Key:
Meaning. See the relationship and oracle or story of the Neteru – Put word list together to tell a story.

Meaning:
- Lemuria is the mirror of the Image and Likeness of God
- Lemuria is called the Lost Continent
- Because *it* is what sank from awareness when we lost 'contentment'
- In the Image and Likeness of God that
- We are and have always been from the beginingless beginning
- In our Psycho/Spiritual Journey in Unfolding Consciousness
- We became dis-content with the image and likeness of God and
- Our identification with and as the One True Self – Ausar Ba
- No longer content with the image of
- All in allness - and the - Seeing of the One True Self in all Selves
- We began to see and delight in a lesser self
- We wanted a more 'personalized' image
- *Our own original*
- Something we could call our own
- *As if we could improve upon God's Design*
- In time we would come to see this distorted and truncated image
- Reflected in the mirror
- We frightened ourselves
- And because we could no longer see the One True Self in our own image
- We could not see The One True Self in others *and*
- We were frightened of others
- When Lemuria sank in our consciousness we lost access to the elixir of life

- The substance from which all is made brand new
- This elixir of life is what the Kamitians call Nu or Nun
- It is the Spirit-Matter continuum from which all creation arises
- It is the Fount of All Possibility
- 5th Root Race (Aryan/European) man has made the Nu-clear Bomb
- Instead of focusing in meditation upon how to return to the Nu-Clear Balm
- To access the Nu-Clear Balm, the elixir of Life, is to be set back to '0'
- The Zero or sphere 0 – AMEN in the Tree of Life
- It is G-round '0' on the Higher Turn of the Spiral
- We need have no fear of this G-round '0'
- It is our Ausarian – Home, with unlimited access to
- 'O'mnipotence, 'O'mniscience, and 'O'mnipresence
- It is the g-round '0' on a lower turn of the spiral that we need to have fear
- It is annihilation and destruction of the Nuclear Bomb and the events of '9/11'
- Which direction are we heading in as a Planetary Family?
- What part are you playing?

Again, the sinking of the continents Lemuria and Atlantis may be understood allegorically as the sinking or loss of contentment with the One True Self. The following is suggestive of evidence and the need for further research on the 3rd Root Race Afrikan/Negro/Lemurian. Wallace Budge, *The Gods of The Egytians, V. ll,* p. 288-289.

> A Nubian god of interest and of some local importance is Merul or Meril, or who was the son of Horus and Isis; he was the third member of the triad of the city of Termes, or Telmes, a city the site of which is marked by the modern village of Kalabsheh in Nubia, situated about thirty-five miles to the north of Syene. At Dabod also he was the third member of the local triad, which consisted of Seb, Nut, and Merul. In the figures of the god reproduced by Lanzone he is depicted in the form of a man, with or without a beard, and he wears the White Crown with plumes, or the triple crown with horns and uraei, or a crown composed of a pair of horns, with two plumes and a solar disk between them, and uraei. His titles are: **"Great god, governor (or dweller in) the White Mountain,"** "son of Horus, great god, lord of Telmes," "Great Sekhem, governor of the two lands of the West," "Beautiful boy who proceedeth from the son of Isis," and "holy child of the son of Osiris,". A text quoted by Brugsh speaks of Merul as coming from Ta-Neter, i.e., the land on both sides of the southern end of the Red Sea, and the coast of Africa which is further to the south. Thus it seems that Merul is not of Egyptian origin, and it is probable that the worship of the god is very ancient. The variant forms of his name are: Menruil, Menlil, Meruter; from the first two of these was formed the classical name of the god-Mandulis.

If we dispell the words Merul, Meril, Menruil, etc. they quickly reveal the word Lemuria.

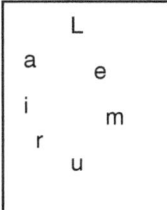

Derived Word List:
Lemuria

Also note in the above quote that Merul or Meril is the 3rd member or third in a triad. This Great god in the White Mountain is likewise referred to in the definition of the word Meru which is expressed accordingly: H.P. Blavatsky. *Theosophical Glossary*, p. 213.

> Meru - "...Geographically accepted, it is an unknown mountain north of the Himalayas. In tradition, Meru was the "Land of Bliss" of the earliest Vedic Times. It is also referred to as Hemadri "the golden mountain"Ratnasanu, "jewel peak" kanikachala, "lotus mountain", and Amaradri and Deva-parvata, **"the mountain of the gods"**. The Occult teachings place it in the very centre of the North Pole, pointing it out as the site of the first continent on our earth, after the solidification of the globe.

Our Story Continues...
We go forward empowered by the words of one of our chiefs accordingly:
Chancellor Williams. *Destruction of Black Civilization,* p. 31.

> That is why I urge those students who intend to accept the great challenge of basic research in this discipline to go into "enemy territory, linger there, study and critically analyze their lectures and their "scholarly" writings, for they are some of the most rewarding sources for African history, precisely because in shrewdly attempting to delete, disguise or belittle the role of Blacks in World history, they often reveal the opposite of what was intended. They are fruitful sources of unconscious evidence, supplying the very evidence they thought to suppress or recording facts the significance of which they were totally ignorant."

We refer now to two quotes from the Esoteric literature accordingly: *Rosicrucian Cosmo-Conception.* p. 304.

> The Negroes and the savage races with curly hair, are the last remnants of the Lemurians.

And likewise said accordingly: The Tibetan. *Esoteric Healing,* p. 221.

> In considering disease and its basic causes, we have dealt particularly with those which concern our Aryan race [read here: Aryan/European] and modern humanity; these are largely astral in origin and might be described as Atlantean [read here: Semitic] in nature. We have briefly considered also the various diseases which originate upon the mental plane; these are more strictly Aryan and involve also the ills to which disciples are prone. Infectious diseases and those which are fundamental in the planetary substance have a potent effect upon those races (still among us) which are the oldest on our planet, and which are related to the fast dying out Lemurian types; Negroes are specially prone to infectious epidemics.

Both of these are important quotes, the second being *especially* so when understood within the wider context, expressed as follows:

1. As you continue to read this text and other texts of the, *Ausarianization in Consciousness Tablet Series*, you will be able bear witness to the fact that the many quotes cited in these books contain the splinters of 'Our Stuff' and Our story.
2. The words Lemuria and Lemurian are used 23 and 149 times respectively in the 24 books by the Tibetan. The word Negro and Negroes are used 35 and 16 times respectively. Yet, the above quote is one of just two times in the *entire* work where the word Lemurian and Negro are *allowed* to appear in the same paragraph, and even *contiguous* in a sentence.
3. Also, take note in this quote of the simultaneous admission that *Lemurians are Negroes* and are the *oldest inhabitants on our Planet*.
4. Take notice also, of the arrogant attitude about the 'dying' out of the older races. The statement about being more prone to infectious epidemics bears research by those who are sincere in working for the greater good of humanity. If this statement has *any* validity, how has it been used, abused, i.e. A.I.D.S. etc.? To say that the Negro, or Lemurian is on its way to extinction - without raising the same kind of Global alarm if the whale for example, where becoming extinct, is *unconscionable!*

Black Race people are the Fathers and Mothers of the Human Kingdom. What may be the impact on the Planet if large populations are affected or 'allowed' to die out in large numbers without ameliorative intervention? This brings us to return to a previous -

> **Metaphysical Law Key:**
> The Law of Correspondence
> As above, so below; as below, so above

This is also the law of correspondence. (Kamitic Law of Tehuti - See The Kybalion). Again this law guides us to examine from the level or plane that *you do know* - to that which - *you do not as yet know that you know*. Let's pay a Metaphysical visit to the 2nd Kingdom which is the Vegetable Kingdom to find an answer. Using the Law of Correspondence (Law of Tehuti), let's posit the massive dying off an integral part of the vegetable kingdom and evaluate what magnitude and impact this may have on the Planet. To offer just one example, we are already experiencing the impact to humanity and nature with the destruction of the Rain Forests.

The diminishing canopy of our trees contributes to:
1. Changes in our environmental relationship to the Sun's ultra violet rays.
2. Washing away of soil. Such soil erosion changes the landscape, causes loss of water balance and fertility in our Earth.
3. Changes in the delicate atmospheric balance of carbon dioxide and oxygen.
4. The Ozone hole.
5. The loss of our cornucopia of herbal healing medicines for Earth's inhabitants.
6. The loss/and or displacement of habitat within our Human, Animal, and Mineral Kingdoms.

There is an expression among Black people that states, "If the White man catches a cold, the Black man catches pneumonia."

1. Is this observance based on differing environments and racial segregation which leads to poorer access to health care and poorer living conditions?
2. Are there deeper Metaphysical meanings here?

Metaphysical law would posit that if the lower spiral is true then the higher spiral is true. In other words, if the Black man is healthy, then the White man is healthy or healthier. Who would lose if both Black and White could be healthy? Like the story of the canary and the miner - if you take care of the canary, you take care of the miner. If Blacks are in 'bad shape' or dying out or for any reason, could Whites be far behind in being in bad shape and dying out also? I posit that the entire Earth eco-system will be *upset* if there is massive decimation to the Afrikan population. Let the scientist, researchers, those studying melanin, sound (vibration) energy field theory, etc., come forth to confirm or disprove what is asserted here.

The following analogy may best serves here:
-The vegetation is to the Vegetable kingdom
-What the Black man and woman are to the Human Kingdom
-They blanket the Earth.

★ *Afrikans/Negroes - Blanket the Earth.*

But it goes even deeper than the issue of any propensities toward disease or disparities in living. Those who have access to the Ancient Wisdom and think more Esoterically can offer opportunity for much 'rationalized and justified' abuse of man against man. There is no guarantee that the mind(s) that can understand the greater scheme of things will not go on to *'scheme'* on a greater scale as may be evidenced accordingly: *Rosicrucian Cosmo-Conception*, p. 290-291

> It has been said by white men against the white race that wherever it goes the other races die out. The whites have been guilty of fearful oppression against those other races, having in many cases massacred multitudes of the defenseless and unsuspecting natives-as witness the conduct of the Spaniards towards the ancient Peruvians and Mexicans, to specify but one of many instances. The obligations resulting from such betrayal of confidence and abuse of superior intelligence and power will all have to be paid-yea, to the last, least iota! - by those incurring them. It is equally true, however, that even had the whites not massacred, starved, enslaved, expatriated and otherwise maltreated those older races, the latter would nevertheless have died out just as surely, though more slowly, because such is the Law of Evolution-the Order of Nature. At some future time the white races bodies, when they become inhabited by the Egos who are now embodied in red, black, yellow or brown skins, will have degenerated so far that they also will disappear, to give place to other and better vehicles. Science speaks only of evolution. It fails to consider the lines of Degeneration which are slowly but surely destroying such bodies as have crystallized beyond possibility of improvement.

I will refrain from the major digression that could be made here to 'pull apart' this one passage. Another book could be written. Suffice it to say. There is a 'qualified' admission here of the atrocities committed by Aryan/Whites upon the Afrikans/Negroes - the older Race and other people of color. Yet *something* is wholly and horribly missing in its presentation. A something that when captured - whether subtly or dramatically presented - can be recognized. It is a something that would seek to preserve the *essence* of human life. Even the most off-handed, over the shoulder comment may express that special *something* that is missing in the passage above. Fortunately that something is captured in the story below that is being told by a Black comedian as he stands before an audience. It is as follows:

> The comedian, in his onstage satire, views incredulously all the fusssss that is being made in a movie about a whale entitled 'Free Willy'. He explains that in the movie, everyone is *aaaallll* upset about a captured whale, who longs to be free from the unnatural water cage he has been confined within and made to perform tricks. Skeptically, he tells the audience that people are chanting, Free Willy! Free Willy! The comedian, in his moment of 'black humor' throws his hands in the air and chides, 'Free Willy! Free Willy! *Free my uncle Willy!*

Pointing out the hypocrisy here, he is equating the capturing and confining of the Whale to the capture and imprisonment of the Black man. The question raised is: How could the sincerity to free Willy be believed in one instance while the same sincerity to free the Black man is unwitnessed in the next? Why is it that the Afrikan, the Negro, the Lemurian, the Black man in simple everyday life and expression 'Gets It' - gets in consciousness what the most so called 'privileged and learned' miss? That is - the reverence and sacredness of *Life* no matter what its duration. The serious note struck, even in humor, can not be missed. There can be no doubt about the grieving of our Mother Earth at the treatment of both the oldest human, land mammal - the Negroes, and one of the oldest, sea mammals - the whale. There is an even deeper connection between Afrikans and whales.

Let's dispell the word <u>Whale</u>: (See previous Metaphysical dispelling Keys)

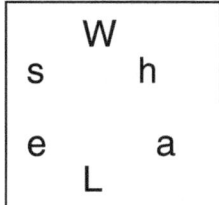

Derived Word list:
Whe(e)ls

Meaning:
Whe(e)ls - Whales are wheels. They swim as Masters of great cycles of time upon the vast ocean expanse. Yet, we are now living in an ever tightening spiral of time in our Earth history.
A narrowing time zone that says:
•Time is up
•Time to return home
•Like the Whale, we have spun out
•We have Beached ourselves.
•Whales come to warn us

The Ausarianization of Consciousness Tablet Series 2 – A.C.T.S. 2
Metaphysical Keys To the Tree of Life & Oracle Keys to Dispelling Illusion
The Psycho/Spiritual Journey of Unfolding Consciousness

- Turn back toward *Home*
- Time to turn our *'outgoing'* footsteps around.
- Like the Whale, we are trapped within the little eddy of time
- No longer attuned to the vast ocean expanse and vast cycles of time
- We are spinning our wheels
- Caught in the ever tightening coil
- In the downward spiral of material consciousness.
- We have lost our bearings.
- We have lost sight of how to navigate the Black Ocean
- The Dark, The Deep – God, Ausarian consciousness
- The Black Man and the Whale must be free.

This Black comedian perhaps was not conscious of the Metaphysical depths from which he spoke because so often as Negroes we speak from the Unitive Unconscious, the Dreamtime, the Trance, that just knows. Unfortunately the racial attitude towards the Negroes by the Western World over 2500 years is captured in the following accordingly: Cheikh Anta Diop. *African Origin of Civilization*, p. 24.

> The modern Negro slave trade was considered an economic necessity prior to the advent of the machine. This would last until the mid-nineteenth century. Such a reversal of roles, the result of new technical relations, brought with it master-slave relationships between Whites and Blacks on the social level. **Already during the Middle Ages, the memory of a Negro Egypt that had civilized the World had been blurred by ignorance of the antique hidden in libraries or buried under ruins.** It would become even more obscure during those four centuries of slavery. Inflated by their recent technical superiority, the Europeans looked down on the Black World and condescended to touch nothing but its riches.
>
> Ignorance of the Black's ancient history, differences of mores and customs, ethnic prejudices between two races that believed themselves to be facing each other for the first time, combined with the economic necessity to exploit - so many factors predisposed the mind of the European to distort the moral personality of the Black and his intellectual aptitudes. Henceforth "Negro" became a synonym for primitive being, "inferior," endowed with a pre-logical mentality. As the human being is always eager to justify his conduct, they went even further. The desire to legitimize colonization and the slave trade-in other words, the social condition of the Negro in the modern World-engendered an entire literature to describe the so-called inferior traits of the Black. The mind of several generations of Europeans would thus be gradually indoctrinated, Western opinion would crystallize and instinctively accept as revealed truth the equation: Negro = inferior humanity. They invoked "the civilizing mission" of the West charged with the responsibility to raise the African to the level of other men [known to us as "the white man's burden"] From then on capitalism had clear sailing to practice the most ferocious exploitation under the cloak of moral pretexts.

Evidences of 'Appearance' of The 6th Root Race

Evidence of the emerging 6th Root Race Consciousness among us can already be glimpsed. It is expressed by those who have moved beyond the boundaries of racial, national, political or religious identification. They identify as citizens and free will agents in the Universe. There will be those who will actually express this inner synthesis in their outward appearance. It is the experience encountered today of going into a store and seeing the clerk behind the counter who looks like he could be from *anywhere in the World and could open his mouth and speak any language in the World.* This is expressed accordingly: Dr. York. *The "Millennium" Book*, p. 218-219.

> **Metaphysical Key To:**
> Evidences of 'Appearance' of
> The 6th Root Race as reflected in the 5th Sub 6th Root Race

> Neutranoids or a Race of People that you can't tell their Nationality, A Neutral Race, A "New Race". If you look at the models inside of magazine, you'll see what I mean. The majority of them look like they can be of a multiple of races. They are also making what it is called the "the New Black Person" on television. No longer do you see dark-skinned African-Americans or even light-skinned African-Americans representing our Race, but what you do see are people who you cannot pinpoint exactly what they are mixed with. However, you can tell there is a little African-American in there somewhere. Before the beginning of the Neutranoid Race Era, when I was living on Mt. Zion at Upstate, New York, I was teaching and talking to the 'Young Disciple', and I told them that soon they will see a Race of Children being brought up whose nationalities would be hard to identify.

Dr York then references an article from the New York Times magazine dated September 29, 1996 entitled: "Race Is Over", by Stanley Crouch. It includes a number of pictures of people who visibly demonstrate the 'inability' one would have in trying to discern their racial origin.
Ibid:

> There is Something that they have to learn to accept, and that is: They can't get rid of African-American because they are holding the planet together! We are the magnets on the planet Ta (Earth). So the Euro-Americans know that they can't totally eliminate African-Americans. If you think they don't know this, you are kidding yourself.

However, what cannot be emphasized enough is that:
- *It is **not** an outer physiological blending that heralds the appearance of the 6th Root Race*
- But *an inner consciousness that is an unbroken circle of synthesis and unity*
- This unitive consciousness will be reflected in all *hues*-of - *man* prevailing in the human family
- Out of the hard won efforts to embrace the underlying unity in diversity,
- Synthesis will result at last
- All the myriad elements are seen as arising out of and returning to the *One Source*

- Earth is seen as a temporary school where lessons are learnt and as preparatory for other fields of Galactic service
- Stationed here on Earth, in our very time and space
- We see the Universal consciousness of the World Servers and Galactic travelors unfolding

Geese Facts

Next fall when you see geese heading south for the winter... flying along in V formation...you might consider what science has discovered as to why they fly that way:

As each bird flaps its wings, it creates an uplift for the bird immediately following. By flying in V formation the whole flock adds at least 71% greater flying range, than if each bird flew on its own.

People who share a common direction and sense of community can get where they are going more quickly and easily because they are traveling on the thrust of one another.

When a goose falls out of formation, it suddenly feels the drag and resistance of trying to go it alone... and quickly gets back into formation to take advantage of the lifting power of the bird in front. If we have as much sense as a goose, we will stay in formation with those who are headed the same way we are.

When the head goose gets tired it rotates back in the wing and another goose flies point. It is sensible to take turns doing demanding jobs...with people or with geese flying south.

Geese honk from behind to encourage those up front to keep up their speed. What do we say when we honk from behind?

Finally...and this is important...when a goose gets sick or is wounded by gunshots, and falls out of formation, two other geese fall out with that goose and follow it down to lend help and protection. They stay with the fallen goose until it is able to fly or until it dies, and only then do they launch out on their own, or with another formation to catch up with their group.

If we have the sense of a goose, we will stand by each other like that.
Author Unknown

A Hunter's Poem

A hunter shot at a flock of geese that flew within his reach.
Two were stopped in their rapid flight and fell on the sandy beach.
The male bird lay at the water's edge and just before he died,
He faintly called to his wounded mate and she dragged herself to his side.
She bent her head and crooned to him in a way distressed and wild.
Carrying her one and only mate as a mother would a child.
Then covering him with her broken wing and gasping with failing breath,
She laid her head against his breast, a feeble honk ... then death.
This story is true, though crudely told. I was the man in this case.
I stood knee-deep in snow and cold, and the hot tears burned my face.
I buried the birds in the sand where they lay, wrapped in my hunting coat.
And I threw my gun and belt in the bay, when I crossed in the open boat.
Hunters will call me a right poor sport and scoff at the thing I did.
But that day something broke in my heart, and shoot again?
God forbid.

Reascension Into Sacredness
from the Elders
Communicated via Dr. Terri Nelson

Reascension into sacredness
All are gathering in
Reascension into sacredness
From the four winds

Our Elders are elated
By the dawning of this hour
They stand in witness to this day
Feel their great power (*repeat 1st verse*)

We emerge from the darkness
Eons long was night
We come now to serve and save
The rising Sun's in sight. (*repeat 1st verse*)

Secrets of Race & Consciousness Afrikan Cosmology of Kamit
with The Spiritual Meaning of The 'N' Word(s)
Neggur - The Goose Goddess who laid the Sun Egg, the Cosmic Egg

Revealed in Ka Ab Ba *(Kabala)* The Tree Of Life   Metaphysical Mysteries Meaning

Select Bibliography & Suggested Reading List

Adler, Vera Stanley. *The Initiation of The World.* York Beach, ME: Samuel Weiser, 1972.
African World History Project. Los Angeles, CA: Association for the Study of Classical African Civilizations, 2002.
Amen, Ra Un Nefer. *Metu Neter, V.I & II.* Bronx, NY: Khamit Corp., 1990.
Arquelles, Jose. *The Mayan Factor.* Santa Fe, New Mexico: Bear & Company, 1987.
Arquelles, Jose. *The Surfers of the Zuvuya.* Santa Fe, New Mexico: Bear & Company, 1989.
Ashby, Dr. Muata. *The Ausarian Resurrection.* Miami, FL: Cruzian Mystic Books, 1995.
Barborka, Geofrey. *The Divine Plan.* London, England: Theosophical Publishing House, 1964.
Ben-Jochannan, Yosef. *Black Man of The Nile and His Family.* Baltimore, MD: Black Classic Press, 1989.
Blavatsky, H.P. (Scribe). *Isis Unveiled, V.I & II.* Pasadena, CA: Theosophical University Press, 1988.
Blavatsky, H.P. (Scribe). *Secret Doctrine, V.I & II.* Theosophical University Press, 1988.
Blavatsky, H.P. *Theosophical Glossary.* Los Angeles, CA: Theosophy Company, 1990.
Bocock Robert. *Freud and Modern Society.* New York, NY: Holmes & Meier, 1978.
Browder, Anthony. *Nile Valley Civilization.* Washington, DC: Institute of Karmic Guidance, 1992.
Budge, E. A. Wallis. *Amulets and Superstitions.* New York, NY: Dover Publications, 1978.
Budge, E. A. Wallis *Prt Em Hru. The Book of Coming Forth By Day.* (Egyptian Book of the Dead). New York, NY: Dover Publications, 1967.
Budge, E. A. Wallis. *Osiris: The Egyptian Religion of Resurrection.* New Hyde Park, NY: University Books, 1961.
Budge, E. A. Wallis. *An Egypian Hieroglyphic Dictionary, V.I & II.* New York, NY: Dover Publications, 1978.
Budge, E. A. Wallis. *The God of The Egyptians, V.I & II.* New York, NY: Dover Publications, 1969.
Burgoyne, Thomas. *The Light of Egypt. The Science of the Soul and the Stars. V.I & II.* Santa Fe, NM: Sun Publishing, 1980.
Churchward, Albert. *Signs and Symbols of Primordial Man.* Brooklyn, NY: A & B Books, 1903.
Churchward, Albert. *Origin and Evolution of the Human Race.* London: George Allen & Unwin LTD. 1921.
Churchward, Albert. *Origin and Evolution of Primitive Man.* London: George Allen & Company, 1912.
Churchward, Albert. *The Arcana of Freemasonry.* London: George Allen & Unwin LTD, 1922.
De Lubicz, Isha Schwaller. *Her-Bak: Egyptian Initiate.* Rochester, VT: Inner Traditions International, 1967.
De Lubicz, Isha Schwaller. *The Opening of The Way.* New York, NY: Inner Traditions International, 1981.
Diop, Cheikh Anta. *African Origin of Civilization: Myth or Reality.* Chicago, IL: Lawrence Hill Books, 1974.
Diop, Cheikh Anta. *Civilization or Barbarism.* Brooklyn, NY: Lawrence Hill Books, 1991.
Hall, Manly P. *Freemasonry of the Ancient Egyptians.* Los Angeles, CA: Philosophical Research Society, 1965.
Heindel, Max. *The Rosicrucian Cosmo-Conception.* Oceanside, CA: Rosicrucian Fellowship, 1988.

Hassan-El, Kashif Malik. *The Wilie Lynch Letter and The Making of a Slave.* Chicago: Lushena Books. 1712, 1999.
Hurtak. J. J. *The Book of Knowledge: The Keys of Enoch.* Los Gatos, CA: Academy for Future Science, 1973.
Jackson, John. *Introduction to African Civilizations.* Secausus, NJ: Citadel Press, 1970.
Jackson, John. *Man, God and Civilization.* Secausus, NJ: Citadel Press, 1972.
James, George, G. M.. *Stolen Legacy.* San Francisco CA: Julian Richardson Assoc.1954, 1985.
Karenga,. Dr. Malauana. *The 7 Principles of Kwaanza.* Los Angeles, CA: University of Sankore Press, 1988.
Krummenaker, Daniel. *Where Were Atlantis And Lemuria?*
Kuhn, Alvin Boyd. *The Lost Light.* Henry Holt & Company,1931.
Lawlor, Robert. *Voices of The First Day.* Rochester, Vermont: Inner Traditions International, Ltd., 1991.
Ligon, A. Black Knostic Study Teachings of Dr. Ligon. (Private Group Study).
LEVI. *Aquarian Gospel of Jesus The Christ.* Marina Del Rey, CA: DeVorss & Co, 1982.
Mackenzie, Donald.*Egyptian Myths and Legends.* Avenel, NJ: Random House Value, 1980.
Massey, Gerald. *Ancient Egypt, The Light of The World V.I & II.* Baltimore, MD: Black Classic Press, 1992.
Massey, Gerald. *A Book of the Beginnings. V.I & II.* Secaucus, NJ: University Books, 1974.
Mead, G.R.S. *Thrice Greatest Hermes.* York Beach, ME: Samuel Weiser, 2001.
Martin, Tony. *Marcus Garvey.* Dover, MA: The Majority Press, 1986.
National Council For Geocosmic Research, 93rd edition.
Nelson, Terri Nelson. *KaAbBa Building The Lighted Temple. Academy Kamitic Education. 2000.*
Nelson, Terri Nelson. *On The Way To Finding Your Soulmate. Academy Kamitic Education. 1996.*
Parfitt, Will. *The Living Qabalah.* Longmead: Element Books, 1988.
Ponce, Charles. *Kabbalah.* Wheaton, IL: The Theosophical Publishing House, 1973.
Regardie, Israel. *The Tree of Life.* York Beach, ME: Samuel Weiser, 1972.
Robbins, Michael. *Infinitizing of Selfhood.* Mariposa, CA: University of The Seven Rays, 1997.
Robbins, Michael.*Tapestry of the Gods. V.I & II.* Jersey City Heights, NJ: University of The Seven Rays, 1988.
Rogers J.A. 100 *Amazing Facts About the Negro.*Helga M. Rogers, St. Petersburg, FL: 1957.
Satguru Sivaya Subramuniyaswami. *Lemurian Scrolls.* India: Himalayan Academy, 1998.
Three Initiates. *The Kybalion, Hermetic Philosophy* Chicago, IL: Yogi Publication Society, 1940.
Tyberb, Judith. *Sanskrit Keys to the Wisdom Religion.* San Diego, CA: Point Loma, 1976.
Tibetan (scribe, A. Bailey). Twenty-Four Books of Esoteric Philosophy, CD-ROM, New York: Lucis Publishing Company, 1998.
Tibetan (scribe, A. Bailey). *Cosmic Fire. Esoteric Astrology. Esoteric Psychology, V.I & II. Rays And Initiations. Initiations Human and Solar.* See 24 Books as reference source.
Westcott , William Wynn. *Collectanea Hermetica.* York Beach, ME: Samuel Weiser, 1998.
Williams, Chacellor. *The Destruction of Black Civilization.* Chicago, IL: Third World Press, 1987.
Wilson, Hilary. *Understanding Hieroglyphs.*Barnes & Noble, Inc. New York, NY:B & N,1993.
The American Heritage Dictionary of The English Language. 3rd Edition. Boston, MA: Houghton Miflon 1992.
Microsoft Word Program. *Thesaurus.* 2003.